P9-AFZ-798

PROMOTING YOUTH SEXUAL HEALTH

Promoting Youth Sexual Health, written for preventionists and interventionists who work with children and adolescents across home, school, or community settings, offers guidance on how to promote sexual health among youth. The reader is first introduced to the state of the field, including sexual behaviors in which youth engage, sexual risk and protective factors, standards and professional guidelines for promoting the sexual health of youth, developmental and cultural considerations, and considerations in supporting LGBTQ youth. Evidence-based strategies to support child and adolescent sexual health in homes, schools, and communities are then presented. The book concludes with a proposed model for integrating supports across settings to comprehensively promote youth sexual health.

Gina Coffee, PhD, is an associate professor and program co-chair in the school psychology program at Loyola University Chicago. In practice, teaching, and research, she focuses on the prevention of academic, behavioral, social, emotional, and health difficulties in children through collaboration with educators, parents, and community members. In 2010, she was awarded an Early Career Research Award by the Society for the Study of School Psychology.

Pamela Fenning, PhD, is a professor at Loyola University Chicago. She is a licensed clinical and school psychologist in Illinois and is currently the co-chair of the National Association of School Psychologists' Child and Professions Committee.

Tommy L. Wells, EdS, MSEd, is a doctoral student in the school psychology program at Loyola University Chicago. Before entering the program, he served both as a school counselor and a counselor in private practice.

PROMOTING YOUTH SEXUAL HEALTH

Home, School, and Community Collaboration

Gina Coffee, Pamela Fenning, and Tommy L. Wells

Routledge
Taylor & Francis Group

NEW YORK AND LONDON

First published 2016
by Routledge
711 Third Avenue, New York, NY 10017

and by Routledge
27 Church Road, Hove, East Sussex BN3 2FA

Routledge is an imprint of the Taylor & Francis Group, an informa business

Library of Congress Cataloging-in-Publication Data
Coffee, Gina. Promoting youth sexual health: home, school, and community collaboration/by Gina Coffee, Pamela Fenning, and Tommy L. Wells.
pages cm
Includes bibliographical references and index.
1. Sexual health. 2. Youth—Sexual behavior. 3. Sexual ethics for youth. 4. Sex instruction for youth. I. Fenning, Pamela. II. Wells, Tommy L. III. Title.
RA788.C625 2015
613.9071'2—dc23
2015012464

ISBN: 978-1-138-77463-6 (hbk)
ISBN: 978-1-138-77464-3 (pbk)
ISBN: 978-1-315-77438-1 (ebk)

Typeset in Bembo
by Book Now Ltd, London

Printed and bound in the United States of America by Publishers Graphics, LLC on sustainably sourced paper.

To the children, adolescents, families, mentors, and advocates who have inspired us in writing this book.

—GC, PF, TW

To my partner, Jeff, and my own two adolescents, Abby and Alyssa, with deep love and gratitude.

—PF

CONTENTS

FIGURES

TABLES

1

AN INTRODUCTION TO CHILD AND ADOLESCENT SEXUAL HEALTH

The World Health Organization (WHO) defines sexual health as "a state of physical, emotional, mental and social well-being related to sexuality; it is not merely the absence of disease, dysfunction or infirmity. Sexual health requires a positive and respectful approach to sexuality and sexual relationships, as well as the possibility of having pleasurable and safe sexual experiences, free of coercion, discrimination and violence. For sexual health to be attained and maintained, the sexual rights of all persons must be respected, protected and fulfilled" (2002).

The WHO (2002) further advances that:

- "Sexual health is about well-being, not merely the absence of disease.
- Sexual health involves respect, safety and freedom from discrimination and violence.
- Sexual health depends on the fulfilment of certain human rights.
- Sexual health is relevant throughout the individual's lifespan, not only to those in the reproductive years, but also to both the young and the elderly.
- Sexual health is expressed through diverse sexualities and forms of sexual expression.
- Sexual health is critically influenced by gender norms, roles, expectations and power dynamics."

Within this context, the purpose of this book is to provide school- and community-based health professionals and preventionists/interventionists who work with children and adolescents (e.g., psychologists, social workers, counselors, nurses, educators)—especially those who work collaboratively with homes, schools, and communities—with guidance in promoting sexual health among children and adolescents. In our collective experiences as mental health professionals who work with youth in schools and who collaborate with educators, families, and community members to support youths' health development, it is our belief that the promotion of sexual health among youth is an essential component to overall physical, emotional, cognitive, and social health.

Current State of Promoting Sexual Health among Children and Adolescents

In recent years, there have been many positive trends in the sexual behaviors of American youth (NCSH, 2013). For example, "youth are waiting longer to initiate sex, rates of condom usage have increased, the number of youths' sexual partners has decreased, and the teen pregnancy and birth rates have declined significantly. Many youth today engage in conversations about sex and sexual health with their partners and parents, and most access sexual and reproductive health care services" (2013, p. 2). Notwithstanding these encouraging trends, however, the need for attention to and promotion of sexual health among children and adolescents, if even just from a physical standpoint, continues to be great, as youth are still contracting and transmitting sexually transmitted infections (STIs) and human immunodeficiency virus (HIV), becoming pregnant, and engaging in sexual risk behaviors (see Chapter 2). In fact, some data indicate that youth 15–24 years of age represent 9.1 million of the 18.9 million new cases of STIs annually, and 615,000 adolescents become pregnant each year (Guttmacher Institute, 2014).

Although the sexual health of youth, as well as engagement in sexual risk behaviors, may certainly be influenced by many factors, access to and the provision of comprehensive and effective sexuality education may well be a necessary, though not sufficient, tool for prevention (see Chapter 4). To that end, through the collaborative efforts of the Future of Sex Education (FoSE) initiative, the *National Sexuality Education Standards: Core Content and Skills, K-12* (FoSE, 2012) were recently developed to provide a framework for school-based, developmentally and age-appropriate sexuality education for young people—noting that sexuality education is inconsistently implemented across the nation and school curricula typically only provide a median of 17.2 hours of instruction (across elementary, middle, and high school) devoted to HIV, STIs, and pregnancy prevention (FoSE, 2012). In alignment with the WHO definition of sexual health, the National Sexuality Education Standards have identified seven domains of sexuality education that are essential for youth: anatomy and physiology, puberty and adolescent development, identity, pregnancy and reproduction, sexually transmitted diseases (STDs) and HIV, healthy relationships, and personal safety.

Sexual Health Resources

The development of the National Sexuality Education Standards represents a significant advance in the field, as the standards not only call attention to the sexuality education needs of youth across childhood and adolescence but also provide a guiding framework for health professionals and preventionists/interventionists who wish to develop and/or implement developmentally and age-appropriate sexuality education.

In addition to the National Sexuality Education Standards, a multitude of sexual health resources is available online for health professionals, preventionists/interventionists, families, and youth themselves. That is, government agencies, advocacy groups, and others have developed invaluable and informative resources designed not only to raise awareness of the sexual health needs of youth but also to educate and inform youth and those who work with them of practices and strategies to promote sexual health.

Examples of online resources for sexual health are presented in Tables 1.1 and 1.2. In addition to providing educational materials for its users, the websites presented in Table 1.2 also include databases of youth sexual behaviors. For example, Child Trends (http://www.childtrends.org) is a nonprofit, nonpartisan research center. Among the data compiled and reported regarding teen pregnancy and reproductive health, the Child Trends indicator list includes information about adolescents who have ever been raped, birth control pill use, children and youth with AIDS, condom use, dating, oral sex behaviors among teens, sexually active teens, sexually experienced teens, STIs, and statutory rape. Through an examination of the data available from multiple institutions, the interested reader may stay abreast of the current state of youth sexual health and behaviors.

The purpose of this chapter is to provide an introduction to child and adolescent sexual health. The remainder of this book is broadly structured around two complementary sections. In the first half of the book, we present an introduction to relevant topics surrounding sexual health of youth. In Chapter 2 (Sexual Risk Behaviors of Children and Adolescents), we present the reader with an overview of the sexual risk behaviors in which children and adolescents engage. The chapter begins with a definition and examples of sexual risk behaviors such as engaging in sexual intercourse, engaging in unprotected sexual intercourse, and/or having sex with four or more partners in their lifetime (CDC, 2014a). The chapter concludes with data regarding the prevalence of sexual risk behaviors among children and adolescents. We continue the discussion of sexual risk behaviors in Chapter 3 (Sexual Risk and Protective Factors) by exploring risk and protective factors that may contribute to engagement in sexual risk behaviors (e.g., Kirby & Lepore, 2007). Environmental and individual risk and protective factors known to influence sexual behavior, pregnancy, and STIs are identified and described. Environmental factors include those associated with the community, family, peer, and romantic partner. Individual factors include those associated with biological factors; race/ethnicity; attachment to and success in school; attachment to community; attachment to faith communities; problem or risk-taking behavior; cognitive and personality traits; emotional well-being and distress; sexual beliefs, attitudes, and skills; and relationships with romantic partners and previous sexual

Table 1.1 Online Resources for Sexual Health

	Mission
ACT (Assets Coming Together) for Youth Center of Excellence—http://www.actforyouth.net Advocates for Youth—http://www.advocatesforyouth.org	"ACT (Assets Coming Together) for Youth Center of Excellence connects research to practice in the areas of positive youth development and adolescent sexual health." "Established in 1980 as the Center for Population Options, Advocates for Youth champions efforts that help young people make informed and responsible decisions about their reproductive and sexual health. Advocates believes it can best serve the field by boldly advocating for a more positive and realistic approach to adolescent sexual health. Advocates focuses its work on young people ages 14–25 in the U.S. and around the globe."
Answer: Sex Ed, Honestly—http://answer.rutgers.edu/	"Answer is now an award-winning, national organization, providing invaluable sexuality education resources to millions of young people and adults every year. Our strategic plan for 2013–2017 is an ambitious one that will enable us to revolutionize sexuality education in the United States."
Centers for Disease Control and Prevention (CDC) Adolescent and School Health—http://www.cdc.gov/healthyyouth/sexualbehaviors/index.htm	"CDC promotes the health and well-being of children and adolescents to enable them to become healthy and productive adults."
GSA Network—http://www.gsanetwork.org/sexualhealth	The GSA Network offers resources for the sexual health needs of lesbian, gay, bisexual, and transgender youth.
American Sexual Health Association—http://www.iwannaknow.org/teens/index.html	"iwannaknow.org offers information on sexual health for teens and young adults. This is where you will find the facts, the support, and the resources to answer your questions, find referrals, and get access to in-depth information about sexual health, sexually transmitted infections (STIs), healthy relationships, and more."
Illinois Caucus for Adolescent Health (ICAH)—http://www.icah.org/sexed	"ICAH is a network of empowered youth and allied adults who transform public consciousness and increase the capacity of family, school and healthcare systems to support the sexual health, rights and identities of youth."

National Campaign—http://thenationalcampaign.org

"Our mission is to improve the lives and future prospects of children and families and, in particular, to help ensure that children are born into stable, two-parent families who are committed to and ready for the demanding task of raising the next generation.

Our strategy is to prevent teen pregnancy and unplanned pregnancy, especially among single, young adults."

National Coalition for Sexual Health (NCSH)—http://nationalcoalitionforsexualhealth.org

"The NCSH aims to make sexual health a common part of our national discourse and promote high quality sexual health care services. The NCSH brings together organizations and individuals who have a stake in not just advancing sexual health, but in advancing the overall health of our nation."

The Sexuality Information and Education Council of the United States (SIECUS)—http://www.siecus.org

"SIECUS educates, advocates, and informs.

Educate: We help schools and communities develop comprehensive sexuality education curricula, train teachers to provide high quality sexuality education in the classroom, and help parents talk to their kids about sex.

Advocate: We educate policymakers and their staff about issues related to sexuality and train advocates on the local, state, and national levels to build support for comprehensive sexuality education and access to reproductive health information and services.

Inform: We produce countless resources for a wide variety of audiences—from policymakers to parents, healthcare providers to teens—to ensure that everyone has access to accurate, complete, and up-to-date information about sexuality."

WHO—http://www.who.int/reproductivehealth/topics/adolescence/en/

"WHO is the directing and coordinating authority for health within the United Nations system. It is responsible for providing leadership on global health matters, shaping the health research agenda, setting norms and standards, articulating evidence-based policy options, providing technical support to countries and monitoring and assessing health trends."

Table 1.2 Online Resources for Sexual Health—Data Sources

	Mission
Add Health—http://www.cpc.unc.edu/projects/addhealth	"The National Longitudinal Study of Adolescent to Adult Health (Add Health) is a longitudinal study of a nationally representative sample of adolescents in grades 7–12 in the United States during the 1994–95 school year. The Add Health cohort has been followed into young adulthood with four in-home interviews, the most recent in 2008, when the sample was aged 24–32."
Child Trends—http://www.childtrends.org	"Child Trends is a nonprofit, nonpartisan research center that provides valuable information and insights on the well-being of children and youth. For more than 30 years, policymakers, funders, educators and service providers in the U.S. and around the world have relied on our data and analyses to improve policies and programs serving children and youth."
Guttmacher Institute—http://www.guttmacher.org	"Now in its fifth decade, the Guttmacher Institute continues to advance sexual and reproductive health and rights through an interrelated program of research, policy analysis and public education designed to generate new ideas, encourage enlightened public debate and promote sound policy and program development. The Institute's overarching goal is to ensure the highest standard of sexual and reproductive health for all people worldwide."
Youth Risk Behavior Surveillance System (YRBSS)—http://www.cdc.gov/HealthyYouth/yrbs/index.htm	"The Youth Risk Behavior Surveillance System (YRBSS) monitors six types of health-risk behaviors that contribute to the leading causes of death and disability among youth and adults, including— • Behaviors that contribute to unintentional injuries and violence • Sexual behaviors that contribute to unintended pregnancy and STDs, including HIV infection • Alcohol and other drug use • Tobacco use • Unhealthy dietary behaviors • Inadequate physical activity YRBSS also measures the prevalence of obesity and asthma among youth and young adults. YRBSS includes a national school-based survey conducted by CDC and state, territorial, tribal, and local surveys conducted by state, territorial, and local education and health agencies and tribal governments."

behavior. The chapter concludes with a specific focus on risk and protective factors that are alterable or amenable to change.

With Chapter 4 (Relevant Standards and Professional Guidelines for the Promotion of Sexual Health of Children and Adolescents), we transition from our discussion of sexual risk behaviors to relevant standards and guidelines that inform the promotion of sexual health, as well as developmental and cultural considerations. The purpose of this chapter is to present the reader with a description of relevant standards and professional guidelines for the promotion of sexual health of children and adolescents. The chapter includes a discussion of legal and ethical considerations, as well as an overview of the recently released National Sexuality Education Standards (including the historical context, content of the standards, and implications for sexual health promotion).

In Chapter 5 (Developmental and Cultural Considerations in Promoting Sexual Health), we present an examination of developmental and cultural considerations in the promotion of sexual health among children and adolescents. The first half of the chapter includes an overview of child and adolescent development and details considerations for providing developmentally appropriate sexuality education. For example, sexuality education for younger children may focus on body parts, basic bodily functions, and the development of healthy friendships, whereas sexuality education for youth may focus on the functions of reproductive organs, pregnancy, STIs, and safer sex behaviors. Consideration is also given to best practices for providing sexuality education to children and adolescents with developmental and cognitive disabilities. Then, in the second half of the chapter, we present a discussion of considerations in the delivery of culturally responsive sexuality education. The reader will be guided through a process of assessing the specific needs of youth within a community and using data from the needs assessment to inform adaptations or modifications of sexuality education curricula.

Beginning with Chapter 6 (Promoting the Sexual Health of LGBTQIA Youth), we use the second half of the book to share evidence-based practices in promoting sexual health of youth. In this chapter, we present the reader with a discussion of sexual health among youth who identify as LGBTQIA. The chapter begins with an overview of the sexual risk behaviors and sexual health needs of LGBTQIA youth who may differ from heterosexual youth. For example, LGBTQIA youth may need sexuality education that emphasizes the prevention of STIs rather than unintended pregnancy. As an additional example, given that LGBTQIA youth can be subjected to discrimination within communities and perhaps the lack of healthy same-sex relationship models in their proximity, they may benefit from sexuality education that emphasizes ways to establish and navigate healthy same-sex romantic relationships. Next, an examination of the extent to which existing sexuality education curricula are responsive to LGBTQIA needs is presented. The chapter concludes with evidence-based strategies for promoting the sexual health of LGBTQIA youth. Strategies will address building awareness, conducting needs assessments with sexual minority youth in a given community, using data to inform education efforts, and coordinating efforts between youths' home, school, and community settings.

With Chapter 7 (Promoting the Sexual Health of Children and Adolescents at Home), we begin to explore strategies for use across settings (i.e., home, school, and community). The purpose of this chapter is to present the reader with evidence-based strategies for promoting the sexual health of children and adolescents at home. The first portion of the chapter includes a discussion of the role of parents/guardians and families in sexual health promotion. The chapter continues with an examination of strategies health professionals and prevention-ists/interventionists who work with children and adolescents can use to teach/work with parents/guardians and families to promote their children's sexual health. One example of a strategy may be the use of consultation with parents/guardians and families to teach effective communication between families and children. Another strategy may be the coordination, explanation, and delivery of services and resources among home, school, and community. For example, health professionals and preventionists/interventionists may act as valuable resources for families in accessing and understanding the sexuality education resources available to them at school and in the community and similarly act as a liaison between schools and communities and families.

The purpose of Chapter 8 (Promoting the Sexual Health of Children and Adolescents at School) is to present the reader with evidence-based considerations for promoting the sexual health of children and adolescents at school. The first half of the chapter includes a discussion of the role of schools in sexual health promotion, including system variables that may enhance or impede sexual health promotion within schools. For example, the promotion of sexual health within schools is dependent on federal and state funding, community beliefs and support, the general school curricula, health curricula, teacher preparation, student interest, scheduling, school climate, etc. The chapter continues with an examination of school-based sexuality education programs health professionals and preventionists/interventionists who work in/with schools can implement and evaluate. We conclude the chapter by proposing a model for comprehensively promoting sexual health to meet the needs of all students in schools.

Following the discussion of strategies in home and school settings, in Chapter 9 (Promoting the Sexual Health of Children and Adolescents in the Community), we examine the role of communities in promoting the sexual health of children and adolescents. We begin with a discussion of building community coalitions. We then review the roles community-based organizations, healthcare providers, and faith-based organizations can play in supporting youths' sexual health development.

Finally, we conclude this book with Chapter 10 (Conclusion and Future Directions) by proposing an interdisciplinary, home, school, and community collaborative model to promote sexual health among youth.

References

ACT for Youth. (n.d.). Retrieved January 1, 2015, from http://www.actforyouth.net

Add Health. (n.d.). Retrieved January 1, 2015, from http://www.cpc.unc.edu/projects/addhealth

Advocates for Youth. (n.d.). Retrieved January 1, 2015, from http://www.advocatesforyouth.org

American Sexual Health Association. (n.d.). *I wanna know!: Sexual health and you.* Retrieved January 1, 2015, from http://www.iwannaknow.org/teens/index.html

Answer: Sex Ed, Honestly. (n.d.). Retrieved January 1, 2015, from http://answer.rutgers.edu

Centers for Disease Control and Prevention (CDC). (2014a, June 12). *Adolescent and school health.* Retrieved January 1, 2015, from http://www.cdc.gov/healthyyouth/sexualbehaviors/index.htm

CDC. (2014b, July 9). *Youth risk behavior surveillance system (YRBSS).* Retrieved January 1, 2015, from http://www.cdc.gov/HealthyYouth/yrbs/index.htm

Child Trends. (n.d.). Retrieved January 1, 2015, from http://www.childtrends.org

Future of Sex Education Initiative (FoSE). (2012). *National Sexuality Education Standards: Core Content and Skills, K-12.* Retrieved from http://www.futureofsexeducation.org/documents/josh-fose-standards-web.pdf

Gay-Straight Alliance Network. (n.d.). *LGBTQ youth sexual health information.* Retrieved January 1, 2015, from http://www.gsanetwork.org/sexualhealth

Guttmacher Institute. (2014). *American teens' sexual and reproductive health.* Retrieved January 4, 2015, from http://www.guttmacher.org/pubs/FB-ATSRH.html

Guttmacher Institute. (n.d.). Retrieved January 4, 2015, from http://www.guttmacher.org

Illinois Caucus for Adolescent Health (ICAH). (n.d.). Retrieved January 1, 2015, from http://www.icah.org/sexed

Kirby, D., & Lepore, G. (2007). *Sexual risk and protective factors: factors affecting teen sexual behavior, pregnancy, childbearing, and sexually transmitted disease: Which are important? Which can you change?* Washington, DC: The National Campaign to Prevent Teen and Unplanned Pregnancy.

National Coalition for Sexual Health (NCSH). (2013). *The sexual health of youth in the United States: An audience profile.* Retrieved January 1, 2015, from http://nationalcoalitionforsexualhealth.org/data-research/audience-profiles/document/AdolescentBackgrounder-final.pdf

NCSH. (n.d.). Retrieved January 1, 2015, from http://nationalcoalitionforsexualhealth.org

The National Campaign. (n.d.). *To prevent teen and unplanned pregnancy.* Retrieved January 1, 2015, from http://thenationalcampaign.org

The Sexuality Information and Education Council of the United States (SIECUS). (n.d.). Retrieved January 1, 2015, from http://www.siecus.org

World Health Organization (WHO). (2002). *Sexual health.* Retrieved January 1, 2015, from http://www.who.int/topics/sexual_health/en

2

SEXUAL RISK BEHAVIORS OF CHILDREN AND ADOLESCENTS

As noted in Chapter 1, the national rates of STI contraction are highest among youth, and the rates of unintended pregnancies are equally staggering (Guttmacher Institute, 2014). One way of beginning to understand the origins of these statistics is to explore the sexual risk behaviors in which children and adolescents engage. The purpose of this chapter is to present an overview of these sexual risk behaviors and the prevalence of sexual risk behaviors among children and adolescents.

Sexual risk behaviors are sexual behaviors that are associated with an increased risk of a negative outcome such as the contraction or transmission of a disease or unintended pregnancy. Although many sexual behaviors carry risk, the risk of contracting or transmitting an STI or of becoming pregnant varies, so behaviors can be categorized along a continuum of risk (Hock, 2011). For example, sexual behaviors such as kissing; touching or massage; fondling or body rubbing; fantasy, cybersex, or phone sex; using clean sex toys; and masturbation or mutual masturbation carry a low risk of contracting or transmitting an STI. Of moderate risk on the continuum are sexual behaviors such as manual stimulation of one another, vaginal intercourse with a male or female condom, anal intercourse with a male or female condom, oral sex on a man with a condom, or oral sex on a woman with a dental dam. Finally, sexual behaviors including vaginal intercourse without a condom, anal intercourse without a condom, and oral sex without protection carry a high risk of contracting or transmitting an STI and/or becoming pregnant.

In addition to the above sexual behaviors, behaviors that are more distal to direct sexual contact may also be considered sexual risk behaviors. Examples include early onset of sexual behavior (e.g., before the age of 13 years); having multiple sexual partners; changing sexual partners frequently; having nonexclusive sexual partners; using unreliable contraceptive methods or using contraceptive methods inconsistently; engaging in sexual behaviors with a partner who engages in sexual risk behaviors, who injects drugs, or who has a history of injecting drugs; having sex while under the influence of alcohol or drugs; or exchanging sex for drugs or money.

Although individuals of any age may certainly engage in sexual risk behaviors, the consequences for children and adolescents who engage in risky behaviors can have significant lifelong implications. For example, a girl who becomes pregnant before completing high school is at greater risk of dropping out (Shuger, 2012), which will directly impact her ability to independently progress educationally, vocationally, and financially. Similarly, an adolescent who contracts an STI or HIV could be more susceptible to contracting additional STIs or other infections or illnesses due to a weakened immune system or may experience permanent health consequences (e.g., infertility) as a result of an STI or of an untreated STI. Further, the nature of the STI (e.g., herpes, HIV) influences the risk for transmission of the STI to others across one's lifespan. Given the significant repercussions of child and adolescent engagement in sexual risk behaviors, it becomes especially important to accurately assess engagement in sexual risk behaviors in a manner that can ultimately facilitate prevention and intervention efforts.

Introduction to the Youth Risk Behavior Survey

High School YRBS

The Youth Risk Behavior Survey (YRBS), a component of the Youth Risk Behavior Surveillance System (YRBSS) designed by the U.S. CDC, offers a way to nationally assess priority health risk behaviors, including sexual risk behaviors (Kann et al., 2014). The YRBSS monitors (a) behaviors that contribute to unintentional injuries and violence; (b) tobacco use; (c) alcohol and other drug use; (d) sexual behaviors that contribute to unintended pregnancy and STIs, including HIV infection; (e) unhealthy dietary behaviors; and (f) physical inactivity as well as prevalence of obesity and asthma. Within the YRBSS, national, state, and large urban school district data are collected through the administration of the high school YRBS, a school-based survey that is completed by students in grades 9–12 and is available for administration by the CDC (national high school YRBS), states, or local districts (standard high school YRBS). The national 2013 high school YRBS consists of 86 items on the standard high school YRBS, along with six additional items that measure use of hallucinogenic drugs, engagement in exercises to strengthen or tone muscles, testing for HIV, use of sunscreen, use of indoor tanning devices, and hours of sleep on an average school night.

The survey has been administered every 2 years since 1991, and the sampling is designed to yield nationally representative data. Following administration, data are analyzed and made available the following summer. As such, data from the

2013 administration (September 2012–December 2013) were published during the summer of 2014. The 2013 administration yielded data from the national survey, 42 state surveys, and 21 large urban school district surveys and can be used to present a current snapshot of youth's engagement in health risk behaviors, as well as trends in behaviors since 1991. Further, the YRBS is publicly available at no cost. Therefore, apart from the sites the CDC samples and funds for administration of the YRBS, any district, community, or group may also choose to administer the YRBS.

Among the 104 health risk behaviors assessed by the YRBS, the survey provides a measure of the following sexual behaviors that contribute to unintended pregnancy and STIs, including HIV infection:

- ever had sexual intercourse;
- had sexual intercourse before the age of 13 years;
- had sexual intercourse with four or more persons during their life;
- currently sexually active (within the previous 3 months);
- condom use during last sexual intercourse;
- birth control pill use before last sexual intercourse;
- intrauterine device (IUD) or implant use before last sexual intercourse;
- shot, patch, or birth control ring use before last sexual intercourse;
- birth control pill; IUD or implant; or shot, patch, or birth control ring use before last sexual intercourse;
- condom use and birth control pill; IUD or implant; or shot, patch, or birth control ring use before last sexual intercourse;
- did not use any method to prevent pregnancy;
- drank alcohol or used drugs before last sexual intercourse;
- taught in school about AIDS or HIV infection;
- tested for HIV.

Middle School YRBS

In addition to the YRBS designed for completion by high school students, a 50-item abbreviated version of the high school YRBS is available for administration with middle school students and is designed to assess the health behaviors of students in grades 6–8 (e.g., Shanklin, Brener, McManus, Kinchen, & Kann, 2007). There is, in fact, no national middle school YRBS. Instead, the survey is completed by middle school students in states, cities, territories, and tribal governments that choose to administer the middle school YRBS. The 2013 administration yielded data from 18 states, 14 cities, 4 territories, and 1 tribal government.

Of the 50 items on the middle school YRBS, the following behaviors that may impact unintended pregnancies and/or the contraction or transmission of STIs are assessed:

- ever had sexual intercourse;
- had sexual intercourse before the age of 11 years;
- had sexual intercourse with three or more persons during their life;
- condom use during last sexual intercourse;
- taught in school about AIDS or HIV infection.

Unlike the high school YRBS, the middle school YRBS does not include items assessing multiple methods of contraception, use of alcohol or drugs prior to last sexual intercourse, or testing for HIV.

LGBTQ Youth

Along with general data summarizing youth engagement in sexual risk behaviors across grade or developmental levels, some sites have also elected to include items on the high school YRBS that measure sexual identity, sex of sexual contacts, or both. With regard to sexual identity, youth indicated they identified as heterosexual, gay or lesbian, bisexual, or unsure. Youth further indicated their sexual contacts were of same sex only, opposite sex only, or both sexes. In 2011, a report summarizing these data was published: "Sexual Identity, Sex of Sexual Contacts, and Health-Risk Behaviors among Students in Grades 9-12—Youth Risk Behavior Surveillance, Selected Sites, United States, 2001-2009" (Kann et al., 2011).

Prevalence of Sexual Risk Behaviors among Children and Adolescents

High School YRBS

The national prevalence of sexual risk behaviors among youth in grades 9–12 (n = 13,583) is presented in Table 2.1 (Kann et al., 2014). Data are presented based on gender, race, and grade for the following behaviors: (a) ever had sexual intercourse, (b) had sexual intercourse before the age of 13 years, (c) had sexual intercourse with four or more persons during their life, (d) currently sexually active, (e) did not use any method to prevent pregnancy, and (f) drank alcohol or used drugs before last sexual intercourse. Additionally, the interested reader is referred to Kann et al. (2014) for data specific to select states and large urban school districts.

Ever Had Sexual Intercourse

Nationally, 46.8% of youth who completed the 2013 YRBS reported having had sexual intercourse. The prevalence was 47.5% among males and 46% among females. Across racial groups, the prevalence was 60.6% among Black youth, 49.2% among Hispanic youth, and 43.7% among White youth. Across grade levels, the prevalence among youth was 30% in ninth grade, 41.4% in 10th grade, 54.1%

Table 2.1 Sexual Risk Behaviors—YRBS 2013 (in Percentages)

	Ever Had Sexual Intercourse M	F	Had Sexual Intercourse Before the Age of 13 Years M	F	Had Sexual Intercourse With Four or More Persons during Their Life M	F	Currently Sexually Active (within Last 3 Months) M	F	Did Not Use Any Method to Prevent Pregnancy (during Last Intercourse) M	F	Drank Alcohol or Used Drugs Before Last Sexual Intercourse M	F
Total	46.8		5.6		15		34		13.7		22.4	
	47.5	46.0	8.3	3.1	16.8	13.2	32.7	35.2	11.5	15.7	25.9	19.3
Racial/ethnic groups												
Black	60.6		14.0		26.1		42.1		15.9		22.8	
	68.4	53.4	24.0	4.9	37.5	15.8	47.0	37.6	11.2	21.2	24.9	20.5
Hispanic	49.2		6.4		13.4		34.7		19.7		24.0	
	51.7	46.9	9.2	3.8	16.5	10.5	34.7	34.7	15.4	23.7	27.0	21.3
White	43.7		3.3		13.3		32.8		11.1		21.3	
	42.2	45.3	4.4	2.1	12.4	14.1	29.7	35.9	10.1	11.9	25.1	18.2
Grades												
9	30		5.8		6.7		19.6		16.3		22.0	
	32.0	28.1	8.7	2.9	9.1	4.4	19.3	19.8	14.3	18.1	27.6	16.7
10	41.4		6.0		12.6		29.4		14.1		22.3	
	41.1	41.7	8.7	3.2	14.5	10.7	27.0	31.8	10.2	17.3	22.6	22.0
11	54.1		5.6		18.5		40.2		12.4		23.2	
	54.3	53.9	8.0	3.3	19.1	17.9	39.6	40.7	11.9	12.9	27.8	19.0
12	64.1		4.9		23.4		49.3		13.3		21.9	
	65.4	62.8	7.4	2.5	25.7	21.1	47.8	50.7	10.9	15.5	25.7	18.4

in 11th grade, and 64.1% in 12th grade. Collectively, data for Black males (68.4%) and males in 12th grade (65.4%) represented the highest percentages of youth who reported having had sexual intercourse. Further, with the exception of White youth and youth in 10th grade, a greater percentage of males compared to females within each racial group and grade level reported having had sexual intercourse. Conversely, data for White males (42.2%) and females in ninth grade (28.1%) represented the lowest percentages of youth who reported having had sexual intercourse. Across time, the percentage of youth who have reported having had sexual intercourse decreased from 1991 to 2001 and from 1991 to 2013 and did not change between 2011 and 2013.

Had Sexual Intercourse Before the Age of 13 Years

Nationally, 5.6% of youth who completed the 2013 YRBS reported having had sexual intercourse before the age of 13 years. The prevalence was 8.3% among males and 3.1% among females. Across racial groups, the prevalence was 14% among Black youth, 6.4% among Hispanic youth, and 3.3% among White youth. Across grade levels, the prevalence among youth who reported having had sexual intercourse before the age of 13 years was 5.8% in ninth grade, 6% in 10th grade, 5.6% in 11th grade, and 4.9% in 12th grade. Collectively, data for Black males (24%) and males in ninth and 10th grades (8.7%) represented the highest percentages of youth who reported having had sexual intercourse before the age of 13 years. Further, a greater percentage of males rather than females within each racial group and grade level reported having had sexual intercourse before the age of 13 years. Conversely, data for White females (2.1%) and females in 12th grade (2.5%) represented the lowest percentages of youth who reported having had sexual intercourse before the age of 13 years. Across time, the percentage of youth who reported having had sexual intercourse before the age of 13 years decreased from 1991 to 1997, from 1991 to 2013, and from 1997 to 2013.

Had Sexual Intercourse with Four or More Persons during Their Life

Nationally, 15% of youth who completed the 2013 YRBS reported having had sexual intercourse with four or more persons during their life. The prevalence was 16.8% among males and 13.2% among females. Across racial groups, the prevalence was 26.1% among Black youth, 13.4% among Hispanic youth, and 13.3% among White youth. Across grade levels, the prevalence among youth who reported having had sexual intercourse with four or more persons during their life was 6.7% in ninth grade, 12.6% in 10th grade, 18.5% in 11th grade, and 23.4% in 12th grade. Collectively, data for Black males (37.5%) and males in 12th grade (25.7%) represented the highest percentages of youth who reported having had sexual intercourse with four or more persons during their life. Further, with the exception of White youth, a greater percentage of males rather than females within each racial group and grade level reported having had sexual intercourse with four or more persons during their life. Conversely, data for Hispanic females (10.5%) and females in ninth grade (4.4%) represented the lowest percentages of youth who reported having had sexual intercourse with four or more persons during their life. Across time, the percentage of youth who reported having had sexual intercourse with four or more persons during their life decreased from 1991 to 2003 and from 1991 to 2013 and did not change between 2003 and 2013 or 2011 and 2013.

Currently Sexually Active

Nationally, 34% of youth who completed the 2013 YRBS reported currently being sexually active (within the last 3 months). The prevalence was 32.7% among males and 35.2% among females. Across racial groups, the prevalence was 42.1% among Black youth, 34.7% among Hispanic youth, and 32.8% among White youth. Across grade levels, the prevalence among youth was 19.6% in ninth grade, 29.4% in 10th grade, 40.2% in 11th grade, and 49.3% in 12th grade. Collectively, data for Black males (47%) and females in 12th grade (50.7%) represented the highest percentages of youth who reported currently being sexually active. Further, with the exception of Black and Hispanic youth, a greater percentage of females rather than males within each racial group and grade level reported currently being sexually active. Conversely, data for White males (29.7%) and males in ninth grade (19.3%) represented the lowest percentages of youth who reported currently being sexually active. Across time, the percentage of youth who have reported currently being sexually active decreased from 1991 to 2013, and did not change between 2011 and 2013.

Did Not Use Any Method to Prevent Pregnancy

Nationally, 13.7% of youth who completed the 2013 YRBS reported they did not use any method to prevent pregnancy during last intercourse. The prevalence among males was 11.5% and 15.7% among females. Across racial groups, the prevalence among Black youth was 15.9%, 19.7% among Hispanic youth, and 11.1% among White youth. Across grade levels, the prevalence among youth in ninth grade was 16.3%, 14.1% among youth in 10th grade, 12.4% among youth in 11th grade, and 13.3% among youth in 12th grade. Collectively, data for Hispanic females (23.7%) and females in 9th grade (18.1%) represented the highest percentages of youth who reported they did not use any method to prevent pregnancy. Further, a greater percentage of females rather than males within each racial group and grade level reported they did not use any method to prevent pregnancy. Conversely, data for White males (10.1%) and males in 10th grade (10.2%) represented the lowest percentages of youth who reported they did not use any method to prevent pregnancy. Across time, the percentage of youth who have reported they did not use any method to prevent pregnancy decreased from 1991 to 2007 and from 1991 to 2013, and did not change between 2007 and 2013 and 2011 and 2013.

Drank Alcohol or Used Drugs Before Last Sexual Intercourse

Nationally, 22.4% of youth who completed the 2013 YRBS reported they drank alcohol or used drugs before last sexual intercourse. The prevalence was 25.9% among males and 19.3% among females. Across racial groups, the prevalence was 22.8% among Black youth, 24% among Hispanic youth, and 21.3% among White youth. Across grade levels, the prevalence among youth was 22% in ninth grade, 22.3% in 10th grade, 23.2% in 11th grade, and 21.9% in 12th grade. Collectively, data for Hispanic males (27%) and males in 11th grade (27.8%) represented the highest percentages of youth who reported they drank alcohol or used drugs before last sexual intercourse. Further, a greater percentage of males rather than females within each racial group and grade level reported they drank alcohol or used drugs before last sexual intercourse. Conversely, data for White females (18.2%) and females in 12th grade (18.4%) represented the lowest percentages of youth who reported they drank alcohol or used drugs before last sexual inter-course. Across time, the percentage of youth who reported they drank alcohol or used drugs before last sexual intercourse increased from 1991 to 1999, decreased from 1999 to 2013, and did not change between 2011 and 2013.

The prevalence of sexual risk behaviors among high school youth, as self-reported through the 2013 YRBS, illuminates differences in some behaviors by gender, racial group, and grade level. For example, a greater percentage of males tend to engage in the measured risk behaviors. Of note, however, a greater percentage of females did not use any method to prevent pregnancy during last intercourse, and with the exception of Black and Hispanic youth, a greater percentage of females reported currently being sexually active. Further, a greater percentage of Black youth reported ever having had sexual intercourse, having had sexual intercourse before the age of 13 years, having had sexual intercourse with four or more persons during their life, and currently being sexually active. Of the remaining sexual risk behaviors, a greater percentage of Hispanic youth (particularly Hispanic females) reported not using any method to prevent pregnancy during last intercourse, as well as drinking alcohol or using drugs before last intercourse. Finally, a greater percentage of youth tend to engage in the following sexual risk behaviors as they get older: having had sexual intercourse, having had sexual intercourse with four or more persons in their life, and currently being sexually active.

In addition to the above sexual risk behaviors, the high school YRBS also pro-vides a measure of contraceptive use among youth. Data regarding the use of the following contraceptives are presented in Table 2.2: (a) condom; (b) birth control

Table 2.2 Contraceptive Use—YRBS 2013 (in Percentages)

	Condom			Birth Control Pill			IUD or Implant			Shot, Patch, or Birth Control Ring			Birth Control Pill; IUD or Implant; or Shot, Patch, or Birth Control Ring			Condom and Birth Control Pill; IUD or Implant; or Shot, Patch, or Birth Control Ring		
	Total	M	F	Total	M	F	Total	M	F	Total	M	F	Total	M	F	Total	M	F
Total	59.1	65.8	53.1	19.0	15.1	22.4	1.6	1.3	1.8	4.7	3.7	5.6	25.3	20.1	29.8	8.8	7.2	10.2
Racial/ethnic groups																		
Black	64.7	73.0	55.3	8.2	9.0	7.3	1.1	0.4	1.7	5.7	1.8	10.1	15.0	11.2	19.2	5.6	4.3	7.1
Hispanic	58.3	66.5	50.7	9.0	10.8	7.3	1.3	1.1	1.4	4.3	3.3	5.2	14.5	15.2	13.9	4.5	6.1	3.0
White	57.1	61.8	53.2	25.9	20.1	30.7	1.9	1.8	2.0	4.8	4.8	4.8	32.6	26.6	37.5	11.3	9.2	13.0
Grades																		
9	62.7	69.5	56.5	11.4	7.7	14.7	0.5	0.0	1.0	1.8	0.6	2.9	13.7	8.3	18.6	4.8	2.4	7.0
10	61.7	69.3	55.5	16.7	13.7	19.2	0.9	0.4	1.3	4.5	3.3	5.5	22.1	17.4	26.0	7.0	4.7	9.0
11	62.3	70.6	54.8	19.3	15.1	23.2	1.5	1.3	1.7	5.0	3.3	6.6	25.9	19.7	31.5	11.1	10.5	11.7
12	53.0	58.0	48.4	23.7	19.3	27.6	2.5	2.4	2.5	6.0	5.7	6.3	32.2	27.4	36.5	9.6	7.9	11.1

pill; (c) IUD or implant; (d) shot, patch, or birth control ring; (e) birth control pill; IUD or implant; or shot, patch, or birth control ring; and (f) condom and birth control pill; IUD or implant; or shot, patch, or birth control ring (Kann et al., 2014).

Condom Use

Nationally, of the 34% of youth who reported currently being sexually active, 59.1% reported they or their partner used a condom during last intercourse. The prevalence was 65.8% among males and 53.1% among females. Across racial groups, the prevalence was 64.7% among Black youth, 58.3% among Hispanic youth, and 57.1% among White youth. Across grade levels, the prevalence among youth was 62.7% in ninth grade, 61.7% in 10th grade, 62.3% in 11th grade, and 53% in 12th grade. Collectively, data for Black males (73.0%) and Black females (55.3%) represented the highest percentages of youth who reported they or their partners used a condom during last intercourse. Further, a greater percentage of males rather than females within each racial group and grade level reported they or their partners used a condom during last intercourse. Conversely, data for Hispanic females (50.7%) and females in 12th grade (48.4%) represented the lowest percentages of youth who reported they or their partners used a condom during last intercourse. Across time, the percentage of youth who reported they or their partners used a condom during last intercourse increased from 1991 to 2003 and from 1991 to 2013, decreased between 2003 and 2013, and did not change between 2011 and 2013.

Birth Control Pill Use

Nationally, of the 34% of youth who reported currently being sexually active, 19% of youth reported they or their partner used birth control pills before last intercourse to prevent pregnancy. The prevalence was 15.1% among males and 22.4% among females. Across racial groups, the prevalence was 8.2% among Black youth, 9% among Hispanic youth, and 25.9% among White youth. Across grade levels, the prevalence among youth was 11.4% in ninth grade, 16.7% in 10th grade, 19.3% in 11th grade, and 23.7% in 12th grade. Collectively, data for White males (20.1%) and White females (30.7%) represented the highest percentages of youth who reported they or their partners used birth control pills before last intercourse. Further, a greater percentage of White females than males and females across grades levels reported they or their partners used birth control pills before last intercourse. Conversely, data for Black females (7.3%), Hispanic females (7.3%), and males (7.7%) in ninth grade represented the lowest percentages of youth who reported they or their partners used birth control pills before last intercourse. Across time, the percentage of youth who reported they or their partners used birth control pills before last intercourse decreased from 1991 to 1995, increased between 1995 and 2013, and did not change between 2011 and 2013.

IUD or Implant Use

Nationally, of the 34% of youth who reported currently being sexually active, 1.6% reported they or their partner used an IUD or implant before last intercourse to prevent pregnancy. The prevalence was 1.3% among males and 1.8% among females. Across racial groups, the prevalence was 1.1% among Black youth, 1.3% among Hispanic youth, and 1.9% among White youth. Across grade levels, the prevalence among youth was 0.5% in ninth grade, 0.9% in 10th grade, 1.5% in 11th grade, and 2.5% in 12th grade. Percentages were consistently low across gender, racial, and age groups, with the clearest trend being an increase in use of an IUD or implant before last intercourse with grade level.

Shot, Patch, or Birth Control Ring Use

Nationally, of the 34% of youth who reported currently being sexually active, 4.7% reported they or their partner used a shot, patch, or birth control ring before last intercourse to prevent pregnancy. The prevalence was 3.7% among males and 5.6% among females. Across racial groups, the prevalence was 5.7% among Black youth, 4.3% among Hispanic youth, and 4.8% among White youth. Across grade levels, the prevalence among youth was 1.8% in ninth grade, 4.5% in 10th grade, 5% in 11th grade, and 6% in 12th grade. Collectively, data for Black females (10.1%) represented the highest percentage of youth, and data for Black males (1.8%) represented the lowest percentage of youth who reported they or their partners used a shot, patch, or birth control ring before last intercourse. Further, a greater percentage of females rather than males within each racial group and grade level reported they or their partners used a shot, patch, or birth control ring before last intercourse. Conversely, data for Black males (1.8%) and males in ninth grade (0.6%) represented the lowest percentages of youth who reported they or their partners used a shot, patch, or birth control ring before last intercourse.

Birth Control Pill; IUD or Implant; or Shot, Patch, or Birth Control Ring Use

Nationally, of the 34% of youth who reported currently being sexually active, 25.3% reported they or their partner used birth control pills; an IUD or implant; or a shot, patch, or birth control ring before last intercourse to prevent pregnancy. The prevalence was 20.1% among males and 29.8% among females. Across racial groups, the prevalence was 15% among Black youth, 14.5% among Hispanic youth, and 32.6% among White youth. Across grade levels, the prevalence among youth was 13.7% in ninth grade, 22.1% in 10th grade, 25.9% in 11th grade, and 32.2% in 12th grade. Collectively, data for White females (37.5%) represented the highest percentage of youth, and data for males in ninth grade (8.3%) represented the lowest percentage of youth who reported they or their partners used birth control pills; an IUD or implant; or a shot, patch, or birth control ring before last intercourse. Further, with the exception of Hispanic males, a greater percentage of females rather than males within each racial group and grade level reported they or their partners used birth control pills; an IUD or implant; or a shot, patch, or birth control ring before last intercourse.

Condom Use and Birth Control Pill; IUD or Implant; or Shot, Patch, or Birth Control Ring Use

Nationally, of the 34% of youth who reported currently being sexually active, 8.8% reported they or their partner used condom and birth control pills; an IUD or implant; or a shot, patch, or birth control ring before last intercourse to prevent pregnancy. The prevalence was 7.2% among males and 10.2% among females. Across racial groups, the prevalence was 5.6% among Black youth, 4.5% among Hispanic youth, and 11.3% among White youth. Across grade levels, the prevalence among youth was 4.8% in ninth grade, 7% in 10th grade, 11.1% in 11th grade, and 9.6% in 12th grade. Collectively, data for White females (13%) represented the highest percentage of youth, and data for Hispanic females (3%) represented the lowest percentage of youth who reported they or their partners used condom and birth control pills; an IUD or implant; or a shot, patch, or birth control ring before last intercourse. Further, with the exception of Hispanic males, a greater percentage of females rather than males within each racial group and grade level reported they or their partners used condom and birth control pills; an IUD or implant; or a shot, patch, or birth control ring before last intercourse. Data for males in ninth grade (2.4%) represented the lowest percentage of youth who reported they or their partners used condom and birth control pills; an IUD or implant; or a shot, patch, or birth control ring before last intercourse.

As with the above sexual risk behaviors, the prevalence of contraceptive use among high school youth, as self-reported through the 2013 YRBS, reveals some differences. Of the contraceptive methods measured, condom use during last intercourse was the most common method employed (approximately 50–60%). Black youth were the most likely among all racial/ethnic groups to report condom use. Further, with the exception of a drop in 12th grade, condom use appears to be stable across the high school years. Reported use of birth control pill; IUD or implant; or shot, patch, or birth control ring before last intercourse was the second most common method of birth control among youth (25.3%) followed by use of birth control pills before last intercourse (19%). Of these, White youth represented the greatest percentage of youth who used birth control pills only or birth control pill; IUD or implant; or shot, patch, or birth control ring and reported increased use with grade level. Finally, the fewest percentage of youth who used birth control reported using an IUD or implant (1.6%); shot, patch, or birth control ring (4.7%); or condom use and birth control pill; IUD or implant; or shot, patch, or birth control ring use (8.8%), with use generally increasing across grade levels.

In addition to the measurement of sexual risk behaviors and contraceptive use, the high school YRBS includes items focused on AIDS or HIV infection: (a) taught in school about AIDS or HIV infection and (b) tested for HIV (Kann et al., 2014). Data regarding student responses to these items are presented in Figures 2.1–2.4.

Taught in School about AIDS or HIV Infection

Nationally, 85.3% of youth who completed the 2013 YRBS reported they had been taught in school about AIDS or HIV infection. The prevalence was 85% among males and 85.8% among females. Across racial groups, the prevalence was 81.9% among Black youth, 84.4% among Hispanic youth, and 86.6% among White youth. Across grade levels, the prevalence among youth was 81.3% in ninth grade, 85.3% in 10th grade, 87.4% in 11th grade, and 88% in 12th grade. Percentages were consistent across gender, racial, and age groups, with the clearest trend being an increase with age.

Tested for HIV

Nationally, 12.9% of youth who completed the 2013 YRBS reported having been tested for HIV (excluding tests accompanying blood donations). The prevalence was 11.2% among males and 14.6% among females. Across racial groups, the

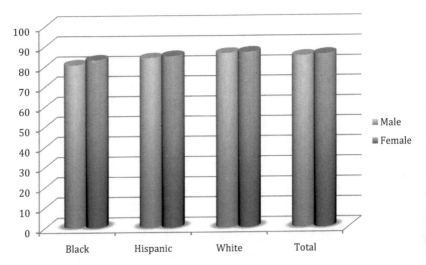

FIGURE 2.1 Taught in school about AIDS or HIV infection (racial groups)—YRBS 2013.

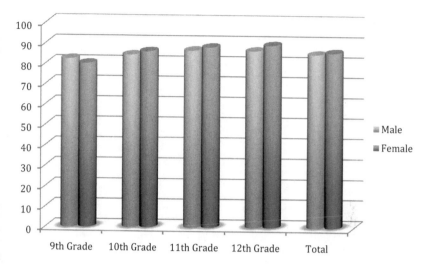

FIGURE 2.2 Taught in school about AIDS or HIV infection (grade levels)—YRBS 2013.

prevalence was 19.8% among Black youth, 12.8% among Hispanic youth, and 10.7% among White youth. Across grade levels, the prevalence among youth was 9.1% in ninth grade, 10.6% in 10th grade, 15.3% in 11th grade, and 17.2% in 12th grade. Collectively, data for Black males (18.7%) and Black females (20.9%) represented the highest percentage of youth who reported having been tested for HIV. Conversely, data for White males (8.7%) and females in ninth grade (7.8%) represented the lowest percentages of youth who reported having been tested for HIV. Further, with the exception of males in ninth grade, a greater percentage of females rather than males within each racial group and grade level reported having been tested for HIV. Across time, the percentage of youth who reported having been tested for HIV did not change between 2003 and 2013 or 2011 and 2013.

The above data certainly begin to provide a glimpse of sexual risk behaviors that high school students exhibit. Nonetheless, in our interpretation, we must consider limitations around the data. First, Kann et al. (2014) note three limitations relevant to data regarding youth sexual behaviors. Specifically, they clarify the data are only representative of youth who attended school during the survey administration period; rates of under- or overreporting cannot be estimated; and certain states (i.e., Georgia, Louisiana, Utah, and Virginia) do not administer items measuring sexual risk behaviors. Additionally, with regard to contraceptive use, we urge the reader to consider potential overlaps in data (e.g., "birth control pills" and "birth control pills; an IUD or implant; or a shot, patch, or birth control ring"), as well as the extent to which males are knowledgeable of their female partners' use of certain contraceptives (e.g., a shot, patch, or birth control ring). Finally, we urge the reader to also consider additional variables (e.g., dosage and quality) around youth's reports of being taught in school about AIDS or HIV infection.

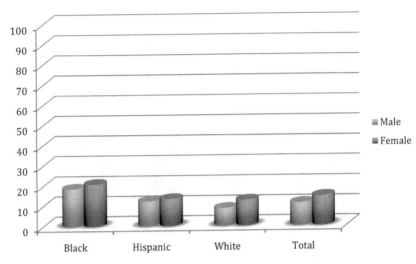

FIGURE 2.3 Tested for HIV (racial groups)—YRBS 2013.

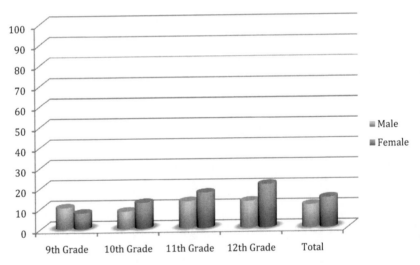

FIGURE 2.4 Tested for HIV (grade levels)—YRBS 2013.

Middle School YRBS

The middle school YRBS assesses sexual behaviors via four items: (a) ever had sexual intercourse, (b) had sexual intercourse before the age of 11 years, (c) had sexual intercourse with three or more persons, and (d) did not use a condom. Further, the middle school YRBS measures whether or not youth in grades 6–8 have been taught in school about AIDS or HIV infection. Given that middle school

YRBS data are available only from states, cities, territories, and tribal governments that choose to administer the middle school YRBS, national data regarding the prevalence of sexual risk behaviors among youth in grades 6–8 are not available. Nevertheless, data regarding the aforementioned behaviors are available for each state, city, territory, and tribal government via Youth Online (http://nccd.cdc.gov/youthonline), an interactive online platform that facilitates analysis of YRBS data.

For example, data collected from youth who completed the survey in 2013 in South Carolina indicated 19.4% of youth had had sexual intercourse, with 11.9% of youth in sixth grade having had sexual intercourse. Of the youth who completed the survey in the District of Columbia, 9.1% indicated they had sexual intercourse before the age of 11 years. In Milwaukee, Wisconsin, 9.3% of youth who completed the survey indicated they had had sexual intercourse with three or more persons (5.9% of youth in sixth grade). Finally, of youth who reported having had sexual intercourse, 48.7% who completed the survey in Hawaii indicated they did not use a condom during last sexual intercourse. In terms of instruction regarding AIDS or HIV infection, 62.7% of youth who completed the survey in Colorado indicated they had never been taught in school about AIDS or HIV infection. It should be noted that these data only represent examples of middle school youth's sexual behaviors in select geographic regions. Still, the data do indicate that young people are engaging in sexual risk behaviors and thereby underscore the importance of early prevention and intervention efforts.

LGBTQ Youth

The prevalence of sexual risk behaviors among LGBTQ youth in grades 9–12 from select sites between 2001 and 2009 (n = 3,733–36,774) is presented in Table 2.3 (Kann et al., 2011). Data are presented by reported sexual identity: gay or lesbian, bisexual, heterosexual, or unsure.

Table 2.3 Sexual Risk Behaviors—YRBS 2001–2009: Select Sites

	Ever Had Sexual Intercourse	Had Sexual Intercourse before the Age of 13 Years	Had Sexual Intercourse with Four or More Persons during Their Life	Currently Sexually Active (within Last 3 Months)	Drank Alcohol or Used Drugs before Last Sexual Intercourse
Gay or lesbian	67.1% (36.6–80.6)	19.8% (13.3–28.5)	29.9% (10.6–39.9)	53.2% (25.0–62.9)	35.1% (21.6–48.0)
Bisexual	69.0% (58.7–82.7)	14.6% (9.0–23.3)	28.2% (22.9–37.0)	52.6% (44.3–61.5)	29.9% (14.2–42.4)
Heterosexual	44.1% (28.4–56.2)	4.8% (4.3–11.2)	11.1% (7.6–20.7)	32.0% (19.3–41.6)	18.7% (14.4–23.9)
Unsure	43.0% (20.5–48.9)	13.1% (5.7–23.6)	18.8% (6.6–23.8)	32.0% (14.3–36.1)	37.9% (27.5–47.6)

Ever Had Sexual Intercourse

Between 2001 and 2009, a median of 67.1% (range 36.6–80.6%) of youth who identified as gay or lesbian, 69% (range 58.7–82.7%) of youth who identified as bisexual, 44.1% (range 28.4–56.2%) of youth who identified as heterosexual, and 43% (range 20.5–48.9%) of youth who reported being unsure of their sexual identity reported having ever had sexual intercourse.

Had Sexual Intercourse before the Age of 13 Years

Between 2001 and 2009, a median of 19.8% (range 13.3–28.5%) of youth who identified as gay or lesbian, 14.6% (range 9–23.3%) of youth who identified as bisexual, 4.8% (range 4.3–11.2%) of youth who identified as heterosexual, and 13.1% (range 5.7–23.6%) of youth who reported being unsure of their sexual identity reported having had sexual intercourse before the age of 13 years.

Had Sexual Intercourse with Four or More Persons during Their Life

Between 2001 and 2009, a median of 29.9% (range 10.6–39.9%) of youth who identified as gay or lesbian, 28.2% (range 22.9–37%) of youth who identified as bisexual, 11.1% (range 7.6–20.7%) of youth who identified as heterosexual, and 18.8% (range 6.6–23.8%) of youth who reported being unsure of their sexual identity reported having had sexual intercourse with four or more persons during their life.

Currently Sexually Active

Between 2001 and 2009, a median of 53.2% (range 25–62.9%) of youth who identified as gay or lesbian, 52.6% (range 44.3–61.5%) of youth who identified as

Table 2.4 Contraceptive Use—YRBS 2001–2009: Select Sites

	Condom Use	Birth Control Pill Use	Depo-Provera Use	Birth Control Pill Use or Depo-Provera Use	Condom Use and Birth Control Pill or Depo-Provera Use
Gay or lesbian	35.8%	10.5%	3.7%	10.5%	4.5%
	(17.2–57.8)	(0.0–15.1)	(0.0–6.3)	(3.7–21.4)	(0.0–15.7)
Bisexual	53.7%	16.2%	3.4%	20.8%	6.2%
	(42.6–54.8)	(7.5–26.4)	(1.1–10.4)	(10–30.8)	(1.7–12.9)
Heterosexual	65.5%	18.0%	3.6%	21.5%	7.6%
	(61.3–72.8)	(6.5–36.9)	(1.4–5.3)	(7.9–41.8)	(3.1–16.7)
Unsure	52.7%	15.5%	5.1%	19.6%	7.2%
	(32.3–73.4)	(4.2–25.2)	(0.0–9.2)	(6.1–31.8)	(0.0–13.0)

bisexual, 32% (range 19.3–41.6%) of youth who identified as heterosexual, and 32% (range 14.3–36.1%) of youth who reported being unsure of their sexual identity reported currently being sexually active (within the last 3 months).

Drank Alcohol or Used Drugs before Last Sexual Intercourse

Between 2001 and 2009, a median of 35.1% (range 21.6–48%) of youth who identified as gay or lesbian, 29.9% (range 14.2–42.4%) of youth who identified as bisexual, 18.7% (range 14.4–23.9%) of youth who identified as heterosexual, and 37.9% (range 27.5–47.6%) of youth who reported being unsure of their sexual identity reported they drank alcohol or used drugs before last sexual intercourse.

Condom Use

Between 2001 and 2009, a median of 35.8% (range 17.2–57.8%) of youth who identified as gay or lesbian, 53.7% (range 42.6–54.8%) of youth who identified as bisexual, 65.5% (range 61.3–72.8%) of youth who identified as heterosexual, and 52.7% (range 32.3–73.4%) of youth who reported being unsure of their sexual identity reported using a condom during last sexual intercourse.

Birth Control Pill Use

Between 2001 and 2009, a median of 10.5% (range 0–15.1%) of youth who identified as gay or lesbian, 16.2% (range 7.5–26.4%) of youth who identified as bisexual, 18% (range 6.5–36.9%) of youth who identified as heterosexual, and 15.5% (range 4.2–25.2%) of youth who reported being unsure of their sexual identity reported using birth control pills before last sexual intercourse to prevent pregnancy.

Depo-Provera Use

Between 2001 and 2009, a median of 3.7% (range 0–6.3%) of youth who identified as gay or lesbian, 3.4% (range 1.1–10.4%) of youth who identified as bisexual, 3.6% (range 1.4–5.3%) of youth who identified as heterosexual, and 5.1% (range 0–9.2%) of youth who reported being unsure of their sexual identity reported using Depo-Provera before last sexual intercourse to prevent pregnancy.

Birth Control Pill Use or Depo-Provera Use

Between 2001 and 2009, a median of 10.5% (range 3.7–21.4%) of youth who identified as gay or lesbian, 20.8% (range 10–30.8%) of youth who identified as bisexual, 21.5% (range 7.9–41.8%) of youth who identified as heterosexual, and 19.6% (range 6.1–31.8%) of youth who reported being unsure of their sexual identity reported using birth control pills or Depo-Provera before last sexual intercourse to prevent pregnancy.

Condom Use and Birth Control Pill or Depo-Provera Use

Between 2001 and 2009, a median of 4.5% (range 0–15.7%) of youth who identified as gay or lesbian, 6.2% (range 1.7–12.9%) of youth who identified as bisexual, 7.6% (range 3.1–16.7%) of youth who identified as heterosexual, and 7.2% (range 0–13%) of youth who reported being unsure of their sexual identity reported using a condom and birth control pills or Depo-Provera before last sexual intercourse to prevent pregnancy.

Taught in School about AIDS or HIV Infection

Between 2001 and 2009, a median of 77.4% (range 72.2–82.5%) of youth who identified as gay or lesbian, 82.8% (range 72.9–89.6%) of youth who identified as bisexual, 87.7% (range 82–91.4%) of youth who identified as heterosexual, and 72.5% (range 56.5–80.7%) of youth who reported being unsure of their sexual identity reported having been taught in school about AIDS or HIV infection.

Similar to the high school YRBS data above, the prevalence of sexual risk behaviors among LGBTQ youth in high school, as summarized across select sites between 2001 and 2009, illuminates differences in some behaviors by sexual identity. In general, it appears that a greater percentage of youth who identified as gay, lesbian, or bisexual (rather than heterosexual or unsure) engaged in the measured sexual risk behaviors.

Similar to the data presented from the 2013 high school YRBS, Kann et al. (2011) identified limitations of the presented data. In addition to limitations noted for the 2013 high school YRBS, Kann et al. (2011) noted that LGBTQ youth may be disproportionately represented among youth who are not in school; the data only represent states and large urban school districts that measured sexual identity, sex of sexual contacts, or both; the data only represent an association between LGBTQ status and risk behaviors, not causality; identification of statistically significant differences among all subgroups, as well as by sex and race/ethnicity, was limited due to small sample sizes; respondents may not have understood the item measuring sexual identity, may not have been aware of their sexual identity, or may have been unwilling to report it; and only sexual identity, rather than sexual attraction, was measured.

The purpose of this chapter was to identify the sexual risk behaviors in which youth engage and the prevalence of the behaviors as measured by the YRBS. Notwithstanding the identified limitations, we believe the YRBS data do begin to shed light on the needs for supports for students across grade levels, racial groups, and sexual orientation. Forthcoming, we will extend this discussion of prevalence to further explore risk/protective factors, legal and ethical standards, and best practice guidelines in the promotion of sexual health, developmental and cultural considerations, needs of LGBTQ youth, and promotion of sexual health across settings.

References

Guttmacher Institute. (2014). *American teens' sexual and reproductive health.* Retrieved January 4, 2015, from http://www.guttmacher.org/pubs/FB-ATSRH.html

Hock, R. R. (2011). *Human sexuality* (3rd ed.). New York, NY: Pearson.

Kann, L., Kinchen, S., Shanklin, S. L., Flint, K. H., Hawkins, J., Harris, W. A., et al. (2014). Youth Risk Behavior Surveillance – United States, 2013. *CDC Morbidity and Mortality Weekly Report, 63*(4), 1–168.

Kann, L., Olsen, E. O., McManus, T., Kinchen, S., Chyen, D., Harris, W. A., et al. (2011). Sexual identity, sex of sexual contacts, and health-risk behaviors among students in grades 9-12 – Youth Risk Behavior Surveillance, selected sites, United States, 2001-2009. *CDC Morbidity and Mortality Weekly Report, 60,* 1–133.

Shanklin, S. L., Brener, N., McManus, T., Kinchen, S., & Kann, L. (2007). *2005 middle school youth risk behavior survey.* Atlanta, GA: U.S. Department of Health and Human Services, Centers for Disease Control and Prevention.

Shuger, L. (2012). *Teen pregnancy and high school dropout: What communities can do to address these issues.* Washington, DC: The National Campaign to Prevent Teen and Unplanned Pregnancy and America's Promise Alliance.

3

SEXUAL RISK AND PROTECTIVE FACTORS

The purpose of this chapter is to present the reader with a description of risk and protective factors that may contribute to engagement in sexual risk behaviors (e.g., Kirby & Lepore, 2007). Environmental and individual risk and protective factors known to influence sexual behavior, pregnancy, and STIs will be identified and described. Environmental factors include those associated with the community, family, peers, and romantic partners, and individual factors include those associated primarily with adolescence and include biological factors; one's attachment to and success in school; attachment to community; attachment to faith communities; problem or risk-taking behavior; cognitive and personality traits; mental health issues, substance abuse, history of sexual/physical abuse, and relationship/dating violence. We consider risk and protective factors together within a particular context (e.g., home, school, community, peer, and individual). Factors related to race and ethnicity, while sometimes considered risk or protective factors, will be addressed in Chapter 5. We make this decision because it is our premise that one's race/ethnicity is not a risk factor but tied to the context or broader community one is a part of and requires specialized attention to cultural and societal factors, such as that within a social-ecological model espoused by the CDC (2014). We further assert that no one risk or protective factor is likely to automatically result in sexual risk behaviors, but such factors work in an interconnected fashion to produce desirable or undesirable health outcomes, as supported by those who argue for a multisystemic and integrated approach to examining risk and protective factors (Kotchick, Shaffer, Forehand, & Miller, 2001). We outline risk and protective factors as a means of arriving at recommendations that are tied to the literature and with the goal of encouraging healthy sexual practices among children and adolescents. After a description of each major category featuring risk and protective factors found in the literature, we provide either a brief case illustration or recommendations that preventionists/interventionists can consider based on this literature. We also provide context-specific recommendations in later chapters covering home, school, and community interventions.

Risk and Protective Factors Defined

Risk and protective factors are important to examine in relation to any health behavior, including sexual health. If risk and protective factors can be identified, they can drive prevention and intervention points. Kirby and Lepore (2007) identified a number of risk and protective factors related to sexual behavior of children and adolescents in their comprehensive report titled "Sexual Risk and Protective Factors: Factors Affecting Teen Sexual Behavior, Pregnancy, Childbearing and Sexually Transmitted Diseases" (under the auspices of ETR Associates and the National Campaign to Prevent Teen and Unwanted Pregnancy). They conducted an extensive literature search of research on the topic and described "risk factors" as

> those that encourage one or more behaviors that might lead to pregnancy or sexually transmitted disease . . . or discourage behaviors that might prevent pregnancy or sexually transmitted disease.
>
> (p. 1)

They defined "protective factors" as

> those that do just the opposite . . . they discourage one or more behaviors that might lead to pregnancy or STD or encourage behaviors that might prevent them.
>
> (p. 1)

Environmental Risk and Protective Factors

Environmental risk and protective factors are an important focus because they are likely ones that are "alterable" (Sinclair, Christenson, & Thurlow, 2005). In other words, they are modifiable based on actions such as prevention, intervention, and support, as opposed to individual factors that may be less amenable to prevention and treatment (e.g., socioeconomic status, gender). In this section, we outline community, family, and peer risk/protective factors followed by recommended strategies and activities in which preventionists/interventionists can engage in to support sexual health. A more detailed description of programing will be addressed in later chapters focused specifically on practices (e.g., see Chapter 7–9).

Community Risk and Protective Factors

An adolescent's connection to the community and neighborhood has been examined as a potential protective factor in reducing the likelihood of health risk behavior, including substance abuse/use and high-risk sexual behaviors. For example, a study conducted in England found that neighborhood connectedness was a protective factor for 15-year-old adolescents engaging in high-risk behavior based on a risk index that included alcohol use and sexual risk behavior of not using a condom during sexual intercourse (Brooks, Magnusson, Spencer, & Morgan, 2012). Cooper et al. (2014) examined community involvement and beliefs of community empowerment (e.g., perceptions that one has control and impact in the community) in a sample of African American adolescents participating in a Midwestern pregnancy prevention program. They measured risk behaviors that included substance use and sexual risk behaviors of ever having engaged in sexual intercourse and having multiple sexual partners. Community involvement did not have a direct but had an indirect impact on sexual risk behaviors through empowerment beliefs. In other words, community involvement was associated with higher empowerment beliefs. Empowerment beliefs, in turn, were associated with fewer sexual risk behaviors. These associations were not found for substance use. Markham et al. (2010) conducted a comprehensive literature review focused on the impact of connectedness made by adolescents in a range of settings on high-risk sexual behaviors. They employed the following stringent criteria for including studies in their analyses: (1) a multivariate analysis, (2) a sample size of over 100, and (3) publication in a peer-reviewed journal. Markham et al. (2010) found inconsistent evidence for a direct association of community connectedness as a protective factor to sexual risk behaviors, but also found no evidence for it as a risk factor. They suggested that more conclusive and methodologically sound research be done due to the limited number of studies available at the time they published their findings and due to significant findings for some racial/ethnic subgroups but not others. They cited one study (Crosby, DiClemente, Wingood, Harrington, Davies, & Oh, 2002, as cited in Markham et al., 2010) which found that connection to the community was a protective factor for African American females not engaging in the sexual risk behaviors of having had recent sex, having a high number of sexual partners, and failing to use contraception. Therefore, these findings suggest that the impact of community involvement on high-risk sexual behaviors is perhaps complex and merits further study. How community involvement was defined tended to vary, and in some cases, there were only a few items that measured the construct since connections in other contexts (e.g., school) were assessed at the same time. Further intervention work should be completed that evaluates the degree to which structures that support community involvement of adolescents as well as give them voice in decisions may impact sexual health decisions they make in the short term and across time.

Kirby and Lepore (2007) completed a comprehensive analysis of studies examining a multitude of risk and protective factors for sexual risk behaviors, and their work is pioneering and highly cited. They employed very specific inclusionary criteria for a particular factor to be classified as a risk or protective factor, which included documentation that it was statistically significant in at least three studies using multivariate analyses conducted in the United States. Please see Kirby and Lepore (2007) for a full description of the inclusionary criteria they employed. Using these criteria, Kirby and Lepore reported that faith communities served as a protective factor for avoiding high-risk sexual behaviors, which we situate in this discussion of community. They found support for the notion that connection to a faith community was associated with being less likely to initiate sex, as was attendance at religious services, but the direction of the relationship was determined to be unclear. It was not evident whether the religious affiliation promoted the lower likelihood of sexual initiation or the relationship was in the other direction.

With respect to community risk factors, Kirby and Lepore (2007) found that community risk factors such as living in a disorganized environment, defined as having high rates of community violence, substance abuse, and hunger, were associated with high-risk sexual behaviors. Although it may be considered outside of the realistic reach of preventionists/interventionists, community leaders, adolescents, and their extended families to modify large-scale systemic community factors, we argue that those working toward facilitating sexual health of youth need to do just that. Following is a brief set of recommendations to address community risk and protective factors that place children and adolescents in harm's way for sexual risk behaviors.

- Provide outlets for youth voice to be heard in decisions about their community, such as models enacted to empower youth voices. For example, prevention and intervention programs and youth empowerment strategies would be potential models to follow (Wilson, Dasho, Martin, Wallerstein, Wang, & Minkler, 2007).
- Work on facilitating activities that engage youth in community service activities and projects to increase their sense of control over their environment. For example, youth can participate in service projects within their community by assisting elders, reading to young children, and engaging in joint activities such as planting gardens and beautifying the neighborhood.
- Coordinate efforts to address needs in the community, such as combating hunger. For example, youth can coordinate and lead efforts at a local food pantry as part of efforts to build the community and cooperation among residents. When youth are involved in such efforts, community residents may work with adolescents in a positive way that dispels myths and stereotypes that may exist about teenagers in a particular community.
- Advocate for the delivery of mental health services such as substance abuse prevention and intervention, given the relationship of these significant issues to sexual risk behaviors and to community disorganization, which will be described more fully in relation to substance use issues. Parents and community members can work with one another to prevent, to the degree possible, access to alcohol and marijuana. Preventionists/interventionists, in collaboration with

drug and alcohol counselors and local law enforcement, can educate parents and extended family members about alcohol and drug use. For example, in a community that one of the authors is familiar with, there has been a breakout of heroine. One way of combating this is for parents and extended family members to be educated as to what types of behaviors and mood changes one might look for in a teenager. Open dialogue and sharing of information among community residents and parents is important, and adults need to give a common message to youth about the risk factors associated with substance use, not only as it relates to sexual health but with respect to other potential dire consequences as well. We contend, for instance, that parents who engage in behaviors such as buying alcohol for their children for parties at home are contributing to problems with substance use and sending unclear messages to young people.

School-Based Risk and Protective Factors

Schools and those who work within them can facilitate positive growth in adolescents, even in situations where other environments like home might not be perceived as supportive (Brooks et al., 2012). For example, lack of school connectedness is a risk factor associated with sexual risk behaviors. Researchers out of Nova Scotia, Canada (Langille, Asbridge, Azagba, Flowerdew, Rasic, & Cragg, 2014), found that low school connectedness, defined as feeling a part of the school, being connected to teachers, fellow students and reported happiness in school, was associated with sexual risk behaviors of having more sexual partners in the last year, not using a condom at last sexual intercourse, and having unplanned sexual intercourse among sexually active boys in grades 10 through 12. However, these findings were not significant for girls. Markham et al. (2010), in their exhaustive literature review of connectedness in adolescent sexual health behavior, found a direct role for school connectedness as a protective factor for early sexual debut in two longitudinal studies they reviewed (Paul, Fitzjohn, Herbison, & Dickson, 2000, as cited in Markham et al., 2010; Resnick et al., 1997, as cited in Markham et al., 2010). Please see Markham et al. (2010) for the other types of sexual risk behaviors associated with school connectedness.

Teachers play an important protective role as key adults in ameliorating sexual risk behaviors of adolescents. McNeely and Falci (2004), in their analysis of adolescent risk behaviors based on the National Longitudinal Study of Adolescent Health completed in 2005, found that teacher support was a protective factor against transitioning to first sexual intercourse among a sample of adolescents surveyed. The magnitude of the effect for teacher support was large for all health behaviors studied, which included factors in addition to adolescent sexual risk behaviors such as violence, substance abuse, suicidality, tobacco and marijuana use. McNeely, Nonnemaker, and Blum (2002) analyzed the National Longitudinal Study of Adolescent Health Survey with a sample of adolescents enrolled in grades 7 to 12 during the 1994–1995 school year. Administrators additionally completed surveys about school policies, procedures, and school characteristics. McNeely et al.'s (2002) findings were that student-reported school connectedness was associated with positive classroom management and discipline practices as well as smaller school size and youth participation in extracurricular activities. Although this study was not a direct assessment of adolescent sexual risk behaviors, the results help to inform school-based practices that can improve school connectedness, which is associated with sexual health. In the earliest study completed using the National Longitudinal Study of Adolescent Health Survey with adolescents, school connectedness was protective of early sexual debut, but not pregnancy history (Resnick et al., 1997). School connectedness has been consistently documented as a potentially alterable protective factor that preventionists/ interventionists can target as a point of intervention in addressing the sexual health needs of adolescents. If teachers are made aware of the important role they play in addressing sexual health, then they can work toward building positive relationships with students. On a system-wide level, schools can ensure that every student has made a connection with at least one teacher or staff member in the building. In some schools, small learning communities are established so that teachers can attend to the needs of a more manageable number of students in large schools.

School connectedness, and strategies to encourage it, has been the subject of federal documents not necessarily specifically targeting sexual risk behaviors but far-ranging behaviors that put adolescents at risk for undesirable student outcomes. For example, the CDC disseminated "School Connectedness: Strategies for Increasing Protective Factors among Youth" (2009) to address a range of adolescent high-risk behaviors, including building adult supports, aligning with a positive peer group, being committed to education, and creating a positive school environment that includes the physical environment. More recently, the U.S. Department of Education (2014) released "Guiding Principles: A Resource Guide for Improving School Climate and Discipline." This document provided schools with guidelines for creating proactive school climates and engaging in equitable and nonbiased discipline efforts that involve removing students from the classroom only as a last resort and disseminating recommendations for implementing other proactive efforts to build school climate. These recommendations were inclusive of communicating acceptance of all students and striving to be an inviting school community that is nondiscriminatory and equitable. Although connectedness to school might be considered an individual factor that an adolescent brings to the table, we would articulate that schools can have a heavy hand in creating a climate that facilitates connections that adolescents make to schools. These connections can serve as a buffer to prevent sexual risk behaviors. Given the federal policy and research-based recommendations for facilitating school connectedness and building positive school climates, preventionists/interventionists along with students, family and community members, and school staff can take measures to capitalize on the potential protective factor of the school environment. The following hypothetical school scenario provides a snapshot of how this might happen.

Washington High School is a large high school located in an urban environment in the northeastern part of the United States. There are roughly 1,600 students enrolled in the school, which is at risk for closing due to declining enrollments, as many families have left the area or gone to private or charter schools. A large industrial plant in the area has recently closed, and there are high unemployment rates in the community. The student population is very diverse, with approximately 40% Hispanic students, 35% Black, 20% White, and 5% Asian/Pacific Islander. In terms of socioeconomic status of the community, about 90% of the student population qualify for free or reduced lunch. Graduation rates have been declining over the years, and enrollment, attendance, tardies, and failure rates are a matter of significant concern. The community experiences gang issues, which contribute to related school safety issues for students coming to school in the morning and leaving school at the end of the day. The school itself is generally fairly safe, with most discipline concerns being for minor infractions, such as tardies and truancy, as well as for classroom-based issues, such as disrespect. Students generally take public transportation to the school, and this often contributes to class tardies and first period being missed. Metal detectors are in the building for students to pass through in the morning. Each student must show identification when entering the building, which sometimes contributes to escalating confrontations between students and security personnel, leading to office disciplinary referrals and subsequent removal through suspension and expulsion. There is a high pregnancy rate among the students, primarily in the Latino population. Although there is a health clinic at the school staffed with a physician, a social worker, and a nurse practitioner, the clinic staff is not allowed to dispense condoms due to school policy regulations. Prenatal care is provided. Female patients to the clinic feel responsible for obtaining birth control, but are reluctant to do so in the event they see a relative at the community pharmacy and would become embarrassed. Therefore, many female patients report not using birth control.

The school faculty, under the leadership of the school principal, is not content with the current structure of the school policies and system. They want to take some action, but are not sure where to start and consult the school-based mental health staff, inclusive of the school social worker, school psychologist, and school counselor. In addition, the school staff holds a meeting with the school-based health center personnel, who are equally as frustrated about the health services they are providing as they feel that they are always "responding to crises" rather than preventing sexual risk behaviors, which was a component of their original focus and mission. Both groups (school-based personnel and health center staff) think that it might be useful to collect some data. First, they decide to disseminate a school climate survey to the students, staff, and parents to assess feelings of safety, security, school climate, and health services they or their children are receiving. The school staff collects and organizes discipline referrals disaggregated by race and ethnicity, as recommended in the literature (Losen & Martinez, 2013). They form a team that is inclusive of school-based mental health staff (e.g., school counselor, school psychologist, school social worker) and the health center staff (e.g., nurse practitioner, health center social worker, and physician when available) to begin reviewing these data and to make an action plan for moving forward to improve the school climate and health center services. Their review of the school climate data reveals that students do not feel safe walking to and from school and during unstructured time, such as passing periods. They would also like more say in how the school rules are formed and feel that they are sometimes not treated in a just manner when it comes to school discipline. Students also report that the health clinic is helpful, but they would like some assistance in approaching their parents to discuss sexuality and contraception. Parents report that they would like some flexibility in school arrival times because of transportation issues and child care responsibilities their adolescents often have in getting younger siblings to school while they work. Classroom teachers report that they would like to receive more professional consultation with classroom management issues and in addressing academic deficiencies and organizational issues that they believe their students have. They attribute these behavioral and academic concerns to failing grades for many students who give up hope, stop coming to school, and become or contribute to students becoming pregnant and engaging in sexual risk or status offenses such as alcohol or drug use, gang activity, all factors that contribute to subsequent drop-out. A cursory review of the discipline data reveals disproportionate representation among minority students, particularly the African American males being reported for primarily classroom-based and subjective offenses, which is a finding consistently borne out in the literature for five decades (Children's Defense Fund, 1975; Skiba, Horner, Chung, Rausch, May, & Tobin, 2011). Based on these data, the team begins to address school climate by finding ways to build student connections to the school through a variety of means that includes assigning mentors or a staff member to provide oversight of enrolled students. They also start to examine the types of school-based health services offered currently and consider ways to expand supports based on the survey data. In addition, they establish a plan to

(Continued)

(Continued)

address school-based behavioral and academic needs through the availability of psychologist and health services staff to provide ongoing consultation (Gregory, Cornell, & Fan, 2011). The newly formed team believes that the students are at a higher risk for a range of health risk behaviors and school concerns. To address these issues and the findings from the data they collected, they consider implementing the following action plan over the next 3 to 5 years as part of a systemic approach to comprehensively prevent sexual risk behaviors among their students:

1   Systematically collect and review school climate data as well as discipline referrals disaggregated by ethnicity over time. Use these data to help plan and build schoolwide behavioral structures that are prevention-oriented and focus on defining and teaching behavioral expectations rather than focusing on removal and punishment, such as that aligned with Schoolwide Positive Behavior Support and culturally responsive approaches (Vincent, Randall, Cartledge, Tobin, & Swain-Bradway, 2011). In addition, the team will consider adopting a system-wide restorative justice approach in which the focus is on preventing and addressing ongoing school and classroom concerns through a relationship focus. The emphasis in restorative justice practices is on restoring relationships among individuals who may have been harmed by a certain act, rather than engaging in retaliation and punishment or removal of the student from the classroom through suspension (Ashley & Burke, 2009; Morrison, 2002). Along with the schoolwide systems of behavioral supports that are being considered, teachers may benefit from classroom-based support through a school-based consultation model in meeting the behavioral and academic needs of their students. For example, as briefly described above, teachers may benefit from a school- or clinic-based mental health professional observing the teacher and then providing ongoing direct consultation and feedback related to classroom management throughout the year (Gregory et al., 2011). Support of teachers in addressing the needs of diverse learners and those from culturally and linguistically diverse backgrounds that may differ from teaching staff is critical to effective school discipline and a nonpunitive approach that is more aligned with a positive and accepting school culture (Gregory et al., 2011).

2   In addition to the collection of behavioral referral data as described above, the school can begin to organize and review direct academic information (failures, particularly in critical classes such as algebra) and academic-related data (e.g., tardies, truancy, credit accrual) into a tracking system that can be used for early identification of students

who are at risk for school failure and dropping out, which tends not be an isolated event but occurs over time with long-term absences, spotty attendance, and cutting. These academic-related concerns and risk for academic failure place children and adolescents at risk for health-related issues, including high-risk sexual behavior and entry to the criminal justice system (Losen & Martinez, 2013). Removal from the classroom for academic or behavioral reasons is often referred to as the "school to prison pipeline" (Losen & Martinez, 2013; Norbury, Wong, Wan, Reese, Dhillon, & Gerdeman, 2012; Shapiro, Rodriguez, & Telip, 2014). Adolescents with low grades and those who have been retained in school are at higher risk of becoming sexually active (Small & Luster, 1994, as cited in Bogenschneider, 2002). In contrast, having high educational goals is a protective factor in delaying sexual activity (Small & Bogenschneider, 1991, as cited in Bogenschneider, 2002). To identify students early on in the trajectory toward academic failure and dropping out of school and to increase the probability of keeping students in school, recent attention has been focused on "early academic warning systems" at the high school level (Norbury et al., 2012). Norbury et al. (2012), under the auspices of the Institute of Educational Sciences, created an early warning system that included the collection of data typically already available in high schools, such as attendance and credit accrual. These data are important to review when adolescents are freshman and not on-track-to-graduate so that academic supports and attention can be given to them before the academic issues escalate to the point where more intensive interventions are required and/or students are already in the pipeline toward dropping out of school and being at risk for incarceration, in part, because of unidentified academic as well as special education needs (Shapiro et al., 2014). We argue that an early warning system by which data are collected on an ongoing basis is aligned with a multitiered system of support (MTSS; Burns & Gibbons, 2012) and population-based, school-based mental health models (Doll & Cummings, 2008). These aforementioned models are typically applied to behavioral, academic, and social-emotional, school-based issues, but could be adapted to examine supports for sexual health of adolescents and the evaluation of outcomes related to sexual risk behaviors. Our proposed model, adapted from MTSS and school-based mental health models, is described more fully in Chapter 8 related to school-based supports of sexual health.

3   The mental health professionals based at the school can consult with the health service providers within the clinic in a more systematic and

(Continued)

(Continued)

structured manner. The formation of a team that includes the expertise of personnel from both sites is already a step in the right direction to facilitate dialogue and coordination of services. It is the experience of the author that, while school-based health centers might be housed within a school building and have enormous potential, there are often challenges with respect to communication and collaboration due to various structural issues and policies within both settings that are not aligned. This is surprising as the school and health clinic are providing services to the same population of students often with issues and concerns that overlap across both contexts. In this case, many potential collaborations could be built, and service delivery could be provided in a more unified manner rather than one that is disjointed and fragmented (Adelman & Taylor, 2007). For example, the school and health center staff could jointly facilitate a group with families focused on the prevention of sexual risk behaviors, as recommended by the WHO (2014). Accurate and factual information about STIs, HIV/AIDS, and reliable contraception could be part of the curriculum that would need to be delivered in a culturally sensitive fashion (Rouvier, Campero, Walker, & Caballero, 2011). A component of the group could be focused on ways to facilitate information between children and families about sexual activity. Literature suggests that adolescents would like to speak with their parents about sexual activity, including obtaining accurate information about contraceptive methods. Further, their parents often want to have such conversations, but may not have the knowledge, modeling, or comfort level to have effective dialogue (Rouvier et al., 2011). Due to the high rates of pregnancy among the Latino population, having culturally sensitive conversations that are respectful yet factual would be important (Rouvier et al., 2011). More specific information about facilitating home and family supports of sexual health is provided in Chapter 7 of this book.

The school-based recommendations in this case example can be modified based on the priorities, needs, and demographics of each particular school setting. The focus on meeting academic and behavioral needs of youth in a prevention-oriented and proactive manner with the goal of facilitating school connectedness is a common denominator. Creating positive school climates is an overall theme that can address many of the school-based risk factors that lead to adolescent sexual risk behaviors, such as risk factors related to academic concerns (e.g., failing grades, not being on-track-to-graduate, being retained), and serve as protective factors of school and community connectedness.

Family Risk and Protective Factors

Parents and adult caregivers play an important role in the sexual risk-taking behavior of adolescents. Protective factors related to parenting behaviors include parental communication (Jaccard & Dittus, 1993, as cited in Whitaker & Miller, 2000), parental monitoring (Huebner & Howell, 2003), and parent–family connectedness (Resnick et al., 1997). Markham et al. (2010), in their exhaustive literature review that included family connectedness as one of the variables studied, found that adolescents with a strong family connection, strong parental general communication about sexual health, and ongoing parental monitoring were protected from some sexual risk behaviors examined in the research, but not others. In Chapter 7, which focuses on promoting home-based support for sexual health, we offer a more in-depth analysis of research related to parental communication and parental monitoring, as well as recommendations for parents and preventionists and interventionists to facilitate parental communication and parental monitoring.

Kotchick et al. (2001), in their review of the literature on a range of variables purported to influence adolescent sexual risk-taking behavior, examined family-related variables such as socioeconomic status, family structure (e.g., living with one or both parents), and parenting variables. They located at least one study that documented the role of low socioeconomic status in conjunction with students experiencing academic problems as jointly predicting early pregnancy (Gordon, 1996, as cited in Kotchick et al., 2001). More recently, Price and Hyde (2009) examined the impact of numerous risk factors, including living in an intact family, across 2 years on sexual debut using a sample of 13–15-year-old adolescents. Their findings for family variables were that, for girls, poor parental relationships, living in a nonintact family, and having parents with lower educational levels were risk factors for having an early sexual debut. For boys, the sole family risk factor found in the study was poor parental relationships predicting the sexual risk behavior of early sexual debut.

We would articulate that when considering family and parenting variables that significantly predict adolescent sexual risk behaviors, alterable variables that preventionists and interventionists may have more ability to impact are parenting behaviors rather than structural family variables, such as living arrangements and socioeconomic status. At the same time, preventionists/interventionists such as healthcare providers and school-based health and mental health professionals can pay particular attention to the needs of families living in poverty that they work with on a daily basis. Unfortunately, adolescents and families living in poverty or facing financial issues may not seek out health supports, resulting in having inaccurate information about pregnancy prevention, STIs, HIV/AIDS, and effective contraception. Therefore, healthcare and school-based professionals could prioritize establishing free clinics and those that work on a sliding scale in the community, advocate for school-based health settings, and establish relationships with universities that could provide services through training of medical interns, residents, other healthcare providers, and school-based mental health professionals. Preventionists/interventions can prioritize providing accurate and accessible information (e.g., in one's primary language) through consultation supports and outreach when working in communities that are impacted by poverty because adolescents and families residing in them may be a particularly vulnerable population.

Peer Risk and Protective Factors

Influence of Peer Groups

Although parents have more influence on their adolescent's sexual choices than they may think (CDC, 2012), peers begin to take a prominent role in the choices that emerging and older adolescents make. Peer factors for adolescent sexual risk behaviors include associating with deviant peers. For example, international research using a high school sample of adolescents ranging in age from 14 to 18 years in Tehran, Iran, revealed that student-reported parental monitoring of high-risk behaviors was a protective factor that was mediated by self-reported association with deviant peers. In the study, deviant peers were defined as those who engaged in drug or alcohol use, carried a weapon such as a knife or gun, or engaged in physical fighting (Ahmadi, Khodadadi Sangdeh, Aminimanesh, Mollazamani, & Khanzade, 2013). Ahmadi et al. (2013) used three rating scales, one related to sexual attitudes, a second that assessed parental monitoring, and a third focused on association with deviant peers. A scale of sexual attitudes rather than actual sexual practices was used because of the cultural issues in the country associated with overt reporting of sexual behaviors. Kirby and Lepore (2007) in their exhaustive review of literature summarized peer influences on adolescent sexual risk behaviors by concluding that adolescents are more likely to be sexually active if they have older friends and if their friends partake in status offenses such as alcohol or drug use or engage in other nonstatus delinquent offenses. Miller-Johnson, Costanzo, Coie, Rose, Browne, and Johnson (2003) examined the sociometric peer acceptance and leadership status of seventh-grade African American early adolescents in relation to engaging in early sexual activity. Peer group leadership was characterized in two ways: (1) unconventional or "peers who are leaders and good to have in charge" (Miller-Johnson et al., 2003, p. 378); and conventional or "persons who are leaders and good to have in charge" (p. 378). Peer groups with unconventional leadership were at increased risk for beginning sexual activity earlier relative to peer groups with conventional leadership. Being in a deviant peer group, however, was not predictive of early sexual activity in the Miller-Johnson et al. (2003) study. Adolescent perceptions of peers favoring safer sexual practices may serve as a protective factor for consistent condom use and having multiple sexual partners, as Kapadia, Frye, Bonner, Emmanuel, Samples, and Latka (2012) documented that adolescent perceptions of peer beliefs about the importance of these safe sexual practices was associated with engaging in the practice of condom use and a diminished probability of having multiple sexual partners. Kapadia et al.'s study was conducted with a sample of Latino, 16–19-year-old adolescents who reported already being sexually active. The range of findings with respect to the impact of peer groups on safe sexual practices supports the notion that adolescent peer relationships are complex and multifaceted in their own right. Depending perhaps, in part, on how peer groups are defined and examined in literature and the sexual risk behaviors measured, a differential impact on sexual risk behaviors may be found. However, taken together, the research literature does support the conjecture that peer groups have a role in the sexual decision making of adolescents, and peer relationships could serve as a useful point of intervention for preventionists/interventionists.

Romantic Relationships with Older Partners

Adolescents who are in a relationship with a romantic partner who is older have been found to have high rates of sexual risk behaviors compared to those in relationships with peers their own age. Marin, Kirby, Hudes, Coyle, and Gomez (2006) surveyed middle school students in California on an annual basis from seventh to ninth grade. Males who reported having a girlfriend their age in seventh grade were more likely to be sexually active in ninth grade. The same held true for females. However, females with older boyfriends were at an even higher risk for being sexually active in ninth grade relative to girls who had boyfriends their same age. In a more recent study, Morrison-Beedy, Xia, and Passmore (2013) surveyed sexually active urban adolescent girls between the ages of 15 and 19. Girls in a romantic relationship with older romantic partners reported more episodes of sexual instances relative to girls in same-age relationships. In addition, girls in relationships with older partners had significantly more reported risk factors that included earlier initiation of sexual activity, having more lifetime sexual partners, having higher incidents of STIs, and being more reluctant to discuss condom use with sexual partners compared to girls in same-age relationships. Markham et al. (2010), in the same comprehensive literature review of connectedness and sexual risk behaviors described above under Community Risk and Protective Factors, examined the issue of connection with one's partner. They reported that partner connectedness was a protective factor for using contraception among females in a romantic relationship, based on consistent findings across at least two longitudinal studies that met the criteria for inclusion in their systematic literature review (e.g., see Ford, Sohn, & Lepkowski, 2001, cited in Markham et al., 2010; see Manlove, Ryan, & Franzetta, 2004, cited in Markham et al., 2010).

Following is a brief set of recommendations that preventionists/interventions can engage in using the knowledge base related to peer risk and protective factors:

- Encourage school staff and parents to monitor peer groups and any changes to those groups. It is common for peer group affiliations to change throughout adolescence, and parents and caregivers need to be knowledgeable about who their children are associating with and should meet them. They should be aware of which peers are in attendance during outings. Parents could also set up a system with their adolescents whereby they need to communicate when they change locations or the members of the groups with whom they are associating. For example, given that many adolescents go out in "groups," ensuring that youth communicate when they would go from a football game to having ice cream at another location is important because peer groups may become reorganized throughout one evening or across time.

- School staff and community leaders can work on providing opportunities for youth to have voice and representation in decisions made at the school and community level, particularly as decisions relate to young people. Controversial peer group leaders can perhaps have their energies rechanneled to productive pursuits. Often adolescents "on the fringe" within schools are not selected for student- and community-directed committees, and they should be sought out because they have influence over other peers and may not always facilitate the best choices if left to their own devices. In many cases, the authors have found that adolescents "on the fringe" or not necessarily aligning with school norms have excellent leadership abilities and skills that could be channeled in a constructive way if given an opportunity to have their voices heard.

- Adolescents should be consulted about the best means of meeting their sexual health needs. They have strong ideas, and school- and community-based groups that involve peers from various social circles could be assembled to discuss teen issues, including sexual health choices they may make.

- Adolescents with older romantic partners are at a higher risk of engaging in sexual risk behaviors, such as early sexual debut and not using a condom. Therefore, parents and other adults in their lives need to be aware of who their adolescents are in romantic relationships with and ensure that they receive accurate information about sexual health issues and prevention that are part of recommended standards, such as those distributed by the WHO (2014).

- Social media is a common form of communication among adolescents, and group chats among peers are very common. Parents and other adult caregivers should be knowledgeable about these communication systems and monitor the communication, as will also be described in Chapter 7 related to home supports. Adolescents need information about the permanency of their electronic communication and an understanding of the impact that this correspondence can have on their future and that of their peers. For example, "sexting" among peers and among partners in romantic relationships has resulted in many unfortunate and negative consequences for the adolescents involved, including legal issues. Sadly, many adolescents on the receiving end of cyberbullying have experienced significant mental health issues and, in highly publicized cases, even ended their lives. Although these incidents were not necessarily related to sexual choices, they highlight the need for understanding that adolescents may use social media in an impulsive moment without thinking about the consequences of their actions. Therefore, adolescents need information about the significant impact that group chats among peers and other forms of social media can have on their lives and that of others. Collaboration among all adults involved in adolescents' lives, including parents, school personnel and administrators, mental health professionals, community members, and local law enforcement, is critical.

Individual Risk and Protective Factors

Biological Factors

Early age of maturity has been associated with sexual risk behaviors. For example, L'Engle, Jackson, and Brown (2006) surveyed seventh and eighth graders across 2 years with respect to sexual expectations and beliefs about sexual activity. Participants categorized as "highly susceptible" to initiating sexual activity were more physically mature relative to those in the categories of "not susceptible" or having "low susceptibility." Other individual characteristics were also predictive of early sexual debut in the study. These characteristics include having sexual feelings and perceived competencies as related to sexual activity, perceiving that peers were sexually active, and having less positive connectedness to parents. Downing and Bellis (2009), in a UK-based survey of risk taking in a sample of participants ranging in age from 16 to 45 years, found that early puberty (menarche in females and onset of puberty in boys) was associated with a range of health risk behaviors that included the sexual risk behaviors of sexual debut and unprotected sex prior to the age of 16.

Cognitive and Personality Traits

Hoyle, Fejfar, and Miller (2010) conducted a comprehensive literature review of studies that examined the relationships between personality dimensions and high-risk sexual behaviors; most of the studies included were published between 1990 and 1999 and not specifically conducted with adolescents. They included studies that had a standard measure for the personality domain assessed and those that evaluated an association between the personality variable and actual sexual risk behaviors rather than beliefs or attitudes. Overall, sensation seeking was a personality characteristic that was positively associated with the three sexual risk behaviors of unprotected sex, having multiple sexual partners, and engaging in high-risk sexual encounters. Agreeableness was a characteristic that was correlated with the three areas of sexual risk behaviors measured, while conscientiousness was specifically associated with condom use.

In a longitudinal study using the National Longitudinal Survey of Youth, maternal ratings of their children's personality prototypes at age 5 or 6 were used to predict sexual risk behaviors of failure to use contraception and a condom at a follow-up when the youth were aged 17 or 18 (Atkins, 2008). Adolescents with the personality prototype of "overcontrolled" at age 5, such as being shy and withdrawn (aligned with internalizing problems), was predictive of less sexual risk behaviors in adolescence. The other personality profiles evaluated were resiliency (e.g., positive emotionality, being social adept) and being undercontrolled (e.g., impulsive, difficulty with social interactions, alignment with externalizing problems).

In recent neuroscience research, Goldenberg, Telzer, Lieberman, Fulingi, and Galvin (2013) conducted a study with a small sample of sexually active adolescents. They completed MRIs on participants while being engaged in an impulse control task. Information about self-reported sexual risk behaviors was also collected. The findings were that activation of the prefrontal cortex during the MRI was negatively associated with elevated sexual risk behavior ratings. The authors interpreted the findings as support for neurologically based impulse control having a role in sexual risk behaviors among adolescents.

Mental Health Issues

Brown et al. (2010) conducted a study with adolescent participants in mental health treatment that included exposure to three variations of a health promotion program (e.g., HIV intervention with their family, HIV intervention for adolescents only, and a general health promotion intervention). Adolescents and their parents completed the Computerized Diagnostic Interview Schedule for Children to evaluate psychiatric symptoms. Their findings were that adolescents who met the diagnostic criteria for externalizing disorders (e.g., oppositional defiant disorder, conduct disorder, attention deficit hyperactivity disorder) or internalizing disorders (major depression, generalized anxiety disorder, posttraumatic stress disorder) that were comorbid with externalizing disorders were more likely to have reported a lifetime history of sex (vaginal and/or anal). In addition, mania was predictive of sexual risk behaviors of having two or more sexual partners in the last 3 months or having an STI. The authors discussed the findings as having implications for paying particular attention to adolescents who have these disorders during a screening process and for providing treatment related to sexual health for this population of students as indicated. For preventionists/interventionists, changes in behavior are potentially observable because, if they are professionals working in schools or community-based clinics, they see the adolescent frequently and can detect whether the adolescent is acting differently than is typical on a day-to-day basis. Parents and adult caregivers should also be given information about mental health disorders such as mania as their children reach adolescence, which is a likely time that these mental health concerns can arise. For example, parents can observe changes in sleeping patterns, eating, agitation, etc. Although these behaviors clearly do not necessarily mean the adolescent has a psychiatric disorder, parents can receive consultation and assistance. Early identification of mental health issues can facilitate information about sexual health behaviors being communicated as soon as possible. Further, supports for families that entail strategies for increased parental monitoring of all health risk behaviors, including sexual risk behaviors, as well as referrals to appropriate mental health agencies and/or hospital settings for appropriate care can occur.

Substance Use

Although one might automatically assume that substance use, inclusive of alcohol, marijuana, and hard drugs, has a causal relationship with sexual risk behaviors by lessening behavioral inhibitions and control among adolescents, the issues are not as clear-cut as they may seem (Schantz, 2012). Under the auspices of the ACT for Youth Center of Excellence collaboration among Cornell University, University of Rochester, and New York State Center for School Safety, a summary and interpretation of the literature examining potential associations between substance use and sexual risk behaviors was completed (Schantz, 2012). The findings of this work were that drug and alcohol use was consistently associated with early sexual initiation, engaging in unprotected sex, and—consistently predictive across studies reviewed—having multiple sexual partners (Schantz, 2012). Other researchers have examined this association. For example, Caminis, Henrich, Ruchkin, Schwab-Stone, and Martin (2007) used longitudinal data collected through the Social and Health Assessment across 3 years (beginning in 2001) with an early adolescent sample enrolled in sixth grade at the start of the study. Caminis et al. evaluated internalizing and externalizing problems, as well as substance use across time to evaluate sexual debut 2 years later. They found that externalizing issues of substance use and what they described as "violent delinquency" predicted sexual initiation in eighth grade. Further, consistent substance use over the course of the middle school years was predictive of sexual risk behaviors.

Tapert, Aarons, Sedlar, and Brown (2001) compared reported sexual risk behaviors in a sample of adolescents receiving substance abuse treatment to those of a nonclinical community-based sample. Their findings were that those in the treatment sample were more likely to engage in a range of sexual risk behaviors as follows: (1) early onset of sexual activity, (2) a higher number of sexual partners, and (3) less consistent use of condoms. These sexual risk behaviors remained for the treatment sample as they transitioned from adolescence to young adulthood, and most participants also reported continued substance use after the substance abuse treatment concluded.

Sexual and Physical Abuse

Reported abuse in the adolescent population has also been implicated as playing a role in adolescent sexual risk behaviors. For example, Stock, Bell, Boyer, and

Connell (1997) used the 1992 Washington State Survey of Adolescent Health Behaviors with girls in middle (grade 8) and high schools (grades 10 and 12). Girls who reported being sexually abused were over two times as likely to have had sexual intercourse relative to those who did not report sexual abuse. Sexual risk behaviors of having had intercourse before the age of 15, not using birth control during the last sexual intercourse, and having had more than one sexual partner were more likely among females reporting sexual abuse. Saewyc, Magee, and Pettingell (2004) examined subtypes of sexual abuse in a study with sexually experienced teenagers in Minnesota. Participants were surveyed about their risk behaviors and whether they had experienced incest, nonfamilial sexual abuse, or both types of abuse. Adolescents who reported abuse of any type were more likely to report risk behaviors and pregnancy involvement compared to participants who did not report abuse. Adolescents who experienced both types of abuse had the highest odds ratio for predicting high-risk behaviors. Gender differences were found in that the disparity between boys who experienced abuse versus those who did not was greater in comparison to the differences found among girls. Lalor and McElvaney (2010) completed a comprehensive literature review and analysis pertaining to the implications of childhood sexual abuse and incorporated numerous studies conducted throughout the world. They concluded that evidence clearly existed for the pathway of childhood sexual abuse to long-term sexual risk behaviors of having multiple sexual partners and being sexually promiscuous. Their analysis also included literature that documented the association of early onset of consensual sexual activity and unprotected sexual experiences among women, as well as an increased prevalence of STIs and prostitution among both men and women. They called for improvement in the methodology of studies. One of the possible mechanisms that they hypothesized to potentially explain this association is the possibility that sexual abuse may disrupt normal physical and emotional development (Stoltz, Shannon, Kerr, Zhang, Montaner, & Wood, 2007, as cited in Lalor & McElvaney, 2010). This hypothesis has implications for sexual health education in that understanding the developmental and mental health needs of adolescents when providing sexual health education and other supports is very important, as will be described more fully within Chapter 5. The provision of appropriate and factual information about preventive sexual health practices should be done with the sensitivity that there may be specially needed accommodations for those who experienced sexual abuse. These individuals are a uniquely high-risk population of youth that have experienced childhood trauma in the form of sexual abuse. Therefore, when the general health curriculum is delivered, it needs to be done with careful observation and support of the potential reactions of these individuals. Support from school-based and/or community-based mental health professionals should be available to health educators.

In an early study, Luster and Small (1994) examined a range of risk factors among a sample of sexually active adolescent females in the Midwest. Included among the risk factors was sexual and physical abuse. Participants were categorized as "high" versus "low" risk takers. High risk takers engaged in behaviors such as having multiple sexual partners and not using a condom during sexual intercourse. There was a higher percentage of individuals who had reported being sexually abused in the high-risk category (31% in high-risk compared to 15% in the low-risk category). A history of physical abuse also distinguished the two groups, as 40% of high-risk females reported physical abuse, compared to 12% of those in the low-risk category.

These findings collectively call for specific attention from preventionists/ interventionists in terms of the care that must be taken to meet the sexual health needs of potentially vulnerable populations of youth such as those who experienced sexual or physical abuse. Participating in the general sexual health curriculum may be beneficial, but perhaps not enough to serve the needs of those who experienced sexual abuse. Service providers with knowledge of those who have been sexually abused should approach the topic with sensitivity and should be aware of their needs to provide more individualized supports. For instance, those who experienced sexual and/or physical abuse may have experienced trauma and the topic of sexuality may bring memories and distress to the adolescents. Therefore, mental health professionals should be in a position to consult with health educators and others in the classroom who might not be in a position to identify and respond to the signs of trauma. Mental health professionals should also be positioned to conduct follow-up assessment and provide or refer out for mental health services, as necessary. Continual collaboration among a team that includes the expertise of mental health staff, such as school psychologists, school social workers, and counselors, along with health educators and administrators in school or healthcare environments is critical.

In addition, another consideration that may arise when working with those who have been abused may be that if an adolescent was removed from the home at some point during the school years due to abuse, then there would be frequent school changes as a result of multiple foster care placements. From the experience of one of the authors, females in a residential treatment setting reported not being exposed to the health curriculum due to gaps in their educational experiences. Health curriculums are often delivered in units across one to two quarters, and it is possible that this short window of time may be missed if there are multiple school transitions due to frequent moves. These types of unique issues may arise in working to meet the needs of a population of youth who experienced abuse and are in critical need for appropriate and sensitive sexual health education and potentially related mental health supports to facilitate sexual health among this particularly high-risk group. We need to ensure that these youth receive the services they deserve and are not overlooked in school and community systems due to the potential transient nature of their lives.

Dating Violence Victimization

Rizzo et al. (2012) completed a path analysis of dating violence victimization and its impact on sexual risk behaviors, defined as unprotected sexual activities. A sample of adolescents with mental health issues participating in a HIV prevent program participated in the study. Dating violence victimization was defined as whether the respondents had been hit, slapped, or forced into sex by a partner. Using various models to evaluate outcomes, a direct effect of dating violence victimization significantly predicted self-reported unprotected sex. In addition, an "indirect pathway" from experiencing dating violence was found. Dating violence was associated with elevated scores for depression, which in turn impacted efficacy for condom use (feeling that one has the ability to effectively use a condom). Condom use then impacted unprotected sexual acts. These findings underscore the importance of incorporating information about dating violence and helping teens to recognize it as part of the sexual health curriculum. Both males and females should have opportunities for dialogue and space to discuss healthy relationships and ways to foster them. They should be taught warning signs for unhealthy relationships and given problem-solving skills for how to navigate through them and seek help from an adult if they feel they are in an abusive or unhealthy relationship. As stated in Chapter 7 on home supports, having opportunities for open communication with parents is very important, as well as having access to resources in the community and school environments. Chapter 8 provides more description of the content that could be covered within a comprehensive sexual health curriculum.

We have just summarized numerous studies that have documented individual risk and some protective factors that likely predispose adolescents to engage in sexual risk behaviors. These factors include biological, personality and behavioral characteristics, mental health needs, substance abuse, sexual and physical abuse, and dating victimization. Given the range of specialized needs of adolescents who are at elevated risk for sexual risk behaviors, and the disparities between the need for mental health services among adolescents and the percentage that ultimately receive them (U.S. Department of Health and Human Services, Office of Adolescent Health, 2014), we make the following recommendations for preventionists/interventionists to consider as part of a MTSS (State of Florida, 2012) approach to addressing the sexual health needs of youth. MTSS will be described in more detail as a school-based model that can be applied to sexual health in Chapter 8. In short, MTSS (often used synonymously with Response to Intervention—RTI) is a model of service delivery that has been widely implemented in schools to meet academic, behavioral, and social-emotional needs of students by providing universal/Tier 1 prevention-oriented supports to all in the building, followed by supplemental supports to students who need additional assistance at the group or supplemental level (Tier 2), and then delivering more individualized intensive supports to those who have the most needs (Tier 3) (Burns & Gibbons, 2012).

- Conduct social-emotional screening of behavior and social-emotional concerns at the school level as part of a continuum of mental health and social-emotional supports aligned with MTSS (State of Florida MTSS, 2012) and implemented on a system-wide school level. The screening could include questions that assess the types of behaviors and mental health concerns (e.g., externalizing and comorbid internalizing issues) that put students at risk for sexual risk behaviors. States and school districts vary with respect to procedures for parents providing either active or passive consent, and this would need to be considered by the team before moving forward. Using the individual risk behaviors just outlined, utilizing screening results that assess these issues, and then determining what levels of support are needed for particular students based on factors that may put them at a higher risk for sexual risk behaviors is one approach that can be utilized. A population-based approach to mental health services is also aligned with school-based models of MTSS/RTI given that both approaches are drawn from a public health model in some capacity (Doll & Cummings, 2008). Having a system of universal screening that identifies students in need of further evaluation and supports would be a potential model that could be informed by the individual risk and protective factors reviewed above.

- Similar to a model of MTSS/RTI, the "universal" application of the sexual health curriculum should be as robust as possible (State of Florida MTSS, 2012). Chapter 4 outlines best practice national guidelines that promote developmentally appropriate and evidence-based sexual health instruction. This curriculum should be delivered to all students in the population. However, after completing screening and examining the degree to which a particular community or school population might be more likely than the general population for risky sexual behaviors (e.g., in a community with high rates of alcoholism, poverty, etc.), supplemental supports or increased intensity of universal supports could be delivered to the entire population, as aligned with population-based mental health service delivery (Doll & Cummings, 2008). For instance, groups related to substance abuse prevention could be delivered to adolescents and their families if this is an identified need or issue since substance use is a risk factor for sexual risk behaviors in the adolescent population. If child abuse and community violence is present, then group supports could be delivered to families and adolescents to meet their specific needs, along with information and supports tailored to specialized needs as they relate to sexual health.

- Despite the best efforts at universal (Tier 1) and secondary (Tier 2) supports, there will be individual children who will have intensive needs. These individuals may have or currently experience sexual and/or physical abuse, disruptive home lives, multiple foster care/residential placement, or have depression, anxiety, or posttraumatic stress disorder. As a result, individualized supports for adolescents who have intensive mental health, behavioral, and academic issues should be instituted along this continuum and MTSS (State of Florida, 2012) and population-based mental health models (Doll & Cummings, 2008) could serve as the service delivery framework. Collaboration between school-based mental health and community mental health providers will most likely be necessary to adequately deliver the intensive supports needed by adolescents who are most at risk for sexual risk behaviors (Adelman & Taylor, 2007). Models of wraparound that provide integrated supports to youth with the most intensive needs could be considered, such as those described by the National Wraparound Initiative (2014).

• Also related to the tenets of MTSS (Burns & Gibbons, 2012) and aligned with a population-based approach to mental health applied to sexual risk behaviors (Doll & Cummings, 2008), data should be collected and used to evaluate children and adolescents' responsiveness to the sexual health curriculum and any additional supports delivered along the continuum. Such data should be collected on an ongoing and formative basis (Burns & Gibbons, 2012) to inform practice. Outcomes such as the percentage of students who drop out of school due to pregnancy or related sexual health issues and overall on-track-to-graduation rates could be considered as possible formative data collection points.

Overall Summary and Future Practice Directions

In this chapter, we have reviewed the literature documenting a range of risk and protective factors across the multiple contexts that adolescents interact with, including community, school, family, peer, as well as the individual risk and protective factors that adolescents bring to these multiple environments. We purport that by addressing these risk and protective factors through use of an integrated public health model such as MTSS/RTI (Burns & Gibbons, 2012) and population-based mental health delivery (Doll & Cummings, 2008), we will be in a better position to meet the sexual health needs of adolescents and to address the challenging statistics that have consistently documented the high rates of sexual risk behaviors among youth (e.g., HIV/AIDS, STIs, unwanted pregnancy, dating violence victimization) through proper sexual health supports delivered along a continuum and tied to need.

References

Adelman, H., & Taylor, L. (2007). *Fostering school, family and community involvement: Effective strategies for creating safer schools and community involvement.* Washington, DC: The Hamilton Fish Institute on School and Community Violence and Northwest Regional Educational Laboratory.

Ahmadi, K., Khodadadi Sangdeh, J., Aminimanesh, S., Mollazamani, A., & Khanzade, M. (2013). The role of parental monitoring and affiliation with deviant peers in adolescents' sexual risk taking: Toward an interactional model. *International Journal of High Risk Behaviors & Addiction, 2*(1), 22–27. doi:10.5812/ijhrba.8554

Ashley, J., & Burke, K. (2009). *Implementing balanced and restorative justice: A guide for schools.* Chicago, IL: Illinois Criminal Justice Information Authority.

Atkins, R. (2008). The association of childhood personality on sexual risk taking during adolescence. *Journal of School Health, 78*(11), 594–600. doi:10/1111/J.1746-1561.2008.00351.X

Bogenschneider, K. (2002). *Risk-focused prevention of early teen sexual activity: Implications for policymakers.* Wisconsin Family Impact Seminars. Retrieved from http://familyimpactseminars. org/s_wifis07c02.pdf

Brooks, F. M., Magnusson, J., Spencer, N., & Morgan, A. (2012). Adolescent multiple risk behavior: An asset approach to the role of family, school and community. *Journal of Public Health, 34*(1), i48–i56. doi:10.1093/pubmed/fds001

Brown, L. K., Hadley, S. W., Stewart, A., Lescano, C., Whiteley, L., Donnenberg, G., et al. (2010). Psychiatric disorders and sexual risk among adolescents in mental health treatment. *Journal of Consulting and Clinical Psychology, 78*(4), 590–597. doi:10.1037/a0019632

Burns, M. K., & Gibbons, K. (2012). *Implementing response-to-intervention in elementary and secondary schools: Procedures to assure scientific-based practice* (2nd ed.). New York, NY: Routledge.

Caminis, A., Henrich, C., Ruchkin, V., Schwab-Stone, M., & Martin, A. (2007). Psychosocial predictors of sexual initiation and high-risk sexual behaviors in early adolescence. *Child and Adolescent Psychiatry, 1*(14), 1–12. Retrieved from http://www.capmh.com/content/1/1/14

CDC. (2009). *School connectedness: Strategies for increasing protective factors among youth.* Atlanta, GA: U.S. Department of Health and Human Services.

CDC. (2012). *Monitoring your teen's activities: What parents and families should know.* Retrieved from http://www.cdc.gov/healthyyouth/protective/pdf/parental_monitoring_factsheet.pdf

CDC. (2014). *Social-ecological model: A framework for prevention.* Retrieved from http://www.cdc.gov/violenceprevention/overview/social-ecologicalmodel.html

Children's Defense Fund. (1975). *School suspensions: Are they helping children?* Cambridge, MA: Washington Research Project.

Cooper, S. M., Johnson, R. W., Griffin, C. B., Metzger, I., Avery, M., Eaddy, H., et al. (2014). Community involvement and reduced risk behavior engagement among African American adolescents: The mediating role of empowerment beliefs. *Journal of Black Psychology*. doi:10.1177/0095798414536225

Crosby, R. A., DiClemente, R. J., Wingood, G. M., Harrington, K., Davies, S., & Oh, M. K. (2002). Activity of African-American female teenagers in black organizations is associated with STD/HIV protective behaviours: A prospective analysis. *Journal of Epidemiological Community Health, 56*, 549–550.

Doll, B. A., & Cummings, J. A. (2008). *Transforming school mental health services: Population based approaches to promoting the competency and wellness of children.* Thousand Oaks, CA: Corwin Press/NASP.

Downing, J., & Bellis, M. A. (2009). Early pubertal onset and its relationship with sexual risk taking substance use, and anti-social behaviour: A preliminary cross-sectional study. *BMC Public Health, 9*, 446. doi:10.1186/1471-2458-9-446

Ford, K., Sohn, W., & Lepkowski, J. (2001). Characteristics of adolescents' sexual partners and their association with use of condoms and other contraceptive methods. *Family Planning Perspectives, 33*, 100–105, 132.

Goldenberg, D., Telzer, E. H., Lieberman, M. D., Fulingi, A., & Galvin, A. (2013). Neural mechanisms of impulse control in sexually risky adolescents. *Developmental Cognitive Neuroscience, 6*, 23–29.

Gordon, C. P. (1996). Adolescent decision-making: A broadly based theory and its application to the prevention of early pregnancy. *Adolescence, 31*, 561–584.

Gregory, A., Cornell, D., & Fan, X. (2011). The relationship of school structure and support to suspension rates for Black and White high school students. *American Educational Research Journal, 48*, 904–934.

Hoyle, R. H., Fejfar, M. C., & Miller, J. D. (2000). Personality and sexual risk taking: A quantitative review. *Journal of Personality, 68*(6), 1203–1231.

Huebner, A. J. & Howell, L. W. (2003). Examining the relationship between adolescent sexual risk taking and perceptions of monitoring, communication and parenting styles. *Journal of Adolescent Health, 33*(2), 71–78.

Jaccard, J., & Dittus, P. J. (1993). Parent-adolescent communication about premarital pregnancy. *Families in Society, 74*, 329–343.

Kapadia, F., Frye, V., Bonner, S., Emmanuel, P. J., Samples, C. L., & Latka, M. H. (2012). Perceived peer safer sex norms and sexual risk behaviors among substance-abusing Latino adolescents. *AIDS Education Prevention, 24*(1), 27–40. doi:10/1521/aeap.2012.24.1.27

Kirby, D., & Lepore, G. (2007). *Sexual risk and protective factors: factors affecting teen sexual behavior, pregnancy, childbearing, and sexually transmitted disease: Which are important? Which can you change?* Washington, DC: The National Campaign to Prevent Teen and Unplanned Pregnancy.

Kotchick, B. A., Shaffer, A., Forehand, R., & Miller, K. S. (2001). Adolescent sexual risk behavior: A multisystem perspective. *Clinical Psychology Review, 21*(4), 493–519.

Lalor, K., & McElvaney, R. (2010). Child sexual abuse, links to later sexual exploitation/high-risk sexual behavior, and prevention/treatment programs. *Trauma Violence Abuse, 11*(4), 159–177.

Langille, D. B., Asbridge, M. Azagba, S., Flowerdew, G., Rasic, D., & Cragg, A. (2014). Sex differences in associations of school connectedness with adolescent sexual risk-taking in Nova Scotia, Canada. *The Journal of School Health, 84*(6), 387–395.

L'Engle, K. L., Jackson, C., & Brown, J. D. (2006). Early adolescents' cognitive susceptibility to initiating sexual intercourse. *Perspectives on Sexual and Reproductive Health, 38*(2), 97–105.

Losen, D. J., & Martinez, T. E. (2013). *Out of school and off track: The overuse of suspensions in American middle and high schools.* Retrieved from http://civilrightsproject.ucla.edu/resources/projects/center-for-civil-rights-remedies/school-to-prison-folder/federal-reports/out-of-school-and-off-track-the-overuse-of-suspensions-in-american-middle-and-high-schools/OutofSchool-OffTrack_UCLA_4-8.pdf

Luster, T., & Small, S. A. (1994). Factors associated with sexual risk taking behaviors among adolescents. *Journal of Marriage and Family, 56*(3), 622–633.

Manlove, J., Ryan, S., & Franzetta, K. (2004). Contraceptive use and consistency in US teenagers' most recent sexual relationships. *Perspectives on Sexual and Reproductive Health, 36*(6), 265–275.

Marin, B. V., Kirby, D. B., Hudes, E. S., Coyle, K. K., & Gomez, C. A. (2006). Boyfriends, girlfriends, and teenagers' risk of sexual involvement. *Perspectives on Sexual and Reproductive Health, 38*(2), 76–83.

Markham, C. M., Lormand, D., Gloppen, K. M., Peskin, M. F., Flores, B., Low, B., et al. (2010). Connectedness as a predictor of sexual and reproductive health outcomes for youth. *Journal of Adolescent Health, 46*, S23–S41.

McNeely, C. A., & Falci, C. (2004). School connectedness and the transition into and out of health risk behavior among adolescents: A comparison of social belonging and teacher support. *Journal of Adolescent Health, 74*(7), 284–293.

McNeely, C. A., Nonnemaker, J. M., & Blum, R. W. (2002). Promoting school connectedness: Evidence from the National Longitudinal Study of Adolescent Health. *Journal of School Health, 72*(4), 138–146.

Miller-Johnson, S., Costanzo, P. R., Coie, J. D., Rose, M. R., Browne, D. C., & Johnson, C. (2003). Peer social structure and risk-taking behaviors among African American early adolescents. *Journal of Youth Adolescence, 32*(5), 375–384.

Morrison, B. (2002). *Bullying and victimisation in schools: A restorative justice approach* (Report No. 219). Australian Institute of Criminology. Retrieved from : http://aic.gov.au/media_library/publications/tandi_pdf/tandi219.pdf

Morrison-Beedy, D., Xia, Y., & Passmore, D. (2013). SI-SRH Sexual risk factors of partner age-discordance in adolescent girls and their male partners. *Journal of Clinical Nursing, 22*, 3289–3299. doi:10.1111/jocn.12408.

National Wraparound Initiative (2014). *National wraparound basics.* Retrieved from http://www.nwi.pdx.edu/wraparoundbasics.shtml

Norbury, H., Wong, M., Wan, M., Reese, K., Dhillon, S., & Gerdeman, R. (2012). *Using the freshman on-track indicator to predict graduation in two urban districts in the Midwest Region* (Issues & Answers Report, REL 2012–No. 134). Washington, DC: U.S. Department of Education, Institute of Education Sciences, National Center for Education Evaluation and Regional Assistance, Regional Educational Laboratory Midwest. Retrieved from http://ies.ed.gov/ncee/edlabs

Paul, C., Fitzjohn, J., Herbison, G., & Dickson, N. (2000). The determinants of sexual intercourse before age 16. *Journal of Adolescent Health, 27*, 136–147.

Price, M., & Hyde, J. (2009). When two isn't better than one: Predictors of early sexual activity in adolescence using a cumulative risk model. *Journal of Youth and Adolescence, 38*(8), 1059–1071.

Resnick, M. D., Bearman, P. S., Blum, R. W., Bauman, K. E., Harris, K. M., Jones, J., et al. (1997). Protecting adolescents from harm: Findings from the National Longitudinal Study on Adolescent Health. *Journal of the American Medical Association, 278*(10), 823–832.

Rizzo, C. J., Hunter, H. L., Lang, D. L., Oliveira, C., Donnenberg, G., DiClemente, R. J., et al. (2012). Dating violence victimization and unprotected sex acts among adolescents in mental health treatment. *Journal of Child and Family Studies, 21*, 825–832. doi:10.1007/S 10826-011-9543-3

Rouvier, M., Campero, L., Walker, D., & Caballero, M. (2011). Factors that influence communication about sexuality between parents and adolescents in the cultural context of Mexican families. *Sex Education, 11*(2), 175–191. doi:10.1080/14681811.2011.558425

Saewyc, E. M., Magee, L. L., & Pettingell, S. E. (2004). Teengage pregnancy and associated risk behaviors among sexually abused adolescents. *Perspectives on Sexual and Reproductive Health, 36*(3), 98–105.

Schantz, K. (2012). *Substance use and sexual risk-taking in adolescence.* ACT for Youth Center of Excellence. Retrieved from http://www.actforyouth.net/resources/rf/rf_substance_0712.pdf

Shapiro, R., Rodriguez, A., & Telip, R. (2014). *Disability rights consortium: Improving educational outcomes for court-involved youth with disabilities.* Presentation at the Disability Rights Consortium at Equip for Equality-Juvenile Justice and Students with Disabilities, Chicago, IL.

Sinclair, M. F., Christenson, S. L., & Thurlow, M. L. (2005). Promoting school completion of urban secondary youth with emotional and behavioral disabilities. *Exceptional Children, 71*(4), 465–482.

Skiba, R. J., Horner, R. H., Chung, C., Rausch, M. K., May, S. L., & Tobin, T. (2011). Race is not neutral: A national investigation of African American and Latino disproportionality in school discipline. *School Psychology Review, 40*(1), 85–107.

Small, S. A., & Bogenschneider, K. (1991). *Youth at risk for early sexual activity and teenage parenthood* (Wisconsin Youth Futures Technical Report No. 11). Madison, WI: University of Wisconsin-Madison.

Small, S. A., & Luster, T. (1994), Adolescent sexual activity: An ecological, risk-factor approach. *Journal of Marriage and the Family, 56*, 181–192.

State of Florida's MTSS. (2012). *MTSS implementation components: Ensuring common language and understanding.* Florida's Positive Behavior Support Project/University of South Florida. Retrieved from http://www.florida-rti.org/educatorResources/MTSS_Book_ImplComp_012612.pdf

Stock, J. L., Bell, M. A., Boyer, D. K., & Connell, F. A. (1997). Adolescent pregnancy and sexual risk taking among sexually abused girls. *Family Planning and Perspectives, 29*, 200–203, 227.

Stoltz, J. A. M., Shannon, K., Kerr, T., Zhang, R., Montaner, J., & Wood, E. (2007). Associations between childhood maltreatment and sex work in a cohort of drug-using youth. *Social Science and Medicine, 65*(6), 214–221.

Tapert, S. F., Aarons, G. A., Sedlar, G. R., & Brown, S. A. (2001). Adolescent substance use and sexual risk-taking behavior. *Journal of Adolescent Health, 28*, 181–189.

U.S. Department of Education. (2014). *Guiding principles: A resource guide for improving school climate and discipline.* Washington, DC: U.S. Department of Education.

U.S. Department of Health and Human Services, Office of Adolescent Health. (2014). *Access to mental health care.* Retrieved from http://www.hhs.gov/ash/oah/adolescent-health-topics/mental-health/access-mental-health.html

Vincent, C. G., Randall, C., Cartledge, G., Tobin, T. J., & Swain-Bradway, J. (2011). Toward a conceptual integration of cultural responsiveness and schoolwide positive behavior support. *Journal of Positive Behavior Interventions, 13*(4), 219–229.

Whitaker, D. J., & Miller, K. S. (2000). Parent-adolescent discussions about sex and condoms: Impact on peer influences of sexual risk behaviors. *Journal of Adolescent Research, 15*(2), 251–273.

Wilson, N., Dasho, S., Martin, A. C., Wallerstein, N., Wang, C. C., & Minkler, M. (2007). Engaging young adolescents in social action through photovoice: The youth empowerment strategies (YES!) project. *The Journal of Early Adolescence, 27*(2), 241–261. doi:101177/0272431606294834

WHO. (2014). *Adolescents: Health risks and solutions fact sheet.* Retrieved from http://www.who.int/mediacentre/factsheets/fs345/en

4

RELEVANT STANDARDS AND PROFESSIONAL GUIDELINES FOR THE PROMOTION OF SEXUAL HEALTH OF CHILDREN AND ADOLESCENTS

The purpose of this chapter is to discuss the relevant standards and professional guidelines for the promotion of sexual health of children and adolescents. Additionally, the National Sexuality Education Standards (NSES) will be reviewed, inclusive of its historical context, content, and implications for sexual health promotion. In reviewing professional guidelines and standards, we begin with identifying current state laws regarding sexual education and HIV education, focusing on information gathered from the National Conference of State Legislatures (NCSL) (2014) and the Guttmacher Institute (2014). We highlight which state laws appear to capture the most comprehensive approach to sexual education. In the second half of the chapter, the NSES is reviewed, emphasizing core concepts for students by grade level. We identify strategies that provide the most comprehensive and ideal guidelines that support best practices for educators.

Recent assessment of sexual behavior among teenagers continues to prompt the need for comprehensive sexual education. According to the CDC (2014), there are "many young people [who] engage in sexual risk behaviors that can result in unintended health outcomes" ("Sexual Risk Behavior" section, para. 1). For example, among high school students in the United States surveyed in 2013:

- 46.8% had ever had sexual intercourse.
- 34.0% had had sexual intercourse during the previous 3 months, and, of these 40.9% did not use a condom the last time they had sex.
- 15.0% had had sex with four or more people during their life.

(CDC, 2014)

It is clear that young people are engaging in sexual behaviors, and it is essential that they receive sexual education prior to engaging in these behaviors.

Currently there are no federal laws regarding sexual education; these decisions are entrusted to each state. State laws about sexual education and HIV education laws can greatly differ, and some states have no requirements to teach these topics.

Legal and Ethical Standards

State Laws

In promoting relevant standards and guidelines for sexual health of children and adolescents, it is important to review state laws regarding sexual education. The NCSL and the Guttmacher Institute have both reviewed the current status of sexual education across the United States. According to the NCSL (2014), they are a national organization that was created in 1975 to "support, defend, and strengthen state legislatures" ("Our Story" section, para. 1). This organization often provides information regarding the creation of state laws, as well as any changes or updates. The Guttmacher Institute (2014) "advances sexual and reproductive health and rights through an interrelated program of research, policy analysis and public education designed to generate new ideas, encourage enlightened public debate and promote sound policy and program development" ("Mission" section, para. 1). The Guttmacher Institute frequently reports on state laws regarding sexual education. In 2014, the NCSL and the Guttmacher Institute reported on these laws as of December 2014. Some states require sexual education and/or HIV education, whereas other states only provide guidelines if a district decides to teach sexual education. A summary of state laws follows:

- Presently, 22 states and the District of Columbia require public schools teach sexual education.
  - o There are 20 of these states and the District of Columbia mandate sexual education *and* HIV education.
    (Guttmacher Institute, 2014; NCSL, 2014)

- Additionally, 33 states and the District of Columbia require students receive instruction about HIV/AIDS.
    (Guttmacher Institute, 2014; NCSL, 2014)

- Lastly, 27 states and the District of Columbia mandate that, when provided, sexual and HIV education programs meet certain general requirements.
  - o There are 13 states require that the instruction be medically accurate.
  - o Further, 26 states and the District of Columbia require that the information be appropriate for the students' age.

○   Eight states require that the program must provide instruction that is appropriate for a student's cultural background and not be biased against any race, sex, or ethnicity.

○   Two states prohibit the program from promoting religion.

(Guttmacher Institute, 2014)

The Guttmacher Institute and the NCSL also reviewed state laws that define parents' rights concerning sexual education. These laws provide an overview of parents' ability to exclude their children from sexual education, to allow parent involvement in the programs, and to allow parents reasonable access to education materials.

State laws regarding parental rights and sexual education are summarized as follows:

- There are 37 states and the District of Columbia that require school districts to allow parental involvement in sexual education programs, HIV education, or both.

(Guttmacher Institute, 2014; NCSL, 2014)

- Three states require parental consent before a student can participate in sexual education or HIV education.

(Guttmacher Institute, 2014; NCSL, 2014)

- There are 35 states and the District of Columbia which allow parents to exclude their children from participation in the sexual education curriculum.

(Guttmacher Institute, 2014; NCSL, 2014)

Most states requiring sexual education have similar laws. As noted above, many state laws indicate that sexual education must be medically accurate and age-appropriate, though these terms may have varying definitions. According to an Oregon state law, for example, "medically accurate" is defined as "information that is established through the use of the 'scientific method.' Results can be measured, quantified, and replicated to confirm accuracy, and are reported or recognized in peer-reviewed journals or other authoritative publications," and it defines "age-appropriate" as "curricula designed to teach concepts, information, and skills based on the social, cognitive, emotional, and experience level of students" (Oregon Administrative Rule, 2009). Similar terminology that applies to most state laws helps to make sexual education and/or HIV education more streamlined and coherent across the country. The existence of common language across states is beneficial for educators and students who may relocate to a different state. Providing national guidelines and standards would be ideal, as it would ensure that all students are receiving the same content. NSES (FoSE, 2014), described later in this chapter, would be an example of nationwide standards. Just like the *Common Core State Standards for English Language Arts and Mathematics*

(National Governors Association, 2010), the NSES offers the same benefits of equal education to all students. The Common Core State Standards (2014) were designed to "establish clear, consistent guidelines for what every student should know and be able to do in math and English language arts from kindergarten through 12th grade" ("What Parents Should Know" section, para. 1). Presently, there are 43 states, the District of Columbia's four territories, and the Department of Defense Education Activity that have adopted the Common Core State Standards (2014). It is hoped that the NSES will be similarly adopted across the United States.

Comprehensive Standards

Of the states that require sexual education, some provide more comprehensive laws and guidelines than others. It is important to note that generally these laws apply to public schools; administrators from private schools can make their own decisions about providing sexual education. We believe that having laws that incorporate an array of topics such as abstinence, contraception, healthy relationships, decision making, sexual orientation, and cultural considerations are ideal. Presently, many state laws (e.g., Alabama, described later) are undeveloped and/or outdated, lacking both research-based practices and inclusive guidelines. In 2009, the state of Oregon (Oregon Administrative Rule, 2009) created comprehensive and inclusive standards that are provided as an example below.

STATE OF OREGON HUMAN SEXUALITY EDUCATION

- Each school district shall teach an age-appropriate, comprehensive plan of instruction focusing on human sexuality education, HIV/AIDS and sexually transmitted disease prevention in elementary and secondary schools as an integral part of health education and other subjects. Course material and instruction for all human sexuality education courses that discuss human sexuality in public elementary and secondary schools shall enhance students' understanding of sexuality as a normal and healthy aspect of human development. In addition, the HIV/AIDS and sexually transmitted disease prevention education and the human sexuality education comprehensive plan shall provide instruction at least annually, for all students grades 6-8 and at least twice during grades 9-12.
- Parents, teachers, school administrators, local health department staff, other community representatives, and persons from the medical community who are knowledgeable of the latest scientific information and effective education strategies shall develop the plan of instruction required by this rule cooperatively.

- Local school boards shall approve the plan of instruction and require that it be reviewed and updated biennially in accordance with new scientific information and effective education strategies.
- Any parent may request that his/her child be excused from that portion of the instructional program required by this rule under the procedures set forth in ORS 336.035(2).
- The comprehensive plan of instruction shall include information that:

  (a) promotes abstinence for school-age youth and mutually monogamous relationships with an uninfected partner for adults as the safest and most responsible sexual behavior to reduce the risk of unintended pregnancy and exposure to HIV, Hepatitis B/C, and other sexually transmitted infectious diseases;

  (b) allays those fears concerning HIV that are scientifically groundless;

  (c) is balanced and medically accurate;

  (d) provides balanced and accurate information on the risks and benefits of contraceptive and other disease reduction measures which reduce the risk of unintended pregnancy, exposure to HIV, hepatitis B/C and other sexually transmitted infectious diseases;

  (e) discusses responsible sexual behaviors and hygienic practices which may reduce or eliminate unintended pregnancy, exposure to HIV, hepatitis B/C and other sexually transmitted diseases;

  (f) stresses the high risks of contracting HIV, hepatitis B and C and other infectious diseases through sharing of needles or syringes for injecting drugs including steroids, for tattooing, and body-piercing;

  (g) discusses the characteristics of the emotional, physical and psychological aspects of a healthy relationship and a discussion about the benefits of delaying pregnancy beyond the adolescent years as a means to better ensure a healthy future for parents and their children. Students shall be provided with statistics based on the latest medical information regarding both the health benefits and the possible side effects of all forms of contraceptives, including the success and failure rates for prevention of pregnancy;

  (h) stresses that HIV/STDs and hepatitis B/C can be serious possible hazards of sexual contact;

  (i) provides students with information about Oregon laws that address young people's rights and responsibilities relating to childbearing and parenting;

  (j) advises pupils of the circumstances in which it is unlawful under ORS 163.435 and 163.445 for persons 18 years of age or older to

(Continued)

(Continued)

have sexual relations with persons younger than 18 years of age to whom they are not married;

(k) encourages family communication and involvement and helps students learn to make responsible decisions;

(l) teaches that no form of sexual expression is acceptable when it physically or emotionally harms oneself or others and not to make unwanted physical and verbal sexual advances;

(m) teaches that it is wrong to take advantage of or exploit another person;

(n) validates through course material and instruction the importance of honesty with oneself and others, respect for each person's dignity and well-being, and responsibility for one's actions; and

(o) uses culturally and gender sensitive materials, language, and strategies that recognize different sexual orientations and gender roles.

- The comprehensive plan of instruction shall include skills-based instruction that:

  (a) assists students to develop and practice effective communication skills, the development of self-esteem and the ability to resist peer pressure;

  (b) provides students with the opportunity to learn about and personalize peer, media and community influences that both positively and negatively impact their decisions to abstain from sexual intercourse;

  (c) enhances students' ability to access valid health information and resources related to their sexual health;

  (d) teaches how to decline unwanted sexual advances, or accept the refusal of unwanted sexual advances, through the use of refusal and negotiation skills;

  (e) is research-based and/or best practice; and

  (f) aligns with the Oregon Health Education Content Standards and Benchmarks.

- All human sexuality education programs shall emphasize that abstinence from sexual intercourse, when practiced consistently and correctly, is the only method that is 100 percent effective against unintended pregnancy, HIV infection (when transmitted sexually), hepatitis B/C infection, and other sexually transmitted diseases. Abstinence is to be stressed, but not to the exclusion of other methods for preventing unintended pregnancy, HIV infection, sexually transmitted diseases, and hepatitis B/C. Such courses are to acknowledge the value of abstinence while not devaluing or ignoring those students who have had or are having sexual relationships. Further, sexuality education materials, instructional strategies, and activities must not, in any way, use shame or fear based tactics.

- Materials and information shall be presented in a manner sensitive to the fact that there are students who have experienced sexual abuse.

(Oregon Administration Rule, 2009)

Oregon's approach to sexual education is comprehensive because it covers a wide range of topics, including contraception, abstinence, and sexual orientation, as well as life skills, such as avoiding coercion, healthy decision making, and family communication. It promotes research-based materials that are sensitive to the needs of different students, including those of varying sexual orientations and victims of sexual abuse. Additionally, HIV/AIDS education is mandated, and along with general sexual education, the standards are to be age-appropriate, medically accurate, and culturally appropriate and unbiased. Lastly, Oregon's law considers parental rights (Guttmacher Institute, 2014).

Conversely, there are states that do not have laws related to sexual education in place; however, there are some states with movement toward creating such laws. For example, Massachusetts does not currently require sexual education; however, in 2012, Bill H. 3793, an Act relative to healthy youth, was proposed that addresses sexual education requirements. This proposed bill provides a first approach to creating laws for school districts. Below are the contents of the proposed bill:

MASSACHUSETTS PROPOSED HB 3793

Section 1

- Each school district or public school that offers sexual health education shall provide medically accurate, age-appropriate education. Sexual health education under this section shall: teach the benefits of abstinence and delaying sexual activity; stress the importance of effectively using contraceptives and barrier methods to prevent unintended pregnancy and sexually transmitted infections, including HIV/AIDS; teach students the skills to effectively negotiate and implement safer sexual activity; help students develop the relationship and communication skills to form healthy, respectful relationships free of violence, coercion, and intimidation and make healthy decisions about relationships and sexuality; and be appropriate for students regardless of gender, race, disability status, or sexual orientation.

(Continued)

(Continued)

Section 32A

- Every city, town, regional school district or vocational school district implementing or maintaining curriculum, which primarily involves human sexual education or human sexuality issues shall adopt a written policy ensuring parental or legal guardian notification of the comprehensive sexual health education that the school will provide and the right of the parent or legal guardian to withdraw his or her child from all or part of the instruction, and the process by which said withdrawal is communicated to the school. Said policy shall also advise parents and legal guardians that instruction materials and related items for said curriculum shall be made reasonably accessible to parents and guardians for inspection and review, and shall specify when and where such materials will be available.

Section 3

- No sooner than the academic year 2015-2016, each school district and Commonwealth charter school shall file a report regarding sexual health education in the district with the department every year by a date and in a format determined by the board. Said report shall include, but not be limited to, the following data for each public school district and Commonwealth charter school, by grade level:

  o A description of any sexual health education curricula offered;
  o The approximate number of hours spent on sexual health education;
  o The number of students receiving sexual health education; and
  o The number of students who withdraw from sexual health education, pursuant to section 32A.

  (Massachusetts Bill, 2012)

Though not as comprehensive as Oregon's current approved law related to sexual education, Massachusetts takes an important step in moving toward empirically supported practices by highlighting the need for data collection via reports that must be filed to the state. It is important to collect data regarding what is being taught and to which students because it can help determine efficacy and enhance management of sexual education programs as well as ensure consistency in adoption and teaching across school districts.

State Laws Regarding Sexual Education Content

The Guttmacher Institute collected information regarding the content of sexual education and HIV education from all states. Common topics include abstinence, contraception, pregnancy, sexual orientation, healthy relationships, and decision making. Some states require more information to be taught than others.

The required content across states is summarized as follows:

- There are 18 states and the District of Columbia that require information on contraception be provided.
- Additionally, 37 states require that information on abstinence be provided.
  - There are 25 states that require abstinence be stressed, compared to 12 states that require abstinence be covered.

- There are 19 states that require instruction on the importance of engaging in sexual activity only within marriage be provided.
- Only 12 states require discussion of sexual orientation.
  - Currently, 9 states require that discussion of sexual orientation be inclusive.
  - Furthermore, 3 states require only negative information on sexual orientation, including Alabama, South Carolina, and Texas. Negative information could include that homosexuality is a criminal offense.

- Currently, 13 states require the inclusion of information on the negative outcomes of teen sex and pregnancy.
- Lastly, 26 states and the District of Columbia require the provision of information about skills for healthy sexuality (including avoiding coerced sex), healthy decision-making, and family communication.
  - Presently, 20 states and the District of Columbia require that sexual education include information about skills for avoiding coerced sex.
  - In addition, 20 states require that sexual education include information on making healthy decisions around sexuality.
  - Only 11 states require sexual education instruction on how to talk to family members, especially parents, about sex.

(Guttmacher Institute, 2014)

The following summarizes the content requirements when HIV education is taught:

- Only 19 states require information on condoms or contraception.
- There are 39 states require that abstinence be included.
  - There are 27 states require that abstinence be stressed, compared to 12 states require that abstinence only to be covered.

(Guttmacher Institute, 2014)

In some instances, states and/or school districts offer abstinence-only pro-grams. If abstinence programs are in place, there can be several required laws to follow. Under Section 510 of the Social Security Act, there are several guidelines that need to be addressed by an abstinence program to qualify for federal funds.

Content requirements for abstinence-only programs to qualify for federal funds are summarized as follows:

- Contents has as its exclusive purpose, teaching the social, psychologi-cal, and health gains to be realized by abstaining from sexual activity;
- Content teaches abstinence from sexual activity outside marriage as the expected standard for all school-age children;
- Content teaches that abstinence from sexual activity is the only certain way to avoid out-of-wedlock pregnancy, sexually transmitted diseases, and other associated health problems;
- Content teaches that a mutually faithful monogamous relationship in the context of marriage is the expected standard of human sexual activity;
- Content teaches that sexual activity outside of the context of marriage is likely to have harmful psychological and physical effects;
- Content teaches that bearing children out-of-wedlock is likely to have harmful consequences for the child, the child's parents, and society;
- Content teaches young people how to reject sexual advances and how alcohol and drug use increases vulnerability to sexual advances;
- Lastly, content teaches the importance of attaining self-sufficiency before engaging in sexual activity.

(Social Security Act, 2010)

Although abstinence is the only way to ensure that unwanted sexual health out-comes do not occur, programs that only address abstinence have limited efficacy. For example, in 2007, Mathematic Policy Research Inc., on behalf of the U.S. Department of Health and Human Services, conducted a study on Title V abstinence-only-until-marriage programs. Title V includes over 700 abstinence-only-until-marriage programs. The study investigated four of these programs that were said to demonstrate the most positive results (Trenholm, Devaney, Fortson, Quay, Wheeler, & Clark, 2007).

The study's results are as follows:

- Evaluation found no evidence that abstinence-only-until-marriage programs increased rates of sexual abstinence.
- Students in the abstinence-only-until-marriage programs had a similar age of first sex and similar numbers of sexual partners as their peers who were not in the programs.
- The average age of sexual debut was the same for the abstinence-only-until-marriage participants and control groups (14 years, 9 months).

(Trenholm et al., 2007)

In a second example, the National Campaign to Prevent Teen and Unplanned Pregnancy released Emerging Answers in 2007 (Kirby, 2007). This report examined what programs successfully worked in preventing teen pregnancy and STDs, including HIV. The authors found strong evidence that abstinence-only-until-marriage programs do not have any impact on teen sexual behavior (Kirby, 2007). Key findings were as follows:

- "In sum, studies of abstinence programs have not produced sufficient evidence to justify their widespread dissemination. Instead, efforts should be directed toward carefully developing and evaluating these programs" (p. 15).
- "At present, there does not exist any strong evidence that any abstinence program delays the initiation of sex, hastens the return to abstinence, or reduces the number of sexual partners. In addition, there is strong evidence from multiple randomized trials demonstrating that some abstinence programs chosen for evaluation because they were believed to be promising actually had no impact on teen sexual behavior" (p. 15).

(Kirby, 2007)

Lastly, Underhill, Montgomery, and Operario (2007) conducted a meta-analysis on data examining the results of 13 abstinence-only trials that included approximately 16,000 students. Findings were as follows:

- Abstinence-only-until-marriage programs were ineffective in changing any of the behaviors that were examined including the rate of vaginal sex, number of sexual partners, and condom use. The rates of pregnancy and sexually transmitted infections among participants in abstinence-only-until-marriage programs were unaffected.
- As a result of this meta-study, the researchers concluded that recent declines in the United States rate of teen pregnancy are most likely the result of improved use of contraception rather than a decrease in sexual activity.

(Underhill et al., 2007)

From a review of existing state laws, it is significant to note that over half of the states do not require sexual education. Interestingly, more states require education about HIV/AIDS than sexual education. The following states currently have no indication of providing sexual education laws or guidelines: Alaska, Kansas, Nebraska, South Dakota, and Wyoming. The following states do not require sexual education: Alabama, Arizona, Arkansas, California, Colorado, Connecticut, Florida, Hawaii, Idaho, Illinois, Indiana, Louisiana, Massachusetts, Michigan, Missouri, New Hampshire, New York, Oklahoma, Pennsylvania,

Texas, Virginia, Washington, and Wisconsin (Guttmacher Institute, 2014). Though some states may not require sexual education, several of them do have content requirements if it is taught, such as Alabama, California, Colorado, Hawaii, Illinois, Virginia, and Washington (Guttmacher Institute, 2014).

Special Considerations

The Guttmacher Institute also highlights that several states have sexual education that provides information inclusive of different sexual orientations. As LGBT youth are disproportionally affected by negative sexual health outcomes (CDC, 2014; Gilliam, 2001), it is important to include LGBT components to sexual education. States that currently include programing for LGBT youth are California, Colorado, Delaware, Iowa, New Jersey, New Mexico, Oregon, Rhode Island, and Washington (Guttmacher Institute, 2014). Conversely, there are states such as Alabama, South Carolina, and Texas that teach sexual orientation negatively.

For example, there is an Alabama law that was written in 1992: "An emphasis, in a factual manner and from a public health perspective, that homosexuality is not a lifestyle acceptable to the general public and that homosexual conduct is a criminal offense under the laws of the state" (Alabama Code, 1992). Though Alabama does not require that schools teach sexual education, if it is provided, this law is still applicable. Having these values taught to students who may identify as LGBT can have a significant negative impact: "It not only prevents LGBT students from learning the information and skills they need to stay healthy, but it also contributes to a climate of exclusion in schools, where LGBT students are already frequent targets of bullying and discrimination" (Slater, 2013). In a study, Goodenow, Szalacha, Robin, and Westheimer (2008) found that young women who identified as lesbian, gay, or bisexual were at higher risk for pregnancy, STI diagnosis, and coerced sexual contact than young women unsure of their identity or who identified as heterosexual. Additionally, according to the CDC (2014), young gay and bisexual men accounted for an estimated 19% (8,800) of all new HIV infections in the United States and 72% of new HIV infections among youth in 2010. These young men, aged 13–24, were "the only age group that showed a significant increase in estimated new infections—22% from 2008 (7,200) through 2010 (8,800)" ("New HIV Infections" section, para. 2, CDC, 2014). It is clear that LGBT youth are a unique population that requires sexual education that addresses their needs. Laws like the one in Alabama only work to alienate LGBT students. We believe that sexual education should provide the same benefits to all students, regardless of sexual orientation.

It is clear that not all states provide the most accurate, data-based curriculum to children and adolescents about sexual education. There are some states that are in the process of developing new and/or updated laws, like Massachusetts and New York (NCSL, 2014), but half of the country still does not require sexual education. There appears to be a connection between states with rigorous standards to require that education must be medically accurate, age-appropriate, and culturally unbiased with a discussion of contraception. These facets, in addition to being inclusive of LGBT youth, are essential components of a comprehensive program.

Overview of NSES
The Historical Context

The history of the *National Sexuality Education Standards: Core Content and Skills, K-12* is based on the ongoing initiative of the FoSE. FoSE is a "partnership between Advocates for Youth, Answer, and the Sexuality Information and Education Council of the United States (SIECUS) that seeks to create a national dialogue about the future of sex education and to promote the institutionalization of comprehensive sexuality education in public schools" ("Press Room" section, para. 13, FoSE, 2014). Professionals from the fields of health education, sexuality education, public health, public policy, philanthropy, and advocacy convened in December 2008 to create a strategic plan for sexuality education policy and implementation (FoSE, 2014). This group developed the NSES in 2011 to address the inconsistences of sexuality education nationwide. As described earlier, many states enforce different laws regarding sexual education, and some states offer no guidance or requirements at all. The NSES (FoSE, 2014) were developed to provide a national set of standards that encompasses best practices consonant to the most current research related to sexual education.

The goals of NSES (2011) were designed to:

- Outline the minimum, essential content and skills for sexuality education K-12.
- Assist schools in designing sexuality education that is planned, sequential, and part of a comprehensive school health education approach.
- Provide a rationale for teaching that is evidence-based, age-appropriate, and theory-driven.
- Support schools in improving academic performance by addressing content that is highly relevant to students and directly related to high school graduation rates.
- Present sexual development as a normal, natural, healthy part of human development.
- Offer recommendations for school personnel on age-appropriate materials to teach.
- Translate the body of research related to school-based sexuality education into practice.

(FoSE, 2014)

The *National Health Education Standards* (NHES) influenced the development of the NSES (2011). The NHES were first created in 1995 and updated in 2007 by the Joint Committee on National Health Education Standards of the American Cancer Society; however, the NHES (CDC, 2015) do not address any specific health content areas, including content for sexuality education. Additionally, the CDC's *Health Education Curriculum Analysis Tool*, existing state and international education standards on sexual health, the *Guidelines for Comprehensive Sexuality Education: Kindergarten–12th Grade*, and the *Common Core State Standards for English Language Arts and Mathematics* influenced the creation of the NSES (FoSE, 2014).

The overarching goal of the NSES (2011) is "to provide clear, consistent and straightforward guidance on the essential minimum, core content for sexuality education that is age-appropriate for students in grades K-12" ("National Sexuality Education Standards" section, para. 1, FoSE, 2014). Before writing these standards, authors based their work on guiding values and principles, as well as described characteristics of effective sexuality education based on the NHES (1995). There are 10 guiding values and principles, with the first two principles highlighted below:

- "Academic achievement and the health status of students are interrelated, and should be recognized as such."
- "All students, regardless of physical or intellectual ability, deserve the opportunity to achieve personal health and wellness, including sexual health."

(FoSE, 2014, p. 9)

These two principles emphasize the importance of sexual education and that it is a right of all students to receive this information. The eight remaining values and principles address a wide range of ideas, such as having qualified sexual education teachers, encouraging the use of technology to access valid information, and explaining the connection between sexual health and healthcare costs (FoSE, 2014). Importantly, the NSES also describes characteristics of effective sexuality education. The three key characteristics of NSES are that it (1) focuses on specific behavioral outcomes, (2) uses strategies designed to personalize information and engage students, and (3) provides functional knowledge that is basic, accurate, and directly contributes to health-promoting decisions and behaviors (FoSE, 2014). These three characteristics reflect what we believe is most important in developing standards for sexual education. Sexual education should have specific goals for behavior that students will achieve by experiencing a program as a way of documenting the efficacy of the instruction and ways to improve curricular efforts in the future, based on these findings. The program should have flexibility in meeting the needs of all students, regardless of race, ethnicity, gender, gender identity, sexual orientation, etc., as well as provide functional information, including both abstinence and contraception, that allows students to make the best sexual health decisions for themselves that will preserve their dignity and keep them physically and emotionally healthy based on accurate information. Complete lists of the

"Guiding Values and Principles" as well as "Characteristics of Effective Sexuality Education" can be found within the handbook of standards (http://www.future-ofsexed.org/documents/josh-fose-standards-web.pdf).

Professional Guidelines

According to the SIECUS (2014), comprehensive sexual education programs have four primary goals: (1) to provide information regarding sexuality that is accurate, (2) to give adolescents a chance to define and develop their "values, attitudes, and insights about sexuality," (3) to help teens "develop relationships and interpersonal skills," and (4) to help them make responsible decisions about sex ("What Are the Goals of School-Based Sexual Education" section, para. 3, SIECUS, 2014). Included in the final goal are curriculum and instruction on abstinence, peer pressure, use of protection, as well as the following key concepts: (1) human development, (2) relationships, (3) personal skills, (4) sexual behavior, (5) sexual health, and (6) society and culture (FoSE, 2014).

The FoSE also has established the idea of developmental messages. Developmental messages are brief statements that contain specific information that young people need to learn about each topic. For each topic, the *Guidelines* present developmental messages appropriate for four separate age levels that reflect stages of development:

Level 1: middle childhood, ages 5 through 8; early elementary school

Level 2: preadolescence, ages 9 through 12; later elementary school

Level 3: early adolescence, ages 12 through 15; middle school/junior high school

Level 4: adolescences, ages 15 through 18; high school

(FoSE, 2014)

By identifying developmental stages, the NSES provides an age-appropriate approach to sexual education that provides specific goals for learning in each level of development. Like many research-based articles and studies, the NSES is built upon a theoretical framework. This framework guides how a piece of work is created, analyzed, and evaluated. For the NSES, authors based their standards on social learning theory, which recognizes that "learning occurs not merely within the learner but also in a particular social context" (Hedgepeth & Helmich, 1996). The NSES includes several essential concepts within this framework for their standards, which are (1) personalization, (2) susceptibility, (3) self-efficacy, (4) social norms, and (5) skills. For more information regarding these concepts, consult the standards book (FoSE, 2014). Additionally, the NSES reflects both *social cognitive theory* and *social ecological model of prevention*. *Social cognitive theory* (Bandura, 1989) emphasizes self-efficacy as well as motivation and emotional learning. The *social ecological model of prevention* (CDC, 2011) focuses on individual, interpersonal, community, and society influences and the role of these influences on people over time. The intersectionality of these frameworks provides the foundation of the NSES, which we believe promotes a sound methodology to the development of the standards.

Content of Standards

There are seven topics chosen as the minimum, essential content and skills for K–12 sexuality education. These topics highlight the major concepts that students should learn from their sexual education program. The topics and descriptions are as follows:

- *Anatomy and Physiology (AP)* "provides a foundation for understanding basic human functioning" (FoSE, 2014, p. 10).
- *Puberty and Adolescent Development (PD)* "addresses a pivotal milestone for every person that has an impact on physical, social, and emotional development" (p. 10).
- *Identity (ID)* "addresses several fundamental aspects of people's understanding of who they are" (p.10).
- *Pregnancy and Reproduction (PR)* "addresses information about how pregnancy happens and decision-making to avoid a pregnancy" (p. 10).
- *STDs and HIV (SH)* "provides both content and skills for understanding and avoiding STDs and HIV, including how they are transmitted, their signs and symptoms, and testing and treatment" (p. 10).
- *Healthy Relationships (HR)* "offers guidance to students on how to successfully navigate changing relationships among family, peers, and partners. Special emphasis is given in the *National Sexuality Education Standards* (2011) to the increasing use and impact of technology within relationships" (p. 10).
- *Personal Safety (PS)* "emphasizes the need for a growing awareness, creation, and maintenance of safe school environments for all students" (p. 10).

Additionally, the seven topics are organized following the eight standards of NHES. With this framework, each of the seven major topics addresses these eight standards. We believe that the standards cover the most important concepts within the major topics. The standards of NHES are as follows:

- *Core Concepts* (CC) Standard 1—"Students will comprehend concepts related to health promotion and disease prevention to enhance health" (FoSE, 2014, p. 11).
- *Analyzing Influences* (INF) Standard 2—"Students will analyze the influence of family, peers, culture, media, technology, and other factors on health behaviors" (p. 11).

- *Accessing Information* (AI) Standard 3—"Students will demonstrate the ability to access valid information, products, and services to enhance health" (p. 11).
- *Interpersonal Communication* (IC) Standard 4—"Students will demonstrate the ability to use interpersonal communication skills to enhance health and avoid or reduce health risks" (p. 11).
- *Decision Making* (DM) Standard 5—"Students will demonstrate the ability to use decision-making skills to enhance health" (p. 11).
- *Goal Setting* (GS) Standard 6—"Students will demonstrate the ability to use goal-setting skills to enhance health" (p. 11).
- *Self-management* (SM) Standard 7—"Students will demonstrate the ability to practice health-enhancing behavior and avoid or reduce health risks" (p. 11).
- *Advocacy* (ADV) Standard 8—"Students will demonstrate the ability to advocate for person, family, and community health" (p. 11).

Core Content of Standards

We believe that by addressing the eight standards within the NHES (1995), the NSES (2011) provides a comprehensive approach to defining standards for sexual education. The standards provide specific descriptions of the goals presented by both grade level and topic area. We present an overview of core concepts presented by grade level, as detailed in the NSES (FoSE, 2014).

Grades K–2 Overview

By the end of the second grade, it is recommended that students have learned beginning concepts in the topics of *AP, ID, PR, HR,* and *PS.* At this point, it is not recommended to teach concepts within *PD* or *SH.*

Core Concepts for grades K–2 are outlined:

(*AP*)   Uses proper names for body parts, including male and female anatomy.
(*ID*)   Describe differences and similarities in how boys and girls may be expected to act.
(*PR*)   Explain that all living things reproduce.
(*HR*)   Identify different kinds of family structures; describe the characteristics of a friend.
(*PS*)   Explain that all people, including children, have the right to tell others not to touch their body when they do not want to be touched; explain what bullying and teasing are; explain why bulling and teasing are wrong.

Grades 3–5 Overview

By the end of the fifth grade, more core concepts should be covered, including all previous concepts in grades K–2. The categories of *PD* and *SH* are initially taught.

Core Concepts for grades 3–5 include all Core Concepts in grades K–2 plus the following:

(PD) Explain the physical, social, and emotional changes that occur during puberty and adolescence; explain how the timing of puberty and adolescent development varies considerably and can still be healthy; describe how puberty prepares human bodies for the potential to reproduce.

(ID) Define sexual orientation as the romantic attraction of an individual to someone of the same gender or a different gender.

(PR) Describe the process of human reproduction.

(SH) Define HIV and identify some age-appropriate methods of transmission, as well as ways to prevent transmission.

(PS) Define sexual harassment and sexual abuse.

Grades 6–8 Overview

Concepts become more developed as they continue to build upon previous standards. Core Concepts for grades 6–8 include all Core Concepts in grades 3–5 plus the following:

(ID) Differentiate between gender identity, gender expression, and sexual orientation; explain the range of gender roles.

(PR) Define sexual intercourse and its relationship to human reproduction; define sexual abstinence as it relates to pregnancy prevention; explain the health benefits, risks, and effectiveness rates of various methods of contraception, including abstinence and condoms; define emergency contraception and its use; describe the signs and symptoms of a pregnancy; identify prenatal practices that can contribute to a healthy pregnancy.

(SH) Define STDs, including HIV, and how they are and are not transmitted; compare and contrast behaviors, including abstinence, to determine the potential risk of STD/HIV transmission from each; describe the signs, symptoms, and potential impacts of STDs, including HIV.

(HR) Describe the potential impacts of power differences such as age, status, or position within relationships; analyze the similarities and differences between friendships and romantic relationships; describe a range of ways people express affection within various types of relationships; describe the advantages and disadvantages of communication using technology and social media.

(PS) Describe the situations and behaviors that constitute bullying, sexual harassment, sexual abuse, sexual assault, incest, rape, and dating violence; discuss the impacts of bullying, sexual harassment, sexual abuse, sexual assault, incest, rape, and dating violence and why they are wrong; explain that no one has the right to touch anyone else in a sexual manner if they do not want to be touched; explain why a person who has been raped or sexually assaulted is not at fault.

Grades 9–12 Overview

The core content of grades 9–12 standards is mostly reflected in grades 6–8 standards; however, in grades 9–12, there is the opportunity to go further in-depth on these topics.

Core Concepts for grades 9–12 include all Core Concepts in grades 6–8 plus the following:

(*AP*)   Describe the human sexual response cycle, including the role hormones play.

(*PD*)   Analyze how brain development has an impact on cognitive, social, and emotional changes of adolescence and early adulthood.

(*ID*)   Distinguish between sexual orientation, sexual behavior, and sexual identity.

(*PR*)   Identify the laws related to reproductive and sexual healthcare services (i.e., contraception, pregnancy options, safe surrender policies, prenatal care); describe prenatal practices that can contribute to or threaten a healthy pregnancy; compare and contrast the laws relating to pregnancy, adoption, abortion, and parenting.

(*SH*)   Describe common symptoms of and treatments for STDs, including HIV; evaluate the effectiveness of abstinence, condoms, and other safer sex methods in preventing the spread of STDs, including HIV; describe the laws related to sexual healthcare services, including STD and HIV testing and treatment.

(*HR*)   Define sexual consent and explain its implication for sexual decision making.

(*PS*)   Analyze the laws related to bullying, sexual harassment, sexual abuse, sexual assault, incest, rape, and dating violence; explain why using tricks, threats, or coercion in relationships is wrong.

Implications for Sexual Health Promotion

NSES (2011) has implications for sexual health promotion and programing. Because they are intended to provide an inclusive approach to sexuality education, the standards offer a detailed, age-appropriate framework for teaching all students. We believe that the theoretical framework integrating social learning theory, social cognitive theory, and social ecological model of prevention lays a strong foundation for developing comprehensive standards. By identifying the core concepts for content in each grade level, educators can easily monitor what topics have been covered.

States can use the NSES (2011) to determine how closely their standards meet the learning objectives and goals described in the NSES. By analyzing current program standards, lawmakers and school administrators can identify which concepts are being taught in sexual education and make adjustments accordingly. This also allows stakeholders to recognize the limitations and strengths of their program compared to the NSES. Working with the NSES, stakeholders will recognize that it provides a sound framework for instruction that reflects data-based research on sexual education. Overall, we believe the NSES focuses on health promotion, including ideas of abstinence and risk reduction of unsafe sexual behaviors. It teaches not only the biology and physical concepts, but it also includes social-emotional aspects of sexual health.

We advocate that all states adopt sexual health education. NSES (2011) provides foundational guidelines for educators, and school administrators can use the standards to develop a curriculum that best fits their student population. All students deserve sexuality education that addresses their needs, which means that any education provided must be inclusive and sensitive to students from various backgrounds and experiences. Instruction should not alienate groups, such as LGBTQ students, students who have been sexually abused, students with non-conforming gender identities, and asexual students. This will require additional work by school administration to be updated on current research regarding these subgroups.

References

Alabama Code § 16-40A-2. (1992). *Minimum contents to be included in sex education programs or curriculum.* Retrieved from http://alisondb.legislature.state.al.us/alison/codeofalabama/1975/coatoc.htm

Bandura, A. (1989). Human agency in social cognitive theory. *American Psychologist, 44*(9), 1175–1184.

CDC. (2011). *The social-ecological model: A framework for prevention.* Retrieved from http://www.cdc.gov/violenceprevention/overview/social-ecologicalmodel.html

CDC. (2014). *HIV among youth.* Retrieved from http://www.cdc.gov/hiv/risk/age/youth/index.html?s_cid=tw_std0141316

CDC. (2015). *National Health Education Standards.* Retrieved from http://www.cdc.gov/healthyyouth/sher/standards/

Common Core State Standards Initiative. (2014). *What parents should know.* Retrieved from http://www.corestandards.org/what-parents-should-know/

FoSE. (2014). *National Sexuality Education Standards: Core Content and Skills K-12.* Retrieved from http://www.futureofsexed.org/documents/josh-fose-standards-web.pdf

Gilliam, J. (2001). *Young women who have sex with women: Falling through cracks of sexual health care.* Retrieved from http://www.advocatesforyouth.org/publications/552?task=view

Goodenow, C., Szalacha, L. A., Robin, L. E., & Westheimer, K. (2008). Dimensions of sexual orientation and HIV-related risk among adolescent females: Evidence from a statewide survey. *American Journal of Public Health, 98*(6), 1051–1058.

Guttmacher Institute. (2014). *State policies in brief: Sex and HIV education.* Retrieved from http://www.guttmacher.org/statecenter/spibs/spib_SE.pdf

Hedgepeth, E., & Helmich, J. (1996). *Teaching about HIV and sexuality: Principles and methods for effective education.* New York: New York University Press.

Kirby, D. (2007). *Emerging answers 2007: Research findings on programs to reduce teen pregnancy and sexually transmitted diseases*. Washington, DC: The National Campaign to Prevent Teen and Unplanned Pregnancy.

Massachusetts Bill H.3793 (2012). *An Act relative to healthy youth*. Retrieved from http://malegislature.gov/Bills/188/House/H3793

National Conference of State Legislatures (NCSL). (2014). *State policies on sex education in schools*. Retrieved from http://www.ncsl.org/research/health/state-policies-on-sex-education-in-schools.aspx

National Governors Association Center for Best Practices & Council of Chief State School Officers. (2010). *Common Core State Standards*. Washington, DC: National Governors Association Center for Best Practices & Council of Chief State School Officers.

Oregon Administrative Rule 581-022-1440. (2009). *Human sexuality education act of 1993*. Revised Statute 2009. Retrieved from http://www.ode.state.or.us/search/page/?=1452

SIECUS. (2014). *Sexuality education Q & A*. Retrieved from http://www.siecus.org/index.cfm?fuseaction=page.viewpage&pageid%20=521&grandparentID=477&parentID=514

Slater, H. (2013). *LGBT-inclusive sex education means healthier youth and safer schools*. Retrieved from https://www.americanprogress.org/issues/lgbt/news/2013/06/21/67411/lgbt-inclusive-sex-education-means-healthier-youth-and-safer-schools

Social Security Act, §510(b)(2). (2010). *Separate program for abstinence education*. Retrieved from http://www.ssa.gov/OP_Home/ssact/title05/0510.htm

Trenholm, C., Devaney, B., Fortson, K., Quay, L., Wheeler, J., & Clark, M. (2007). *Impacts of Four Title V, Section 510 Abstinence Education Programs* (Final Report). Retrieved from http://www.mathematica-mpr.com/publications/pdfs/impactabstinence.pdf

Underhill, K., Montgomery, P., & Operario, D. (2007). Sexual abstinence only programs to prevent HIV infection in high-income countries: Systematic review. *PLoS Medicine, 4*(9), e275. doi:10.1371/journal.pmed.0040275

5

DEVELOPMENTAL AND CULTURAL CONSIDERATIONS IN PROMOTING SEXUAL HEALTH

The purpose of this chapter is to present the reader with an examination of developmental and cultural considerations in the promotion of sexual health among children and adolescents. The first portion of the chapter will present a brief overview of child and adolescent sexual health development and age-appropriate sexual health education. Consideration will also be given to best practices for providing sexual health education to children and adolescents with developmental and cognitive disabilities. The next portion of the chapter will describe the literature with respect to the sexual health of racial and ethnic minority youth and concomitant recommendations for advocating for and delivering culturally responsive sexual health education. Using multitiered systems of supports (Burns & Gibbons, 2012) and population-based mental health models (Doll & Cummings, 2008) as a data-based decision-making framework to meet the sexual health needs of all youth, recommendations for adaptations and sensitive practices for specialized populations, such as individuals with disabilities and racial/ethnic minority youth, will be interspersed throughout the chapter.

Child and Adolescent Sexual Development

Sexual Development in Childhood

Sexual development is commonly associated with onset of puberty, but begins in infancy and early childhood (Kreipe, 2010). According to the National Sexual Violence Resource Center (2013), sexual development follows a developmental sequence from infancy. As the National Sexual Violence Resource Center (2013) articulates, healthy childhood sexual development follows a developmental trajectory, with milestones such as curiosity and exploration of one's body, including one's genitals (ages 0–2) and playful exploration of bodies with same-age peers (ages 3–5). Subsequently, during the middle childhood years (ages 5–8), children continue to explore their own bodies and perhaps those of others and begin to explore gender roles, which also occurs among those who identify as transgender (National Sexual Violence Resource Center, 2013). Gender identity occurs as early as age 2 or 3, and those who identify as transgender may need additional support in navigating gender expression, particularly when experiencing negative familial or societal reactions (Kreipe, 2010; National Sexual Violence Resource Center, 2013). The National Child Traumatic Stress Network (NCTSN, 2009), in their description of sexual development, describes how sexual behaviors among children are present from birth and can be concerning for parents to observe, but are typically part of normal development. As children reach school age (ages 7–12), they increasingly become more private with respect to masturbation and undressing (NCTSN, 2009). The NCTSN describes childhood sexual behaviors such as "playing doctor" and even touching another's private parts as not "uncommon" and not likely a cause for concern, even though such behaviors may be alarming for adults. NCTSN articulates that most developmentally expected childhood sexual behaviors are tied to curiosity, especially when they are infrequent, spontaneous, voluntary, and occur among similar age-and-size friends who play together often. The NCTSN describes that although such behaviors are common, and not likely a cause for concern, they should not be ignored and do provide for a teachable moment about appropriate sexual boundaries (NCTSN, 2009). Further, the NCTSN provides an outline of specific sexual safety behaviors that should be taught to children by age group. NCTSN recommends a developmental approach for teaching sexual health behaviors by developmental stage from their vantage point of being an agency focused on traumatic stress. Young children (ages 4–6) should be taught that sexual abuse is when someone touches your private parts, or asks you to touch their private parts and it does not matter if they know you (NCTSN, 2009).

Developmentally, young children should be taught the anatomically correct information about body parts and proper terms for bathroom routines (NCTSN, 2009). School-aged children (ages 7–12) should be taught information about proper physical boundaries, dating, sexual reproduction, and basic contraception (NCTSN, 2009). See the NCTSN (2009) document with a specific table that outlines detailed recommended teaching topics by age group, as well as a list of additional resources for parents and caregivers to access when teaching sexual boundaries and content with their children. The NCTSN is an important resource to access when ensuring that children, adolescents, caregivers, and family members have accurate information about developmentally appropriate sexual behaviors and sexual health content that should be covered by developmental level. The NCTSN (2009) also provided guidelines for teaching children sexual safety behaviors and how to seek assistance and support when concerned about potential child sexual abuse or inappropriate sexual boundaries that might be observed in one's own children, other children, or within the classroom setting.

Sexual Development in Adolescence

Strength-based Approach

In later childhood years (ages 9–12), puberty begins along with increased youth awareness of privacy and curiosity about physical development (Kreipe, 2010). Despite sexual development being a process that evolves from infancy, many equate sexual development with adolescence, at which time there are significant physical and emotional changes that coincide with the completion of puberty and the beginning of many important choices related to sexual health. Kreipe (2010), in his ACT for Youth Center of Excellence webinar covering major physical, psychological, and sociocultural factors in adolescent puberty and changes in the teen years, emphasized the need for adults in adolescents' lives to facilitate healthy relationships, rather than focusing solely on the avoidance of STIs. Kreipe's point about the need for a comprehensive approach to sexual health and not one solely based on disease prevention is a prevailing point in prominent publications related to general adolescent health. For instance, a 2009 report sponsored by the Johns Hopkins Center for Adolescent Health (McNeely & Blanchard, 2009) stated that "problem-free is not fully prepared" (Foreword, ix). Rather, McNeely and Blanchard describe the contemporary notion of "positive youth development" in research and recommended policy on the topic. A positive or resiliency approach, as defined by adolescent attainment of assets defined as "Competence, Confidence, Connection, Character, and Caring" (the "five C's," p. 3), is emphasized rather than a model solely based on the avoidance of diseases or high-risk behavior. The prevention of high-risk, health-related behaviors is still viewed by advocates of an asset approach as an important focus, but an additional focus on more comprehensive health instruction that goes beyond simply avoidance of adolescent risk behaviors, such as early-onset sexual activity and not using condoms, is also emphasized. The same thinking on assets and strengths is increasingly being applied to supporting not only general adolescent health but also sexual health in children and adolescents as well. For example, Kreipe (2010) outlines an ecological view when supporting youth undergo pubertal changes that are more comprehensive than singularly focusing on avoiding sexual risk behaviors.

Adolescent Sexual Development

As Kreipe's (2010) webinar outlines, significant hormonal changes mark the start of puberty, which results in a number of physical changes. The major physical changes during puberty, condensed from Kreipe's webinar, are that girls develop breasts typically between the ages of 7 and 13 and menstruation generally occurs generally between the ages of 11 and 13. Additional physical changes in girls are the widening of the hips and increased fat deposits. Physical signs of puberty for boys include the lengthening of the penis, enlargement of testicles, and release of sperm, often in the form of "wet dreams" (ejaculation of sperm during sleep) (Kreipe, 2010). For girls, puberty tends to end somewhere between the ages of 12 and 16, whereas boys reach puberty later, often between the ages of 14 and 20, but may continue growing into their early twenties. Once females begin to menstruate and males ejaculate, one can assume that pregnancy may occur. For females, an initially erratic menstrual cycle does not mean that they cannot get pregnant.

McNeely and Blanchard (2009) provide a similar description of physical pubertal changes as was presented in Kreipe's webinar and corresponding narrated PowerPoint presentation. See Kreipe (2010) for these materials and for a much more detailed overview of the physical changes of puberty than is being summarized here. The Johns Hopkins Center for Adolescent Health document (McNeely & Blanchard, 2009) is another useful resource that outlines physical developmental changes of youth and also provides helpful tips for parents and other concerned adults in helping youth navigate through the physical changes of puberty. These tips include actively listening to teen concerns about the physical changes they are experiencing and their physical appearance, as well as providing strategies for teens to have proper nutrition and combating media portrayals of unrealistic body images (McNeely & Blanchard, 2009). Puberty is a sensitive time for youth and can be a challenging developmental benchmark for parents and other influential adults (e.g., teachers, coaches) that support adolescents during this physical transition time. Teens who identify as transgender may need additional support as these physical changes occur, particularly if they receive negative familial or societal reactions and may have significant confusion about the changes that are occurring in their bodies that do not correspond to their gender identity (Kreipe, 2010).

As Kreipe (2010) and others (e.g., Bearinger, Sieving, Ferguson, & Sharma, 2007; Rouvier, Campero, Walker, & Caballero 2011) emphasize, puberty and sexual development occurs within a broader society in which cultural norms impact all behaviors, including the expression of sexual ones. Kreipe (2010) also stresses that puberty is not solely defined by physical changes, but psychological and psychosocial development as well. In the Johns Hopkins Center for Adolescent Health document (McNeely & Blanchard, 2009), an entire chapter is focused on social relationships that become very important as adolescents learn empathy, which involves the ability to take another's perspective and learning the impact that one has on other people. Parents and adult role models play a significant role in helping teens navigate social relationships, including romantic ones, which increasingly take a prominent role in the lives of teenagers and serve as models for future significant partnerships in the adult world (Kreipe, 2010). The Johns Hopkins document also contains critical information about bullying and specific skills that schools, families, and community agencies can teach to students to prevent and address relationship aggression and bullying when they experience it first-hand or see it (McNeely & Blanchard, 2009). For example, the long-term potential negative impact of bullying should be stressed with youth as well as assertiveness skills in speaking up whether one is being bullied or is an observer. Further, issues of cyberbullying are increasingly becoming more prevalent and the permanency of what is posted on social media needs to be emphasized with youths. Families, parents, schools, community agencies, and the youth themselves need to work with one another to have honest communication about bullying and social media. Social development and relationships among adolescents are taking on new dimensions. Youth need to be taught proper etiquette and the permanently damaging nature and harm that can ensue when poor decisions are made with respect to social media (McNeely & Blanchard, 2009).

Developmentally Appropriate Sexual Health Education

As articulated in Chapter 4 of this book, NSES (FoSE, 2014) has developed developmentally based skills and indicators to guide states, school districts, and schools in designing sexual health curriculum for children across the developmental spectrum from kindergarten through high school. Consistent with the notion that sexual development and sexual behaviors are common to children before the adolescent milestone of puberty is reached, sexual health instruction and support should be initiated early in the school years (FoSE, 2014; NCTSN, 2009). According to the NSES, described in more detail within Chapter 4, early developmentally appropriate sexual health indicators include accurate labeling of body parts, including sexual organs, and safety information conveyed to children about inappropriate touching, establishing healthy boundaries, and the importance of reporting concerns to adults (FoSE, 2014). The most critical information to teach youth at various developmental stages also matches the developmental sexual stage that youth pass through as they grow and mature. The organization that created the NSES (2014) was very clear that the document does not mandate a particular content or specific curriculum. However, there is a focus on knowledge and skill outcomes. For example, as children reach third through fifth grade, appropriate recommended outcomes are an understanding of STIs and adolescent puberty issues (FoSE, 2014). As children get older, a more in-depth understanding of STIs, such as HIV/AIDS, and sexual reproduction, as well as information related to sexual harassment and bullying is indicated between sixth through eighth grade. Once children reach high school, between ninth and twelfth grade, they should have more complex knowledge and understanding of human sexual behavior, legal rights related to sexual health services, sexual orientation, and gender identity (FoSE, 2014). NSES (2014) is organized by the following seven topics standards: (1) anatomy and physiology, (2) puberty and adolescent development, (3) identity development, (4) pregnancy/reproduction, (5) STDs/HIV, (6) healthy relationships, and (7) personal safety. We would articulate that the developmental sequence of knowledge and indicators within the National Sexuality Education Standards (2014) is organized in a very thoughtful manner and would be effective in guiding a universal system-level, developmentally appropriate curriculum for children and adolescents. Each state, school district, and/or school will likely adopt their own curricula based on state laws related to teaching sexual health, community standards, and local curriculum (e.g., see Chapter 4). Individuals residing within a community and attending local public and private schools, inclusive of families, teachers, administrators, mental health personnel, community members, and the students themselves, will have their own priorities and preferences for sexual health instruction, based on their viewpoints, values, and unique needs related to support of sexual health. At the same time, the NSES (2014) and state-mandated guidelines are recommended for those who provide sexual health supports to review in designing universal Tier 1 core curriculum. A universal/Tier 1 curriculum delivered to all students would be aligned within MTSS (Burns & Gibbons, 2012) and population-based mental health models (Doll & Cummings, 2008) familiar to many school districts and community agencies focused on disease prevention. Described elsewhere in this book, particularly in Chapter 8, a universal core curriculum is delivered to all students, whether it be one focused on behavior, academics, social-emotional supports, or—in the case of sexual health—a health-based curriculum in which data are used to evaluate outcomes. The core curriculum could be based on the NSES (2014), along with additional student outcomes considered important within the local environment using population-based models for determining health needs within a community (Doll & Cummings, 2008). For example, in one community, there might be high rates of violence, inclusive of dating violence that might be identified, which would necessitate instruction and accurate information about healthy relationships and setting boundaries. Information related to relationships might be delivered in a more comprehensive manner relative to other settings, given the population statistics (Doll & Cummings, 2008). In another community, high rates of substance abuse, such as heroin addiction, might be an identified risk factor for risky sexual behaviors (Kirby & Lepore, 2007). Using data to guide instruction, a unit could be developed to provide instruction about the sexual health risks associated with substance abuse along with other identified health risk factors that might be identified in a particular setting. Using multitiered systems of supports as a framework, we would recommend that supplemental and individualized supports additionally be provided based on student needs analogous to what would be delivered to address academic, behavioral, and social emotional needs (Burns & Gibbons, 2012). Supplemental supports would need to be considered for youth who do not respond effectively to the core sexual health instruction, potentially including those who have a range of disabilities, including physical, mental health, and academic. Consistent with multitiered systems of supports, evaluation of student skills, expected outcomes, knowledge, perceptions, and behaviors related to sexual health could be collected on an ongoing basis using a team problem-solving model. Within multitiered systems of supports, "progress monitoring" of desired goals and outcomes would be used to determine when an expected benchmark is achieved and, if not, more intensive supplemental or individualized instruction should be provided (Brown-Chidsey & Andren, 2012; Burns & Gibbons, 2012). Possible sources of health-related data collection already available in the school could be grades in health courses, performance on health chapter tests and quizzes, or meeting a school- or district-established health benchmark on a departmental or common core assessment. System-level risk-level data could be pregnancy rate in a particular community, rate of STIs, or school dropout due to pregnancy and child birth. Aligned with the Johns Hopkins Center for Adolescent Health document, one could also evaluate health assets, such as self-efficacy related to health decisions and feelings of competency in social relationships, including romantic ones (McNeely & Blanchard, 2009). The school district and/or community agency that provides sexual health instruction should focus on establishing a health curriculum that meets the needs of all students/clients that they serve with attention to special-ized needs that might be present for those who have disabilities, unique learning needs, or are linguistically/culturally diverse.

Providing Appropriate Sexual Health Education to Youth with Specialized Learning Needs

Youth with developmental disabilities and other learning needs require appropri-ate education in sexual health, and we would recommend that all youth, regardless of disability, be considered as part of the population in a school or community agency that should receive instruction as part of an approach using multitiered systems of supports (Burns & Gibbons, 2012) and a population-based approach (Doll & Cummings, 2008). Advocates for Youth (2006) describe three myths about the sexuality of individuals with disabilities that sometimes result in the erroneous conclusion that sexual health instruction is not necessary for individuals with dis-abilities. These myths include the notion that people with disabilities are asexual and child-like, or, in contrast, people with disabilities are incapable of controlling their sexuality or are characterized as "hypersexual" and, therefore, discussion of the topic through appropriate sexual education should be avoided. Clearly, these myths need to be dispelled, and we would support the prevailing notion among policy makers, researchers, and advocates that individuals with disabilities have the same rights as others to clear and accurate information about their sexual health (Baxley & Zendell, 2011; Murphy & Young, 2005; WHO/UNFPA, 2009).

The aforementioned myths are disputed by research evidence. For instance, there is no evidence to support the notion that individuals with disabilities are any less sexually active than their peers without disabilities. Suris, Resnick, Cassuto, and Blum (1996) studied Minnesota adolescents (grades 7–12) who had visible chronic conditions (e.g., cerebral palsy, muscular dystrophy, and arthritis), nonvis-ible chronic conditions (e.g., diabetes, asthma), and a control sample without diagnosed disabilities. Each participant completed a self-report measure about sexual behavior, use of contraception, being pregnant or causing pregnancy, STI prevalence, reason for not being sexually active, and reported sexual abuse history. The findings were that adolescents with chronic health conditions were equally as likely to report having engaged in sex at least once compared to controls. Males with visual and nonvisual conditions and females with visual conditions were more likely than controls to report ever having an STI. The findings of Suris et al. were that boys with nonvisible conditions were five times more likely to report being sexually abused compared to controls, whereas one out of four girls reported sexual abuse, which was a rate slightly higher than controls. The findings of this study certainly counter the notion that individuals with disabilities are less sexually active than their peers without disabilities. Further, the findings provide evidence that individuals with disabilities are a group particularly at risk for sexual abuse, have a right to receive adequate information related to their sexual health, and to not endure sexual violation or sexual assault just like any other human (Advocates for Youth, 2006). In an article specific to the sexual health of those with developmental disabilities, Murphy and Young (2005) stated, "The presence of a developmental disability does not override the rights of children and adolescents to develop and express their sexuality or to have access to accurate information that permits safe and healthy choices to be made" (p. 643). Unfortunately, adolescents and adults with disabilities are more likely than their nondisabled peers to be excluded from sexual health instruction, despite their status as a high-risk population for sexual trauma and abuse (Rohleder, Braathen, Swartz, & Eide, 2009, cited in WHO, 2011).

Two international agencies collaborated to support the sexual health rights of individuals with disabilities—WHO and United Nations. Together, these two international rights organizations produced the UN Population Fund (UNFPA) Guidance Note (WHO/UNFPA, 2009), which summarized and supported the UN General Assembly adoption of the "Convention on the Rights of Persons with Disabilities" (the "Convention"). The "Convention" was the most rapidly adopted legislation in the history of the United Nations (WHO/UNFPA, 2009). The "Convention" contains specific provisions to support the sexual and reproductive health of individuals with disabilities. These provisions include specific language about equal access to health care, accurate sexual health information and population-based sexual health programing, and protection from sexual abuse and violence. The "Convention" also supports nondiscrimination in personal choices about one's fertility, getting married, entering and sustaining romantic relationships, and family planning (WHO/UNFPA, 2009). The UNFPA Guidance Note also contains recommendations for making sexual and reproductive health services and information accessible for individuals with disabilities. The report notes the importance of physical access to medical facilities and examination rooms (e.g., wheelchair access, lower examination tables), and presentation of sexual health information in an accessible format to those with sensory disabilities (e.g., braille, sign language, or slower presentation of information in multiple modalities), yet also stresses that accessibility and awareness means "more than ramps" (WHO/UNFPA,

2009, p. 17). The report also emphasizes the notion that general population-based health education can often be accessed by individuals with disabilities with only minor adaptations in instruction, which lends support to school-based adoption of multitiered systems of support in the delivery of health instruction for everyone in the population (Burns & Gibbons, 2012). The report provides a checklist for healthcare providers to determine whether their services are accessible to individuals with disabilities and whether healthcare providers have an adequate level of knowledge and training to provide services to individuals with disabilities.

Overall, the sexual health needs of individuals with disabilities, despite being a population particularly at risk for sexual exploitation and abuse, are not being met. Due to multiple factors that relate to stigma, lack of access to physical environments (e.g., healthcare settings and school general instructional environments), and societal bias and stigma, individuals with disabilities are not getting their needs met, beginning from early childhood through adulthood. We articulate that schools and community healthcare agencies and settings can help to facilitate appropriate access to evidence-based sexual health instruction across the developmental trajectory for individuals with a range of behavioral, social-emotional, academic/learning, and physical disabilities using multitiered and population-based models of support (Burns & Gibbons, 2012; Doll & Cummings, 2008). The Individuals with Disabilities Education Act (IDEA, 2004) mandates that individuals with disabilities have access to a fair and appropriate education in the least restrictive environment using reasonable accommodations. We would argue that specific attention be afforded to the content of sexual health and that schools, beginning when children with disabilities are young, are in the best position to provide support of sexual health, with support from community healthcare agencies and settings.

Integrating the Needs of Individuals with Disabilities into Multitiered and Population-Based Systems of Support

We advocate that individuals with disabilities receive instruction in the general education settings and by accessing the general education curriculum, consistent with IDEA (2004) guidelines. Therefore, in the case of sexual health instruction, we recommend that schools and districts provide instruction to individuals with disabilities that are aligned with the NSES (2014) described above. Incorporating multitiered systems of supports as a framework that uses data to guide efforts, core instruction/Tier 1 supports that are intended for the entire population would be a place to begin. Consistent with IDEA (2004) mandates, reasonable modifications to the general education curriculum may be necessary, such as making materials and instruction accessible to individuals with sensory impairments (e.g., braille, sign language interpreters; Advocates for Youth, 2006; WHO/UNFPA, 2009). Other reasonable accommodations that could be made to address learning styles might be presentation of materials in multiple modalities (e.g., visual/auditory/ kinesthetic approaches) and a slower pace of instruction (Advocates for Youth, 2006). Further, sexual health curricula exist that have been developed specifically for individuals with disabilities. These curricula can be delivered in general education environments as part of routine instruction for all students or tailored for groups (Tier 2) or inidividual students (Tier 3) that require more specialized sexual health instruction and supports. For example, Baxley and Zendell (2011) offer a curriculum guide that incorporates instructional materials and adaptations covering developmentally appropriate recommended sexual health topics that are very aligned with the NSES (2014), which we recommend be provided to all students in a way that is accessible to them. The developmentally appropriate skills outlined in Baxley and Zendell (2011) are consistent with those outlined above as part of a developmentally appropriate curriculum that matches the stages of development. For example, developmentally appropriate outcomes such as labeling body parts, developing and sustaining healthy relationships, pubertal changes, sexual reproduction, appropriate touching, and related content covering sexual and physical abuse are part of the curriculum and modified in a user-friendly manner for individuals with a range of specialized learning needs. Materials developed by Baxley and Zendell (2011) include a number of picture cues that facilitate the teaching of concepts to individuals with disabilities using multiple modalities. Visual depictions of public and private body areas, "good and bad touching" are examples of supplementary instructional materials to be presented on their own to individuals with disabilities or integrated into core curricular instruction that is delivered to all students as part of a multitiered approach to health instruction (Burns & Gibbons, 2012). Another excellent resource produced by the Massachusetts Department of Public Health and the Massachusetts Department of Developmental Services contains a very comprehensive set of references and resources that can be used to support the sexual health of youth who have a wide range of disabilities, including books written by individuals with autism spectrum disorders and epilepsy (Massachusetts Department of Public Health, 2014). The topics covered are recommended content for sexual health curriculum and include information pertaining to social skills, relationships, puberty, self-care, sexuality, and individuals with disabilities who identify as LGBTQ. These comprehensive resources can be reviewed and utilized in the development of a specialized sexual health curriculum or as supplemental or individual curriculum that could be delivered in addition to a core curriculum delivered on a universal/Tier 1 basis as described above.

Further, as a component of sexual health instruction specific to individuals with disabilities, teaching self-determination skills may be an appropriate additional component of individualized instruction for individuals with disabilities who have more intensive needs for sexual health instruction and support beyond what can be provided on a universal (Tier 1) or secondary (Tier 2) basis (e.g., see Wehmeyer, 1998). Self-determination theory and skills focus on supporting youth with disabilities to determine their own future orientation and personal goals rather than being directed by others (Wehmeyer, 1998). Another major concept within self-determination is that those within a particular group, such as those having a disability, are the ones that should determine their political stance (Wehmeyer, 1998). Recently, self-determination has been integrated into effective models that support youth with emotional and behavioral disorders to stay in school and avoid dropout as part of the Rehabilitation for Empowerment, Natural Supports, Education, and Work (RENEW) model (Malloy, 2013).

We advocate for a multitiered system of supports in providing appropriate sexual health instruction to individuals with disabilities. Similar to approaches with all students in a population, we would recommend that a universal core curriculum for the entire school population be considered as a first option. Then, the healthcare team can determine if additional supplemental and/or individual supports should be considered for the entire population or a smaller subset with specialized needs (Brown-Chidsey & Andren, 2012; Burns & Gibbons, 2012; Wehmeyer, 1998).

Specialized Supports for Families of Youth with Disabilities

For any child, family members may want to have open communication with their son or daughter about sexual health and behavior but, as described in more detail in Chapter 7, may not feel comfortable or have the confidence or skills to do so (Guzman, Golub, Caal, Hickman, & Ramos, 2013). This potentially uncomfortable topic may be even more unsettling and scary for families with youth who have a disability. However, parents and family members play a prominent role in influencing their youth's decisions about engaging in high-risk sexual behaviors (Kirby & Lepore, 2007). The importance of providing youth with disabilities with accurate information about sexuality cannot be understated, given the unfortunate high rates of sexual abuse for individuals with disabilities (Martinello, 2014). For individuals with intellectual disabilities, the most likely perpetrators are caregivers (Martinello, 2014). Family members and adults who support youth with disabilities will potentially need substantial support in navigating issues related to sexual education and health of this population. Findings from a recent Turkish qualitative study of mothers with children who have intellectual disabilities were that mothers felt that sexual education was needed, but should be delivered in agencies outside of the home (Gurol, Polat, & Oran, 2014). Just like any other child or adolescent, youth with disabilities benefit from frequent, open, and spontaneous communication that begins early and happens over the years, rather than one "big talk" just prior to puberty (Eisenberg, Sieving, Bearinger, Swain, & Resnick, 2006; U.S. Department of Health and Human Services, 2014). Thankfully, there have been numerous resources for parents and preventionists or interventionists that support them in meeting the important sexual health needs of youth with disabilities. As an example, the Alberta Health Services (2009) produced a guide specifically for parents of individuals with disabilities, which contains valuable information about the social and sexual development that all individuals experience, regardless of disability. In addition, the Alberta Health Services guide emphasizes recommendations common to parents of all youth, such as having early conversations and teaching about sexual behaviors and having conversations about the prevention of sexual abuse, using concepts such as "good touch" and "bad touch," which are phrases articulated elsewhere in this chapter. Further, there is an excellent bibliography of books and resources for parents in teaching their children and adolescents with disabilities about sexual health topics, such as care during menstruation and clear information about physical changes that need to be taught to boys and girls as they undergo puberty (Alberta Health Services, 2009). Further, Advocates for Youth (2006) provide an excellent summary of tips for families when discussing sexuality with youth who have disabilities, which include recommended communication strategies discussed above about frequent, early, and spontaneous conversations using "teachable moments" as well as modifications for youth with disabilities such as visual presentation of ideas using photos and repeating information as necessary. Similar to other resources, the Advocates for Youth document provides a number of resources for parents in addressing the sexual health needs of youth with disabilities.

CASE SCENARIO EXAMPLE: ADDRESSING THE SEXUAL HEALTH NEEDS OF A FEMALE WITH DOWN SYNDROME

In this case scenario, we illustrate some recommendations previously described in the literature and policy documents in addressing the sexual health needs of individuals with disabilities.

Emily is a White, 13-year-old female with Down syndrome. She lives with her two parents, Jim and Irene, and her three older siblings in a small rural town in central Illinois. She has a 17-year-old brother, Marcus, and a 16-year-old sister, Karen. Emily has attended the local public school with her siblings since she began in the early childhood program at the age of 3. Her parents both work outside of the home. Her mother works part-time in a local clothing store, and her dad is an English teacher and soccer coach at the local high school. Emily is part of a tight-knit nuclear and extended family. Jim and Irene grew up in the community and are part of a large extended family. There are many cousins, aunts, uncles, and long-time friends and neighbors. Jim and Irene are happy with the school district and the services in the community. They have always believed that Emily has been accepted in the community, and educationally, she has been included in general education classes with some support from her classroom assistant, who has worked

(Continued)

(Continued)

with Emily since she was in kindergarten. Jim and Irene received a letter that the sexual health curriculum was about to be taught in health class and have approached the school principal with some concerns about Emily's participation in the upcoming sexual health curriculum unit. Like all parents in the district in this state, they have the opportunity to "opt out" of the instruction. They are just not sure that she is ready for a discussion of adult topics and do not believe that she will need the information as she is unlikely to have the same type of future like having a family or getting married herself, unlike her siblings (Advocates for Youth, 2006). Emily, on the other hand, has wanted to be with her classmates since an early age and doesn't want to be singled out or removed from participating in the health curriculum unit. The principal has scheduled a meeting with the family and has also invited the health teacher, Emily's classroom assistant, the school psychologist, and school counselor to be part of the initial meeting, with plans for a second subsequent meeting to include Emily. At the meeting, Jim and Irene are very adamant that Emily not receive the sexual health curriculum that her peers are receiving. Although they have always been open to the ideas that the school team has with respect to the Individualized Education Plan goals suggested for Emily, in this case they are initially not in agreement. They remain, however, open to listening to the perspectives of the school staff. They are worried that Emily will get ideas about becoming sexually active, and this will be embarrassing to them with respect to their standing and visibility in the community. The health educator, with support from the school psychologist, reflects and acknowledges their concerns, but also gently provides information that counters myths about sexual behavior of individuals with disabilities (Advocates for Youth, 2006; Murphy & Young, 2005). Jim and Irene remain hesitant, but increasingly are open to being educated about the need for accurate information for all youth, including those who have disabilities (WHO/UNFPA, 2009). When they learn about the high rates of sexual abuse among individuals with disabilities, they begin to agree that Emily needs some instruction in sexual health, but perhaps not in an integrated fashion with her peers. In the end, Jim and Irene agree to allow Emily to have sexual health instruction using the same curriculum as her peers, but make suggestions for modifications that prove to be very useful in helping Emily to understand the concepts. A smaller team, including the health educator, school counselor, school psychologist, and parents, designs supplemental teaching materials that include visual pictures of the major concepts and activities to discuss at home using resources drawn from Alberta Health Services (2009) and the Massachusetts Department of Public Health (2014). A second meeting is conducted that includes the larger team and Emily to review the curricular materials and to incorporate Emily into decisions about her long-term future orientation, goals, and plans, consistent with person-centered planning (Wehmeyer, 1998). Emily would like a future that involves having a boyfriend like her older sister. The school has offered to organize a group for parents of children with disabilities from around the larger community to discuss issues of parenting an adolescent with a disability, and Irene and Jim are part of the group. In fact, they have decided to take a lead role in recruiting other parents and families they know from the larger county area as well as research information on the topic of healthy social and dating relationships among individuals with disabilities!

This case scenario illustrates that there are no easy answers in parenting children and adolescents in general. When a child/adolescent has a disability, there are unique considerations that may emerge. Communication, understanding, and reserving judgment among all parties will ultimately help individuals, regardless of personal situation or disability, in achieving sexual health and the most optimal outcomes and individual control over one's future.

Culturally Responsive Sexual Health Education

When designing and implementing a sexual health curriculum and related supports, one must be particularly sensitive to the cultural background and values of the child and adolescent participants, as well as the families and community members who have a significant impact on the choices they make, including approval of them (Larson, Sandelowski, & McQuiston, 2012).

Cultural issues, norms, and values relating to sexual behavior and choices have a significant impact on sexual health of youth and should be considered in the development of any sexual health strategies, curriculum, or educational supports (Bearinger et al., 2007). Bearinger et al. analyzed international prevalence rates for sexual intercourse, use of condoms, medical birth control (e.g., birth control pills, IUDs, etc.), as well as for presence of STIs, including HIV/AIDS. Their findings, overall, were that adolescents were at a much greater risk for STIs relative to all other age groups. Comparisons across countries for sexual intercourse prevalence revealed that in most countries of the developing world and Sub-Saharan Africa (with the exception of Nigeria and Rwanda), one third or more of unmarried adolescent girls had experienced sexual intercourse. The sexual intercourse rates for girls in other regions of the world (the Philippines, Eastern Europe, and Latin America) were proportionately lower. Unmarried boys in most countries examined had higher rates than girls in comparative countries, with rates on the average of 40% or more, except in a few countries where the rates were less than 30% (e.g., Nigeria, Rwanda, and the Philippines). Overall, across all countries, boys were more likely to have multiple sexual partners. In terms of condom use, increased rates at the time of the study were reported for developing countries and Sub-Saharan Africa, yet were still interpreted by the authors as too small to prevent the spread of STIs. In terms of medical contraception use, adolescent females in the United States were less likely than their peers in the United Kingdom, Canada, and France to report use. Unfortunately, in Sub-Saharan Africa, very low numbers of unmarried adolescent females, aged 15–19, used medical contraception at most recent sexual intercourse. The rates for contraception use among unmarried sexually active females were higher in other regions of the world, inclusive of Latin America and the Caribbean. In terms of STI/HIV rates, the largest numbers of reported infections occurred in Southern/Southeast Asia, and the next highest rates were in Sub-Saharan Africa, followed by the lowest prevalence in Latin America and the Caribbean. The authors also reported the startling finding that marriage created a heightened risk for adolescent girls in developing countries to experience risky sexual intercourse. The authors collectively interpreted the findings that adolescents across the globe are at heightened risk for STIs and high-risk sexual activity and, although the authors noted that it is very difficult to collect accurate prevalence data related to STIs, concluded that the highest rates of STIs occur among young people below the age of 25 (Bearinger et al., 2007). The authors also stressed the notion that adolescents require accurate information and access to proper sexual health care. In the case of young married adolescent females, they may not experience equitable access to sexual heath-related services because of financial dependence on male relatives and their families. We would articulate that gender difference be carefully considered and that steps taken across all communities to allow all adolescents access to accurate information related to contraception, pregnancy prevention, and STIs, which is aligned with the guidelines established and promoted by the WHO (2014) in our increasingly global and international world.

More recent statistics and prevalence rates collected within the United States provide an opportunity to examine disaggregated sexual heath data by race and ethnicity among those living in the United States. Child Trends Data Bank (2014) reported recently collected data through the CDC, using the most recent administration of the High School Youth Risk Behavior Survey (1991–2013) with adolescents (CDC, 2014). The Child Trends Data Bank report contained student-reported rates of sexual intercourse within the last 3 months disaggregated by gender and race/ethnicity across the multiple years in which the High School Youth Risk Behavior Survey was collected. The Child Trends Data Bank findings were that from the years spanning 1991 to 2013, the overall rate of self-reported sexual activity of approximately one third of high school students was very stable across time, with slight fluctuations of 33% to 38% across over 20 years of data collection. When disaggregated by race/ethnicity, the largest decrease was among Black students, as the proportion of sexually active students in this racial subgroup decreased from 59% in 1991 to 42% in 2013 (Child Trends Data Bank, 2014). Overall, males and females reported similar rates of sexual activity in 2013, with

33% of males and 35% of females reporting being sexually active within the last 3 months. There were differences noted when the data were further disaggregated by gender and race/ethnicity (Child Trends Data, 2014). Looking only at the 2013 CDC data, Black male students reported slightly higher rates of sexual activity (at 47%) compared to Black female students (at 38%). For other racial/ ethnic groups, there were no significant differences when the sexual activity prevalence rates were compared between White males and White females, nor for White Hispanic males relative to White Hispanic females. Overall, in 2013, Hispanic students did not differ significantly in their reported sexual activity relative to White or Black students. Racial differences in reported sexual activity were present among males, but not among females. Among males, Black students were most likely to report being sexually active, followed by Hispanic males and then White males.

Racial and ethnic differences with respect to a range of sexual risk behaviors are complex and potentially connected to other factors. For example, Biello, Ickovics, Niccolai, Lin, and Kershaw (2013) examined the potential influence of neighborhood segregation on self-reported age of first sexual intercourse among a sample of Black and White adolescents using National Longitudinal Survey of Youth collected from 1997 to 2005 and U.S. Census data to define metropolitan area. The researchers categorized segregation in the following manner: exposure, concentration, centralization, clustering, and unevenness. The issues were complex, but in essence, adolescents in highly segregated (hypersegregated) areas were more likely to evidence racial disparity in age of first reported sexual intercourse compared to their White adolescent peers. There were no racial disparities in age of first sexual experience in nonsegregated areas. The authors hypothesized that issues connected to neighborhoods with high concentrations of race minorities are associated with long-standing sociocultural and economic disadvantages. This study begins to explore some of the challenges inherent in looking solely at racial/ethnic statistical differences in rates of high-risk sexual behaviors and outcomes. As Biello et al. (2013) state, further research should begin to explore the multiple variables and factors that may help to explain racial/ethnic differences in sexual risk behaviors. We would recommend further research exploring the larger societal and political variables that could account for racial and ethnic differences in sexual risk behavior. One area to further explore is whether disparities in access to adequate health care documented for ethnic minority youth, particularly those who live in poverty and face significant societal issues such as homelessness, have an impact on access to sexual health services (Elster, Jarosik, VanGeest, & Fleming, 2003). Elster et al. (2003), based on a review of the literature, found evidence that health disparities existed for racial and ethnic minority youth in some healthcare areas studied, after controlling for socioeconomic status. However, there were too few studies about reproductive health for conclusions to be drawn. More recently, Flores (2010) completed a systematic literature of studies from 1950 until 2007 related to health disparities in children's healthcare access and health risk behaviors across multiple domains. The overall findings were that there were pervasive disparities in access to health care across multiple dimensions for particular racial and ethnic groups. Several health disparity variables were examined in the Flores (2010) study, and we specifically summarize their reported findings for adolescent health by each racial/ethnic group studied. Adolescent health included indicators for sexual risk behaviors and outcomes, which we are most interested in. See the Flores (2010) study for the comprehensive findings that were reported. Based on the reported Flores (2010) findings, African American females had significantly more adolescent health issues relative to White females, which included being more likely to have an STI. Asian/Pacific Islander adolescents also had significantly greater adolescent health issues not specific to sexual health (e.g., were less likely to use seat belts). Latina adolescents had higher birth rates compared to all other racial/ethnic groups studied, having a rate three times that of their White female counterparts. Latinos were more likely to receive treatment in an emergency department for any STI. These two studies underscore health disparities and higher prevalence rates of sexual risk behaviors and outcomes across multiple ethnic groups. We would argue that preventionists/interventionists can advocate for more systematic research with respect to examining ways to provide equitable access to racial/ethnic minority adolescents in the arena of healthcare overall and specific to the prevention and treatment of sexual risk behaviors and support of health assets, in particular (McNeely & Blanchard, 2009).

Sexual health research focused on Latinos is a particularly significant underexplored area with respect to the sexual health of culturally and linguistically diverse adolescents. Cardoza, Documét, Fryer, Gold, and Butler (2012) conducted a systematic literature of sexual health interventions for Latinos and included those that evaluated impact on critical sexual health outcomes. These outcomes were increased sexual health knowledge, behavior, attitudes or beliefs, abstinence, reduction in sexual risk behaviors, impact on unintended initial or subsequent pregnancies, having STIs, inclusive of HIV/AIDs, and mixed sexual health outcomes. After conducting a systematic literature search of articles on the topic, only 15 articles met the inclusionary criteria the researchers established (Cardoza et al., 2012). The researchers noted the following strengths of sexual health research with Latinos: data measuring important sexual health outcomes (e.g., abstinence, teen pregnancy, STIs) and social ecological issues (e.g., adolescent relationships, attitudes, knowledge). In addition, sexual health programs with this population incorporate varied instructional methods such as home visits, lectures, and discussions in multiple environments, such as schools, neighborhoods, and health clinics. However, the authors identified multiple weaknesses in the literature, which include the limited number of behavioral inventions that focus on promoting Latino adolescent sexual health outcomes. The researchers concluded that there are not enough available studies that specifically evaluate teen pregnancy, as most target STIs/HIV. Further, the researchers additionally concluded that there is a limited focus on building community capacity as an intervention component and that much work has been targeted to Latinas, with limited focus on males (Cardoza et al., 2012).

Larson et al. (2012) conducted qualitative interviews with school personnel and parents in a rural North Carolina sixth-through-eighth-grade setting that had increasing enrollment, primarily due to recent immigration of Latino students to the area. Field observations in the school and community were completed as well. Larson et al. cited CDC data documenting disheartening health outcomes for this population as a rationale for the study, which included statistics documenting that the Latino young adults have the highest rates of AIDS compared to all ethnic and racial groups and Latinas between the ages of 15 and 19 (CDC, 2010a, cited in Larson et al., 2012) and are three times more likely to get pregnant compared to their White peers (CDC, 2009, cited in Larson et al., 2012), yet despite these deleterious outcomes, Latinos were more likely to report not being exposed to sexual health education in schools compared to their White peers (CDC, 2010b, cited in Larson et al., 2012). The aim of the Larson et al. study was to examine how contextual factors of the school may help to explain disparities in sexual health outcomes among Latina youth and to evaluate whether school staff differed from parents in their understanding of the sexual behaviors of these young people. Based on the analysis of the qualitative interviews and field work, three main themes were described by the authors as impacting the sexual behaviors of the Latino youth. The first theme was that the school environment and set-up afforded an opportunity for the Latina youth, being in a sixth-through-eighth-grade setting, to engage in sexual behaviors within the educational arena with older males. As an example, younger Latina middle school girls, who might have been chronologically older, but placed in lower grades because of recent migration or English language learner issues, had unsupervised opportunities to find their way to the high school wing to interact with older boys. In some cases, overt violent behaviors within the school, such as youth bringing weapons to school, overshadowed addressing sexual behaviors. Suspension from school created opportunities for sexual behaviors to occur due to lack of supervision. School personnel were only allowed to provide an abstinence-only curriculum and thus sometimes stayed away from conversations related to overt sexual behaviors, even when they witnessed it. As state employees, they were cautious in going beyond the state-required curriculum. Parents were also reluctant to talk about sexual activity and believed that it was the role of the school, as it was in Mexico, which was the country of origin for many families, to provide the instruction rather than at home. School personnel thought that sexual health education was the parents' role, and therefore, there was a disconnect and misunderstanding between home and school. Another major identified theme by Larson et al. (2012) was the issue of cultural confusion, norms, and stereotypes. Latinas were described as looking older and, in some cases, were older due to being held back. School personnel reported provocative dress among Latinas and were conflicted between ensuring cultural sensitivity and enforcing the school dress code. While school personnel believed that Latinas dating older boys was culturally accepted by the family and tied to a female role of having a family and leaving school, this was not the case when parents were asked about what they desired for their daughter's future.

Overall, the literature and evidence-based interventions available to meet the sexual health needs of diverse students from varying racial and ethnic groups need significant focused attention and more concentrated efforts from policy makers, researchers, and preventionists and interventions who work with diverse youth. We make the following recommendations, based on the knowledge base that is available:

- Continue to evaluate sexual health interventions in schools by collecting sexual risk outcomes disaggregated by race/ethnicity (Biello et al., 2013). Examining disaggregated racial/ethnicity data has been recommended in the educational literature examining disproportionality in discipline and juvenile justice outcomes (Losen & Martinez, 2013). Overall, more systematic research needs to explore the impact of various sexual health interventions among all racial/ethnic minority groups (Biello et al., 2013).
- Integrate the viewpoints and participation of parents, family members, and the extended community into the development and implementation of culturally relevant interventions. Families are important treatment agents in any effective sexual health curriculum and are critical to culturally relevant interventions, in part, because of limited understanding that preventionists/interventionists and healthcare educators have with respect to the belief systems of racially, ethnically, linguistically, and culturally diverse children, adolescents, and their families (Larson et al., 2012). Preventionists/interventionists and health educators run the risk of falling back on cultural stereotypes and assumptions that might not be accurate (Larson et al., 2012). Therefore, individuals, agencies, and schools that address the sexual health needs of diverse populations need to have culturally relevant training and a more in-depth understanding of the cultural needs of the youth and families they serve (Montgomery, 2001).
- Involve the youth themselves as treatment agents and as critical to guiding, evaluating, and sustaining interventions. Participatory action research models, in which goals and priorities are driven from those that are most impacted by the innovation, may be particularly useful models as a framework in creating more culturally relevant and empowering supports (McIntyre, 2007).
- Advocate for equitable access to healthcare services and supports for racial/ethnic minority students and individuals who have been marginalized within our communities, such as youth who are homeless, living in poverty, and at risk or already connected to the juvenile justice system (Elster et al., 2003; Flores, 2010).
- The limited research to date with respect to sexual health interventions for racial and ethnic minority youth appears to be focused on sexual risk factors and outcomes. Although an expansion of this work in terms of identified

sexual health risk factors and outcomes is important, we would additionally articulate that a strength-based approach that focuses on resiliency and assets, which is aligned with the model of competencies discussed earlier through the Johns Hopkins Center for Adolescent Health (McNeely & Blanchard, 2009), would be an important focus with racial/ethnic minority youth.

This chapter presented a developmental overview of sexual development and recommendations for evidence-based sexual health. We continue to advocate, as in other chapters, that a multitiered system of supports (Burns & Gibbons, 2012) and population-based health support model (Doll & Cummings, 2008) is a useful framework for the delivery of appropriate sexual health curriculum, beginning with a universal system core curriculum approach that is evaluated using data to determine the need for additional supplemental and/or individual supports. Further, we described special considerations for individuals with learning issues and diagnosed disabilities, using multitiered systems of support that could be used within a problem-solving framework (Brown-Chidsey & Andren, 2012). Finally, we provided some of the available literature from an international standpoint and for the U.S. population of racial and ethnic minority youth, inclusive of the significant disparities in access to sexual health support among these subgroups. We take the position of the WHO (2011) that all young people are entitled to accurate sexual health information and supports to address their needs regardless of background or learning need. There is a great deal of work to be done with respect to providing developmentally appropriate sexual health instruction to all youth. However, there are a wide range of resources available as documented in this chapter and no reason why the already significant work cannot be expanded in a more comprehensive manner to meet the sexual health needs of all youth, inclusive of those with disabilities, individuals who identify as LGBTQ or are culturally and linguistically diverse, in a comprehensive and asset-based approach to addressing healthy sexual developments that potentially have long-term significant individual and societal outcomes (McNeely & Blanchard, 2009).

References

Advocates for Youth. (2006). *Sex education for physically, emotionally and mentally challenged youth.* Retrieved from www.advocatesforyouth.org

Alberta Health Services. (2009). *Sexuality and disability: A guide for parents.* Retrieved from http://www.arc-spokane.org/PDFs/Sexuality%20and%20Developmental%20Disability%20parent%20guide.pdf

Baxley, D. L., & Zendell, A. L. (2011). *Sexuality across the lifespan for children and adolescents with developmental disabilities: An instructional guide for parents/caregivers of individuals with developmental disabilities.* Tallahasse, FL: U.S. Department of Health and Human Services/Administration on Developmental Disabilities and the Florida Developmental Disabilities Council, Inc.

Bearinger, L. H., Sieving, R. E., Ferguson, J., & Sharma, V. (2007). Global perspectives on the sexual and reproductive health of adolescents: Patterns, prevention and potential. *Lancet, 369,* 1220–1231.

Biello, K. B., Ickovics, J., Niccolai, L., Lin, H., & Kershaw, T. (2013). Racial differences in age at first sexual intercourse: Residential racial segregation and the black-white disparity among U.S. adolescents. *Public Health Reports, 128*(Suppl. 1), 23–32.

Brown-Chidsey, R., & Andren, K. J. (Eds.). (2012). *Assessment for intervention: A problem-solving approach* (2nd ed.). New York, NY: Guilford Press.

Burns, M. K., & Gibbons, K. (2012). *Implementing response-to-intervention in elementary and secondary schools: Procedures to assure scientific-based practice* (2nd ed.). New York, NY: Routledge.

Cardoza, V. J., Documét, P. I., Fryer, C. S., Gold, M. A., & Butler, J. (2012). Sexual health behavior interventions for U.S. Latino adolescents: A systematic review of the literature. *Journal of Pediatric Adolescent Gynecology, 25*, 136–149.

CDC. (2009). Sexual and reproductive health of persons aged 10–24 years, United States, 2002–2007. *Surveillance Summaries, 58*(SS-6), 1–60.

CDC. (2010a). *Sexually transmitted disease surveillance 2009*. Atlanta, GA: U.S. Department of Health and Human Services.

CDC. (2010b). Youth risk behavior surveillance — United States, 2009. *Surveillance Summaries, 59*(SS-5), 1–142.

CDC. (2014). *1991–2013 High school youth risk behavior survey data*. Retrieved from http://nccd.cdc.gov/youthonline

Child Trends Data Bank. (2014, July). *Sexually active teens: Indicators on children and youth*. Bethesda, MD: Child Trends Data Bank.

Doll, B. A., & Cummings, J. A. (2008). *Transforming school mental health services: Population based approaches to promoting the competency and wellness of children*. Thousand Oaks, CA: Corwin Press/NASP.

Eisenberg, M. E., Sieving, R. E., Bearinger, L. H., Swain, C., & Resnick, M. D. (2006). Parents' communication with adolescents about sexual behavior: A missed opportunity for prevention? *Journal of Youth and Adolescence, 35*(6), 893–902.

Elster, A., Jarosik, J., VanGeest, J., & Fleming, M. (2003). Racial and ethnic disparities in health care for adolescents: A systematic review of the literature. *Archives of Pediatric Adolescent Medicine, 157*(9), 867–874.

Flores, G. (2010). Racial and ethnic disparities in the health and health care of children. *Pediatrics, 125*(4), 979–1020.

FoSE. (2014). *National Sexuality Education Standards: Core content and skills, K-12*. Retrieved from http://www.futureofsexed.org/documents/josh-fose-standards-web.pdf

Gurol, A., Polat, S., & Oran, T. (2014). Views of mothers having children with intellectual disabilities regarding sexual education: A qualitative study. *Sex Disability, 32*, 123–133.

Guzman, L., Golub, E., Caal, S., Hickman, S., & Ramos, M. (2013). *Let's (not) talk about sex: Communication and teen pregnancy prevention within Hispanic families*. Retrieved from http://www.childtrends.org/wp-content/uploads/2013/11/2013-50LetsNotTalk-AboutSex.pdf

Individuals with Disabilities Education Act (IDEA), 20 U.S.C. § 1400 (2004).

Kirby, D., & Lepore, G. (2007). *Sexual risk and protective factors: Factors affecting teen sexual behavior, pregnancy, childbearing, and sexually transmitted disease: Which are important? Which can you change?* Washington, DC: The National Campaign to Prevent Teen and Unplanned Pregnancy.

Kreipe, R. E. (2010). *Healthy adolescent sexual development*. Retrieved from http://www.actforyouth.net/resources/n/n_healthy_adol_sx_dev

Larson, K., Sandelowski, M., & McQuiston, C. (2012). It's a touchy subject: Latino adolescent sexual risk behaviors in the school context. *Applied Nursing Research, 25*, 231–238.

Losen, D. J., & Martinez, T. E. (2013). *Out of school and off track: The overuse of suspensions in American middle and high schools*. Retrieved from http://civilrightsproject.ucla.edu/resources/projects/center-for-civil-rights-remedies/school-to-prison-ffolder/federal-reports/out-of-school-and-off-track-the-overuse-of-suspensions-in-american-middle-and-high-schools/Exec_Sum_OutofSchool_OffTrack_UCLA.pdf

Malloy, J. (2013). The RENEW model: Supporting transition-age youth with emotional and behavioral challenges. *Report on Emotional and Behavioral Disorders in Youth, 13*(2), 38–46.

Martinello, E. (2014). Reviewing strategies for risk reduction of sexual abuse of children with intellectual disabilities: A focus on early intervention. *Sex Disability, 32,* 167–174.

Massachusetts Department of Public Health/Massachusetts Department of Developmental Services. (2014). *Healthy relationships, sexuality and disability: Resource guide 2014 edition.* Boston, MA: Massachusetts Department of Public Health-Bureau of Community Health and Prevention.

McIntyre, A. (2007). *Participatory action research (Qualitative research methods).* Los Angeles, CA: Sage.

McNeely, C., & Blanchard, J. (2009). *The teen years explained: A guide to healthy adolescent development.* Baltimore, MD: Center for Adolescent Health at Johns Hopkins Bloomberg School of Public Health.

Montgomery, W. (2001). Creating culturally responsive, inclusive classrooms. *Teaching Exceptional Children, 33*(4), 4–9.

Murphy, N., & Young, P. C. (2005). Sexuality in children and adolescents with disabilities. *Developmental Medicine and Child Neurology, 47*(9), 640–644.

NCTSN. (2009). *Sexual development and behavior in children: Information for parents and caregivers.* Retrieved from http://www.NCTSN.org

National Sexual Violence Resource Center. (2013). *An overview of healthy childhood sexual development.* Retrieved from https://luc.app.box.com/files/0/f/2478209123/1/f_25050195437

Rohleder, P., Braathen, S. H., Swartz, L., & Eide, A. H. (2009). HIV/AIDS and disability in Southern Africa: A review of relevant literature. *Disability and Rehabilitation, 31*(1), 51–59. doi:10.1080/09638280802280585

Rouvier, M., Campero, L., Walker, D., & Caballero, M. (2011). Factors that influence communication about sexuality between parents and adolescents in the cultural context of Mexican families. *Sex Education, 11*(2), 175–191.

Suris, J. C., Resnick, M. D., Cassuto, N., & Blum, R. W. (1996). Sexual behavior of adolescents with chronic disease and disability. *Journal of Adolescent Health, 19,* 124–131.

U.S. Department of Health and Human Services. (2014). *Talking with teens.* Retrieved from http://www.hhs.gov/ash/oah/resources-and-publications/info/parents/conversation-tools/

Wehmeyer, M. L. (1998). Self-determination and individuals with significant disabilities: Examining meaning and misinterpretations. *Research and Practice for Persons with Disabilities, 23*(1), 5–16.

WHO. (2011). *World report on disability* (Chapter 3). Geneva, Switzerland: WHO. Retrieved from http://www.who.int/disabilities/world_report/2011/report.pdf

WHO. (2014). *Adolescents: Health risks and solutions.* Retrieved from http://www.who.int/mediacentre/factsheets/fs345/en/

WHO/UNFPA. (2009). *Promoting sexual and reproductive health for persons with disabilities* (WHO/UNFPA Guidance Note). Geneva, Switzerland: WHO/UNFPA. Retrieved from http://www.who.int/reproductivehealth/publications/general/9789241598682/en/

6
PROMOTING THE SEXUAL HEALTH OF LGBTQIA YOUTH

Introduction

The purpose of this chapter is to present a discussion of sexual health among youth who identify as lesbian, gay, bisexual, transgender, queer, intersex, and asexual (LGBTQIA). The chapter will explore the sexual risk behaviors and sexual health education needs of LGBTQIA youth who may differ from heterosexual youth. This chapter will mainly provide information regarding the needs of LGBTQ youth. Youth who identify as intersex or asexual may have other needs that are outside the scope of our discussion, particularly because of the lack of current research regarding sexual health of these populations. The chapter provides an overview of LGBTQIA terminology, an introduction to needs of LGBTQ youth, and specific topics of importance in promoting sexual health.

Terminology

The LGBTQIA community often is associated with a variety of terminology that can be ambiguous. For example, the acronym LGBTQIA can be extended to LGBTTQQIAAP (2S) subpopulations—lesbian, gay, bisexual, transgender, transsexual, queer, questioning, intersex, asexual, allies, pansexual, and two-spirited. Which terminology to include and how to define them often has been debated, but they encompass a wide range of identities.

> Lesbian: "Term used to describe female-identified people attracted romantically, erotically, and/or emotionally to other female-identified people" (Green & Peterson, 2006, p. 6).

Gay: "1. Term used in some cultural settings to represent males who are attracted to males in a romantic, erotic and/or emotional sense. Not all men who engage in 'homosexual behavior' identify as gay, and as such this label should be used with caution. 2. Term used to refer to the LGBTQI community as a whole, or as an individual identity label for anyone who does not identify as heterosexual" (p. 3).

Bisexual: "A person emotionally, physically, and/or sexually attracted to males/men and females/women. This attraction does not have to be equally split between genders and there may be a preference for one gender over others" (p. 2).

Transgender: "A person who lives as a member of a gender other than that expected based on anatomical sex. Sexual orientation varies and is not dependent on gender identity" (p. 9).

Transsexual: "A person who identifies psychologically as a gender/sex other than the one to which they were assigned at birth. Transsexuals often wish to transform their bodies hormonally and surgically to match their inner sense of gender/sex" (p. 10).

Queer: "1. An umbrella term which embraces a matrix of sexual preferences, orientations, and habits of the not-exclusively-heterosexual-and-monogamous majority. Queer includes lesbians, gay men, bisexuals, transpeople, intersex persons, the radical sex communities, and many other sexually transgressive (underworld) explorers. 2. This term is sometimes used as a sexual orientation label instead of 'bisexual' as a way of acknowledging that there are more than two genders to be attracted to, or as a way of stating a nonheterosexual orientation without having to state who they are attracted to. 3. A reclaimed word that was formerly used solely as a slur but that has been semantically overturned by members of the maligned group, who use it as a term of defiant pride. 'Queer' is an example of a word undergoing this process. For decades 'queer' was used solely as a derogatory adjective for gays and lesbians, but in the 1980s the term began to be used by gay and lesbian activists as a term of self-identification. Eventually, it came to be used as an umbrella term that included gay men, lesbians, bisexuals, and transgendered people. Nevertheless, a sizable percentage of people to whom this term might apply still hold 'queer' to be a hateful insult, and its use by heterosexuals is often considered offensive. Similarly, other reclaimed words are usually offensive to the in-group when used by outsiders, so extreme caution must be taken concerning their use when one is not a member of the group" (p. 7).

Questioning: "For some, the process of exploring and discovering one's own sexual orientation, gender identity, or gender expression" (University of Michigan, 2014).

Intersex: "General term used for a variety of conditions in which a person is born with a reproductive or sexual anatomy that does not seem to fit the typical definitions of female or male" (Intersex Society of North America, n.d.).

Asexual: "Person who is not sexually attracted to anyone or does not have a sexual orientation" (Green & Peterson, 2006, p. 1).

Ally: "Someone who confronts heterosexism, homophobia, biphobia, transphobia, heterosexual and genderstraight privilege in themselves and others; a concern for the well-being of lesbian, gay, bisexual, trans, and intersex people; and a belief that heterosexism, homophobia, biphobia and transphobia are social justice issues" (p. 1).

Pansexual: "A person who is sexually attracted to all or many gender expressions" (p. 6).

Two-spirited: "Native persons who have attributes of both genders, have distinct gender and social roles in their tribes, and are often involved with mystical rituals (shamans). Their dress is usually a mixture of male and female articles and they are seen as a separate or third gender. The term 'two-spirit' is usually considered specific to the Zuni tribe. Similar identity labels vary by tribe and include 'one-spirit' and 'wintke'" (p. 10).

It is important to remember that youth may identify as one, multiple, or none of these terms. For example, someone can identify as transgender and lesbian. Further, not everyone who is involved in the LGBTQIA community will be familiar with all the various subgroups and terminology. As terminology is often evolving, it is essential to continually be informed about changes and variations in definitions and to have ongoing conversations with students and/or youth about the way they would like to be addressed.

Sexual Education and LGBTQ Youth School Experiences

Current sexual education standards fail to provide risk reduction instruction for LGBT youth (Kubicek, 2010), as programs are often focused on heterosexual issues. Because heterosexuality is presented as the social norm, sexual education disregards LGBTQ youth. This leaves LGBTQ youth at risk for sexual violence and engagement in unprotected sex (Bridges, 2007). Additionally, excluding LGBTQ topics in sexual education dismisses the opportunity to teach heterosexual youth about gender and sexual orientation diverse populations. Teaching gender and sexual orientation diversity is an important step in creating a more inclusive school environment. LGBTQ youth often are more subjected to a negative school experience. Surveys on research of youth across the nation have reported high rates of bullying, harassment, and dating violence:

- In 2011, 81.9% of LGBT students reported being verbally harassed, 38.3% reported being physically harassed, and 18.3% reported being physically assaulted at school in the past year because of their sexual orientation.
  (Kosciw, Greytak, Bartkiewicz, Boesen, & Palmer, 2012)

- Surveys show that 8 percent of high school students have been forced to have intercourse, and 9 percent have experienced dating violence.
  (Eaton et al., 2012)

Comprehensive sexual education can help decrease the rate of dating violence and bullying among youth. Research has indicated the positive benefits of including information on healthy relationships into sexual education programs. For example, one study reported that students were 60% less likely to perpetrate forms of dating violence against a partner after being taught a safe dating curriculum (Foshee, Bauman, Arriaga, Helms, Koch, & Linder, 1998). Although no research has been conducted on the benefits of inclusive sexuality education, there is research to indicate that including positive representations of LGBT people, history, and events in school curriculum is associated with a safer, more accepting school climate for LGBTQ youth, as does providing LGBTQ-specific resources (GLSEN, 2011).

In outlining support for LGBTQIA inclusive programs, the American Psychological Association and the National Association of School Psychologists (2014) "affirm that same-sex sexual and romantic attractions, feelings, and behaviors are normal and positive variations of human sexuality regardless of sexual orientation identity" as well as "affirm that diverse gender expressions, regardless of gender identity, and diverse gender identities, beyond a binary classification, are normal and positive variations of the human experience" ("The Role of Mental Health-care Professionals in Schools" section, para. 2–3). The American Psychological Association and the National Association of School Psychologists (2014) outlined the following key points:

- "Support efforts to ensure the funding of basic and applied research, and scientific evaluations of interventions and programs, designed to address the issues of gender and sexual orientation diverse adolescents in the schools."
- "Recommend the continued development and evaluation of school-level interventions that promote academic success and resiliency, that reduce bullying and harassment, that reduce risk for sexually transmitted infections, that reduce risk for pregnancy among adolescents, that reduce risk for self-injurious behaviors, and that foster safe and supportive school environments for gender and sexual orientation diverse students."
- "Recommend that special sensitivity be given to the diversity within the population of gender and sexual orientation diverse students, with new interventions that incorporate the concerns of sexual minorities often overlooked or underserved, and the concerns of racial/ethnic

minorities and recently immigrant children and adolescents who are also gender and sexual orientation diverse students" ("Programs and Interventions" section, para. 13).

- "Promote cross-agency collaboration to create policies that positively affect the health and wellbeing of gender and sexual orientation diverse adolescents and children" ("Policies" section, para. 3).

These guidelines help schools to develop inclusive environments for LGBTQ students who often have negative experiences because of their sexuality, both real and perceived.

Population of LGBT People in the United States

There are varying estimates of the percentage of LGBT adults in the United States. According to Gates (2011), reasons for such variation include "differences in the definitions of who is included in the LGBT population, differences in survey methods, and a lack of consistent questions asked in a particular survey over time" (p. 2). Estimates of the percentage of LGBT individuals are helpful in informing future policies and research, such as creating sexual health education to serve LGBTQ populations.

According to Gates (2011), 2.2% of women identify as bisexual, and 1.1% of women identify as lesbian; 1.4% of men identify as bisexual, and 2.2% of men identify as gay; and 0.3% of individuals identify as transgender. Gates (2011) indicated that some "transgender individuals may identify as lesbian, gay, or bisexual, so it is not possible to make a precise combined LGBT estimate" (p. 6). Gates' (2011) analyses indicate that there are more than 8 million adults in the United States who are LGB, which is 3.5% of the adult population. It is also indicated that there are about 700,000 transgender people in the United States. Combining these figures, Gates (2011) estimates that there are approximately 9 million Americans who identify as LGBT.

Interestingly, Gates (2011) states that among adults who identify as lesbian, gay, or bisexual, the majority identified as bisexuals (1.8% compared to 1.7% who identify as lesbian or gay). Additionally, women are more likely than men to identify as bisexual. In a majority of the surveys given, bisexual women comprise more than half of the lesbian and bisexual population, whereas gay men comprise more than half of gay and bisexual men (Gates, 2011). Another important figure to consider is the number of people who have reported same-sex sexual behavior yet identify as heterosexual. Gates (2011) describes how estimates of people who have had any same-sex sexual behavior or same-sex sexual attraction are significantly higher than estimates of people who actually identify as lesbian, gay, or bisexual. It is estimated that 19 million Americans (8.2%) have engaged in same-sex sexual behavior. In addition, about 25.6 million Americans (11%) acknowledge they have had same-sex sexual attraction (Gates, 2011). Because there are a high percentage of people who engage in same-sex behavior at some point in their lives, we should suggest LGBTQ topics are essential within sexual health education.

In addition to the estimates provided by Gates (2011), there are other estimates given for the LGBTQ population. For example, Ward, Dahlhamer, Galinksy, and Joestl (2014), through the CDC, published results from the 2013 National Health Interview Survey (NHIS). The "2013 data release marks the first time nationally representative data on sexual orientation are available in NHIS, the goals of this report are to present population distributions of sexual orientation and examine prevalence rates of select health indicators across sexual orientation groups" (p. 2). Results indicated that among adults aged 18 and over, 96.6% identified as straight, 1.6% identified as gay or lesbian, and 0.7% identified as bisexual. The other adults surveyed identified as "something else" (0.2%), selected "I don't know the answer" (0.4%), or refused to provide an answer (0.6%) (Ward et al., 2014). Ward et al. also found that more women than men identified as bisexual, similar to the Gates (2011) study. Although these estimates differ from the Gates (2011) study, LGBTQ people represent a significant subpopulation in the United States.

LGBTQ Sexual Health Risks

LGBTQ youth are at greater risk for negative sexual health outcomes than heterosexual peers. In particular, some gender and sexual orientation diverse adolescent subpopulations, including young gay men, homeless adolescents, racial/ ethnic minority adolescents, transgender women of color, and adolescents enrolled in alternative schools, are at heightened risk for STIs, including HIV (CDC, 2012; Markham, Tortolero, Escobar-Chaves, Parcel, Harrist, & Addy, 2003). This is attributed to complex and interacting factors related to stigma, socioeconomic class, and minority stress (Hatzenbuehler, Phelan, & Link, 2013; Meyer, 2003; Phelan, Link, & Tehranifar, 2010). In an overall assessment of negative sexual health outcomes, Blake, Ledsky, Lehman, Goodenow, Sawyer, and Hack (2001) found that lesbian, gay, and bisexual youth who are sexually active reported having first intercourse at an early age, a higher number of sexual partners, a higher use of alcohol or drugs before last sex, and increased pregnancy rates.

LGBTQ adolescents may also be at an increased risk for pregnancy (Goodenow, Szalacha, Robin, & Westheimer, 2008; Russell, Ryan, Toomey, Diaz, & Sanchez, 2011; Ryan, Russell, Huebner, Diaz, & Sanchez, 2010; Saewyc, Poon, Homma, & Skay, 2008). In a study, Goodenow et al. (2008) found that young women who identified as lesbian, gay, or bisexual were at higher risk for pregnancy than young women unsure of their identity or who identified as heterosexual. Moreover, participants who identified as LGBTQ were more likely to have experienced sexual coercion as well as to report behaviors that might increase risk of HIV infection ("Discussion" section, para. 2). Additionally, according to the CDC (2014b), young gay and bisexual men accounted for an estimated 19% (8,800) of all new HIV infections in the United States and 72% of new HIV infections among youth in 2010. These young men, aged 13–24, were "the only age group that showed a significant increase in estimated new infections—22% from 2008 (7,200) through 2010 (8,800)" ("New HIV Infections" section, para. 2, CDC, 2014b). It is clear that LGBTQ youth are experiencing higher rates of negative sexual outcomes. The next section will provide more detailed statistics for lesbians, gay men, bisexuals, and transgender people.

Lesbian Sexual Health Outcomes

For the purposes of this chapter, we will define lesbians as women who have sex with women. Lesbians are a diverse group of women with variations in sexual identity, sexual behaviors, sexual practices, and risk behaviors. Young lesbians are often regarded as being safe from experiencing negative sexual outcomes; however, studies have indicated that young lesbians over their lifetimes experience STIs at similar rates to all women; they experience pregnancy at higher rates than their heterosexual counterparts; and they are less likely to use protection during heterosexual intercourse (McNair, 2005). Goodenow et al. (2008) found that "adolescent females with a bisexual or lesbian identity were more likely than self-identified heterosexuals to have had multiple sexual partners or to have been pregnant" ("Discussion" section, para. 2).

Other studies indicate that some lesbians, particularly adolescents, young women, and women with both male and female partners, might be at increased risk for STIs and HIV as a result of certain reported risk behaviors (Goodenow et al., 2008; Koh, Gomez, Shade, & Rowley, 2005). For example, lesbians are at risk for acquiring bacterial, viral, and protozoal infections from current and prior partners. The risk of experiencing an STI can depend on a particular sexual practice, such as oral-genital sex, vaginal/anal sex using fingers, insertive sex toys, and oral-anal sex (Fethers, Marks, Mindel, & Estcourt, 2000; Marrazzo, Koutsky, Eschenbach, Agnew, Stine, & Hillier, 2002). Sexual practices that involve vaginal/anal sex using fingers, as well as using insertive sex toys, allow the transmission of bodily fluids. Several studies have indicated the efficacy of these transmission routes for infection, including Kellock and O'Mahony (1996) finding a metronidazole-resistant trichomoniasis via masturbation, and Kwakwa and Ghobrial (2003) finding that HIV was transmitted via sex toys. Also, the practice of oral-genital sex among lesbians may cause a higher risk for genital infection with herpes simplex virus type 1 (Marrazzo, Stine, & Wald, 2003). Encouraging healthy sexual practices would help prevent the spread of these types of infections, like describing the need to clean shared sex toys between uses.

Importantly, Goodenow et al. (2008) found that lesbians were more likely to have injected drugs and to have had multiple lifetime sexual partners. They believe that participant illegal injection drug use is a major concern and recommend that health professionals and educators ensure that "prevention efforts are directed toward the full range of health risk behaviors, not just sexual behaviors, that may place these adolescents at risk" ("Discussion" section, para. 5). We agree that sexual health education should include more information than just sexual health risks, such as drugs/alcohol use and healthy relationships.

In an effort to explain why lesbians may have increased negative sexual health outcomes, Goodenow et al. (2008) propose that lesbians may be

> attempting to cope with a heavily stigmatized identity may lead some adolescent females to "heterosexual immersion" (excessive and high-risk sexual behavior with male partners) in an attempt either to "cure" themselves of homosexuality or to prove to themselves or others, by being pregnant, that they are not lesbian.
>
> ("Discussion" section, para. 1)

These factors are important considerations in developing appropriate strategies and interventions for lesbian youth.

Gay Men Sexual Health Outcomes

For the purposes of this chapter, we will refer to men who have sex with men as gay men. Like lesbians, gay men have their own sexual behaviors, sexual practices, and risk behaviors, and they experience a high rate of negative sexual health outcomes. For example, STIs occur at a high rate among sexually active gay men. This includes STIs for which effective treatments are available (e.g., syphilis, gonorrhea, chlamydia, pubic lice, anal papilloma) and for which no cure is currently available (e.g., HIV, hepatitis A or B, human papillomavirus [HPV]). A major concern for gay men's health is HIV/AIDS. Despite recent declines in new HIV infections, there is a rise in infections for young gay men in the United States. HIV infection among young gay men aged 13-24 years increased by 26% over 2008-2011 (CDC, 2012). Moreover, in 2011, an estimated 3,004 youth in the United States and six dependent areas were diagnosed with AIDS, a number that has increased 29% since 2008 (CDC, 2014a). Racial/ethnic minorities are at a higher risk for infection. In 2010, Black youth accounted for an estimated 57% (7,000) of all new HIV infections among youth in the United States, followed by Hispanic/Latino youth at 20% (2,390) and White youth at 20% (2,380). Importantly, almost 60% of youth with HIV in the United States do not know they are infected (CDC, 2014a).

There are several possible reasons for the increase in HIV/AIDS diagnoses among youth. According to the CDC (2014a), potential reasons include low perception of risk, low rates of testing, low rates of condom use, high rates of STIs, older partners, substance use, homelessness, inadequate HIV prevention education, and feelings of isolation. We would like to highlight the challenge of inadequate HIV prevention education. Because some sexual education programs exclude information about sexual orientation, youth are not receiving HIV prevention education necessary to make healthy decisions. The increasing number of HIV diagnoses for young gay and bisexual men necessitates the inclusion of sexual orientation topics in sexual education programs. It is essential that HIV/AIDS be discussed, including information on abstinence and safer sex, to help prevent infection.

A new and possibly controversial topic regarding HIV prevention is the use of PrEP (preexposure prophylaxis). The goal of PrEP is to prevent HIV from replicating and infecting someone who is exposed to the virus (CDC, 2014b). When taken consistently, PrEP has been shown to reduce the risk of HIV infection in people who are at high risk by up to 92% (Grant et al., 2010), and researchers state that PrEP is much less effective if it is not taken consistently. In a second study among men and women in HIV-discordant couples (Baeten et al., 2012), those who received PrEP were 75% less likely to become infected than those on a placebo. Additionally, among those with detectable levels of medicine in their blood, PrEP reduced the risk of HIV infection by up to 90% (Baeten et al., 2012). PrEP is a powerful HIV prevention tool and can be combined with condoms and other prevention methods to provide even greater protection than when used alone. Despite the preliminary promise of PrEP, its use can often be a controversial topic because some people believe that it will decrease the use of condoms, leading to other infections and a belief that condoms are no longer necessary. Koester et al. (2014) conducted interviews with participants who were part of a PrEP study. Koester et al. (2014) found that participants who took PrEP mainly used it as an additional source of reassurance to supplement their current risk management strategy to avoid HIV infection. Once on PrEP, participants generally did not report significant changes in their sexual behaviors except in younger participants, and in most cases, it did not lead to increased sex without a condom (Koester et al., 2014). These qualitative data help support that those who use PrEP are not subsequently engaging in more risky sexual behaviors. We believe that PrEP should be included in sexual education discussions. Similar to other methods of protection against STIs, HIV/AIDS, and unintended pregnancy, it is a strategy to help avoid unwanted sexual outcomes.

A second topic to include in sexual education is the availability of postexposure prophylaxis (PEP). PEP involves taking certain medications within 72 hours after exposure to HIV to decrease the possibility of becoming HIV-positive (CDC, 2014b). These medicines keep HIV from making copies of itself and spreading through one's body. However, PEP is not always effective and does not guarantee that someone will not become infected (CDC, 2014b). Like a morning-after-pill, PEP can be used as a secondary prevention strategy. Although it is not preferred over traditional contraception, it provides an additional tool for those who may be at high risk. This is particularly critical because there is a possibility that traditional methods of contraception are not always effective.

In developing appropriate strategies for prevention, discussion of contraception is critical. Smith, Herbst, Zhang, and Rose (2014) studied the effectiveness of condom use for HIV prevention. Among gay men who reported anal sex with an HIV-positive male partner, consistent condom use yielded 70% effectiveness for HIV prevention compared to those who never used condoms. Though not statistically significant, this estimate of 70% effectiveness was less than the 80% effectiveness previously reported for heterosexuals in HIV-discordant couples reporting consistent condom use. Education about condom use is essential, particularly because only 16% of gay men reported consistent condom use during anal sex with male partners of any HIV status (Smith et al., 2014). Chin et al. (2012) describe how sexual education courses that include information on condoms and communication skills have been shown to increase healthy sexual behavior changes in the general student population.

Another major sexual health concern for gay men is the HPV. HPV causes anal and genital warts as well as increased rates of anal cancers. Gay and bisexual men are estimated to be 17 times more likely than heterosexual men to develop anal cancer (CDC, 2014b). Although treatments for HPV do exist, recurrences of warts and the rate at which the infection can be spread between partners are very high. Gay and bisexual men, people with weakened immune systems, and people living with HIV/ AIDS are also at higher risk for some HPV-related health problems. Tider, Parsons, and Bimbi (2005) found that some gay men did not understand the health consequences of HPV. For example, there is a direct link between HPV and genital warts, but some participants indicated they had genital warts but not HPV. This lack of accurate information among LGBTQ youth is of concern. Youth are unaware of the potential outcomes associated with their sexual behaviors. Continual STI and HIV education is needed among gay men, including programs on abstinence, delaying the initiation of sex, and negotiating safer sex, to help them make healthier decisions.

Bisexual Men and Women Sexual Health Outcomes

Bisexuality is unique because it includes both male and female experiences. As noted earlier, bisexuals comprise a slight majority in adults who identify as LGB (Gates, 2011). Miller, André, Ebin, and Bessonova (2007) highlighted common issues that people who are bisexuals encounter. Miller et al. (2007) first explain the difference between behavior and identity, particularly when describing bisexual people. For example, a person can have a bisexual identity even if he or she has decided to not have sex. On the other hand, a person can be bisexual and also be in a monogamous relationship with a man or a woman. Additionally, there are people who have sex with men and women, yet they can identify themselves as gay, lesbian, heterosexual, or bisexual (Miller et al., 2007). It is important to note that bisexual women's issues are not always the same as those of lesbian women. This is true even for bisexual women who only have sex with women, or for lesbian women who also have sex with men. Similarly, bisexual men's issues are not always the same as for gay men, even for bisexual men who only have sex with men, or for gay men who also have sex with women (Miller et al., 2007). To describe sexual health risks for bisexuals, we will first discuss bisexual women.

Dobinson (2007) indicates that bisexual women are more likely than heterosexual women to report higher risk sexual behaviors. For example, bisexual women are more likely to report engaging in sex with a man who is known to have sex with men, engaging in sex with a man living with HIV, having multiple male sexual partners, engaging in sex with injecting drug users (IDUs), and having a sex partner who has had sex with a prostitute. Additionally, bisexual women report less condom use with casual sex partners and less condom use during anal sex. Moreover, research has also found that bisexual women with larger numbers of female partners are more likely to experience vaginal infections including bacterial vaginosis, trichomonas vaginalis, and herpes (Bailey, Farquhar, & Owen, 2004). Lastly, when compared with heterosexual women and lesbians, bisexual women exhibit the highest rates of combining substance and/or alcohol use with sex (Dobinson, 2007). In general, bisexual women appear to have more negative sexual health outcomes compared to bisexual men.

For bisexual men, data have shown that some groups of bisexual men report less risky sexual behaviors with males, such as less anal sex, but they are more likely than heterosexual men to have sex with female prostitutes and to have anal sex with women. However, bisexual men have reported more condom use than heterosexual men (Dobinson, 2007). Certain groups of bisexual men, such as men living with HIV who are IDUs, have been more likely to engage in unprotected sex, report less education, less income, more anxiety, more hostility, more childhood sex abuse, and greater unemployment than gay and bisexual men who have not used drugs (Ibanez, Purcell, Stall, Parsons, & Gomes, 2005). Overall, Dobinson (2007) found that bisexual and gay men are more likely to report having an STI.

A unique issue for bisexual men and women is the idea of biphobia, which Miller et al. (2007) define as "fear or hatred of bisexual people" (p. 4). Although many other LGBTQ youth experience discrimination, Miller et al. (2007) highlighted that some bisexual people experience internalized biphobia. Some of the negative feelings often experienced by bisexual people struggling with internalized biphobia include the following: (1) "We do not exist; we are invisible; bisexuality is not real." (2) "We are responsible for the spread of AIDS." (3) "We are 'on the fence,' incapable of commitment." (4) "We do not know who we are; we're just 'in a phase.'" (5) "We are hypersexual, 'on the prowl' at all times" (Miller et al., 2007, p. 35). These are internalized issues that may have an impact on well-being. Miller et al. (2007) describe how "biphobia results in debilitating discrimination against bisexuals, which in turn creates a significant impact on bisexual health" (p. 35). We believe biphobia can lead to other health concerns, such as issues with self-esteem and identity. Understanding this facet of bisexuality is helpful for educators to consider, particularly when providing mental health services for youth.

Within comprehensive sexual education, we believe that bisexuality should be its own component and not combined with gay or lesbian topics. Because of unique issues that bisexuals encounter, such as biphobia, there is research to suggest bisexual identity development may be more complicated than sexual identity development for gay men or lesbians (Dworkin, 2006). This is important to consider when developing programs to address the needs of bisexuals.

Transgender Men and Women Sexual Health Outcomes

Transgender people are a gender identity minority (CDC, 2011) rather than sexual minority. CDC (2011) describes gender identity as a person's basic sense of self. This entails identifying as male, female, or some other gender, including transgender, bigender, and intersex. According to the CDC (2011), "transgender refers to people whose gender identity does not conform to norms and expectations traditionally associated with a binary classification of gender based on external genitalia" (p. 1), and it includes "people who self-identify as gender variant; male-to-female (MTF) or transgender women; female-to-male (FTM) or transgender men; many other gender nonconforming people with identities beyond the gender binary; and people who self-identify simply as female or male" (p. 1). Importantly, transgender people can identify with any sexual orientation.

As described by Dragowski (2014), transgender people can have any sexual orientation. This includes heterosexual (attraction to people of their other gender), gay or lesbian, bisexual, queer (attractions that are not aligned with and do not recognize the gender binary), asexual, and pansexual. A significant concern is that transgender youth lack health information regarding their needs. For example, sexual education rarely addresses transgender people's bodies and identities. In a study by Reisner, Perkovich, and Mimiaga (2010), transgender men who have sex with men report a lack of adequate information about their sexual health at rates as high as 93.8%. Lack of appropriate information can lead to negative sexual health outcomes.

Transgender people have the highest risk for HIV infection and STIs according to the CDC (2011). High levels of HIV risk behaviors have been reported among transgender people, including transgender women having multiple sex partners and unprotected receptive and/or insertive anal intercourse (CDC, 2011). Transgender women also report increased levels of alcohol and substance use, which can impair judgment leading to unsafe sexual practices (CDC, 2011). Among transgender men, there is some evidence of multiple male sex partners and unprotected receptive anal or vaginal intercourse with men, though these behaviors have not been reported to increase HIV infection in this population (CDC, 2011). Although not as fully researched, HIV prevalence in transgender men is estimated to range from 2–3%. In the first studies of HIV among transgender female youth, HIV prevalence varied from 19–22%, showing them to be at a high risk for HIV infection (Garofalo, Deleon, Osmer, Doll, & Harper, 2006; Kenagy & Bostwick, 2005; Kenagy & Hsieh, 2005; Rodríquez-Madera & Toro-Alfonso, 2005). Additionally, African American and Latino/a transgender people are at especially high risk for HIV and other STIs (CDC, 2011; Garofalo, et al., 2006; Nuttbrock et al., 2009).

Nuttbrock et al. (2009) found that the most significant risk factor for HIV and STIs for Hispanic and African American transgender women was the social expression of transgender identity, which was measured as gender identity disclosure and dressing in female attire: "Those who presented in the female gender role at an early age, and dress accordingly, were more likely to become infected with HIV or some other STI" ("Discussion" section, para. 5), whereas those who expressed themselves as male did not experience these outcomes. Transgender women sexually who are attracted only to men, termed androphillic, may have an elevated risk for HIV or STIs because of their comparatively frequent sexual contacts with high-risk partners, like men who have sex with men (Bockting, Miner, & Rosser, 2007). In a study by Sevelius (2009), it was found that although HIV prevalence among transgender men who have sex with men was low, their reported sexual behaviors still indicated a high level of risk.

The risk factors associated with HIV and STIs among the ethnic minority transgender women were virtually absent among the Caucasian transgender women in the study by Sevelius (2009). Androphillic sexual orientation, commercial sex partners, and the social expression of transgender identity were consistently associated with HIV among the ethnic minority transgender women, but this was infrequently reported by Caucasian transgender women (Sevelius, 2009). This suggests that the differences in HIV infections among ethnic groups may be attributable to ethnic differences in these risks. These findings indicate that HIV and STI prevention is needed for Hispanics and African American transgender women. Reisner et al. (2010) discuss the lack of culturally relevant and accurate sexual health information tailored to the sexual health needs of transgender men who have sex with men. This puts them at risk for HIV and STIs from inaccurate information, limited support, lack of access to sexual health resources, and lack of sexual partners who are knowledgeable and respectful of their bodies, preferred sexual practices, and identities (Reisner et al., 2010). Prevention should focus on a key risk factor for HIV and STIs in this population, which is the social expression of transgender identity (Sevelius, 2009). Gender identity affirmation can be a central issue for transgender persons. Bockting, Rosser, and Scheltema (1999) state that approaches to HIV prevention should promote the affirmation of gender identity while simultaneously avoiding the high-risk behaviors that are often associated with it.

Transgender men have another major issue regarding sexual health outcomes. Many transgender men who have sex with men are at risk for unintended pregnancy as well as STIs. Transgender men who have sex with men report high rates of unprotected vaginal and anal intercourse (Reisner et al., 2010; Sevelius, 2009), and some transgender men report being more concerned about pregnancy than HIV and other STIs (Reisner et al., 2010). Transgender men need education of pregnancy prevention just like other young women. Reisner et al. (2010) describe why sexual health programs and interventions are needed for transgender men. These programs and interventions should be culturally competent and address the sexual health needs of transgender men who have sex with men, as well as the needs of their nontransgender male sexual partners. In addition, they recommend integrating sexual health information created by transgender men into healthcare services. These services should include peer support, mental health services, Internet-delivered information, and safer sex materials that are more pleasure-focused. Lastly, training for healthcare providers is an important aspect of intervention integrity for this population (Reisner et al., 2010). We believe that these recommendations could be used to supplement current sexual education programing in schools, such as topics of peer support, mental health services, and Internet-delivered information.

LGBTQ Dating Violence

There have only been a few studies regarding dating violence within the LGBTQ community, particularly when focusing on youth. A study by Freedner, Freed, Yang, and Austin (2002) indicated that dating violence was prevalent in all sexual orientation groups. Compared with heterosexuals, bisexual males had greater odds of reporting any type of abuse, and bisexual females had greater odds of experiencing sexual abuse. Additionally, lesbians had greater odds of being scared about their safety compared to heterosexual females. Lastly, both bisexual men and women were more likely to be threatened with outing compared to gay men and lesbians.

More recently, Dank, Lachman, Zweig, and Yahner (2014) conducted a study in which they found that LGB youth showed significantly higher rates of all types of dating victimization and perpetration experiences when compared to heterosexual youth. Specifically, "higher percentages of LGB youth reported being victimized by physical dating violence (43%), psychological dating abuse (59%), cyber dating abuse (37%), and sexual coercion (23%), than did heterosexual youth, who reported rates of 29%, 46%, 26%, and 12%, respectively. Similarly, higher percentages of LGB than heterosexual youth reported perpetrating physical dating violence (33%), psychological dating abuse (37%), cyber dating abuse (18%), and sexual coercion (4%)" ("Results" section, para. 1).

Furthermore, transgender youth reported some of the highest victimization rates for issues including physical dating violence, psychological dating abuse, cyber dating abuse, and sexual coercion. However, transgender youth also reported the highest perpetration rates of physical dating violence, cyber dating abuse, and sexual coercion (Dank et al., 2014). Female youth were second most likely to be victimized by psychological dating abuse, cyber dating abuse, and sexual coercion. Lastly, male youth had the lowest victimization rates with regard to psychological dating abuse, cyber dating abuse, and sexual coercion and "were more likely than female youth to experience physical dating violence as victims and to perpetrate sexual coercion" ("Results" section, para. 2). Importantly, higher proportions of LGB victims of dating violence and abuse sought help (18%), did so within 1 day of the incident (8%), and did so after the first incident of violence (10%), compared to 8%, 3%, and 3% of heterosexual victims.

There are several negative outcomes of dating violence. According to Coker (2007), experiencing dating violence is associated with an increase in sexual risk-taking behaviors, inconsistent condom use or partner refusing to use condoms, reduced use of hormonal contraceptives, and having been diagnosed with an STI. Additionally, dating violence victimization was also associated with having some type of vaginal infection or urinary tract infection, chronic pelvic or abdominal pain, painful menses, and sexual dissatisfaction or lack of sexual pleasure (Coker, 2007). Moreover, dating violence is associated with unwanted pregnancy. Miller, Jordan, Levenson, and Silverman (2010) found that dating violence may also include reproductive coercion and explicit behavior to promote pregnancy that is unwanted by a partner, such as birth control sabotage.

LGBTQ Geographical Considerations

LGBTQ youth in rural areas have a unique set of challenges. According to Palmer, Kosciw, and Bartkiewicz (2012), these youth have limited access to LGBT-related resources and found that "only 11% of rural LGBT students reported having an LGBT-inclusive curriculum (i.e., having been taught positive things about LGBT people, history, or events in their classes), significantly less than the 18% of suburban and 20% of urban students" (p. 23). Additionally, school readings were also less likely to include information about LGBT persons, history, or events than in suburban or urban schools. Lastly, rural students reported less access to LGBT-related content on the Internet using school computers. Palmer et al. (2012) found that 39% of rural LGBT students whose school computers had Internet access said they could access LGBT-related websites, compared to 44% of suburban students and 44% of urban students.

Participants were also asked about the sexual education provided at their school and whether it used an abstinence-only education. Existing research demonstrates that many abstinence-only curricula provide misleading and medically inaccurate information about sexuality and sexual health. Moreover, these programs commonly ignore the needs of LGBT youth who may not receive accurate information about HIV prevention and relevant information on sexual health matters (Ott & Santelli, 2007; Santelli, Ott, Lyon, Roger, Summer, & Schleifer, 2006; Yakush, 2007). Overall, rural and urban students were only slightly less likely than suburban students to have been taught any curriculum about sexual health: 84% of rural students versus 87% of suburban students and 83% of urban students (Palmer et al., 2012). However, rural LGBT students were more likely to have been taught to practice abstinence-only in sexual education. One-third (32%) of rural LGBT students said they were taught an abstinence-only sexual health curriculum, which was greater than the 28% of suburban students and 25% of urban students who were taught abstinence-only (Palmer et al., 2012). Rural school educators should ensure that they are providing appropriate and medically accurate education and services to their LGBTQ populations and take steps to create a positive environment for all students.

Strategies for Sexual Health Promotion

To begin with creating a safer environment for LGBTQ students, we highlight the NASP (2011) position statement that outlines inclusive school-based strategies:

1   Establish and enforce comprehensive nondiscrimination and anti-bullying policies that include LGBTQ issues.
2   Educate students and staff.
3   Intervene directly with perpetrators.
4   Provide intervention and support for those students targeted for harassment and intimidation and those exploring their sexuality or gender identity.
5   Promote societal and familial attitudes and behaviors that affirm the dignity and rights within educational environments of LGBTQ youth.
6   Recognize strengths and resilience.

Additionally, gender and sexual orientation diverse students report increased school connectedness and school safety when school personnel intervene in the following ways: (1) addressing and stopping bullying and harassment; (2) developing administrative policies that prohibit discrimination based on sexual orientation, gender identity, and gender expression; (3) supporting the use of affirming classroom activities and the establishment of gender and sexual orientation diverse–affirming student groups; and (4) valuing education and training for students and staff on the needs of gender and sexual orientation diverse students (Case & Meier, 2014; Greytak, Kosciw, & Diaz, 2009; McGuire, Anderson, Toomey, & Russell, 2010; NASP, 2011; Sausa, 2005).

According to Miller et al. (2007), knowing whether a person identifies as heterosexual, gay, lesbian, or bisexual is not an accurate way to predict whether he or she will have sex with men, women, both, or neither. It also does not indicate or predict what kind of sexual activities they will engage in. Sexual identity must be separated from sexual behavior, which is what people actually do sexually. From an HIV and STI prevention framework, sexual behavior is more important. It is a person's behavior—such as whether they are exposed to HIV or an STI through sexual activity or other behaviors like needle sharing—that puts them at risk (Miller et al., 2007). Successful prevention programing addresses both behavior and identity while always being aware of the differences between the two.

Gowen and Winges-Yanez (2014) conducted a qualitative study on youth perception of LGBTQ-inclusive sexual education. There were several suggestions that participants made to increase inclusivity in sexuality education. These included (1) LGBTQ issues, such as gender diversity, sexual orientation, being queer, stigmatization, and LGBTQ role models; (2) access to resources such as local resources, pamphlets, and online resources; (3) STI prevention, including safer sex and condoms; (4) relationships, including communication, healthy relationships, dating violence; and (5) anatomy, including different body parts, diversity in external appearance, and body acceptance.

Within this study, participants emphasized that discussions of relationships give youth a better understanding of how to "keep yourself safe" and "set boundaries" with sexual partners (Gowen & Winges-Yanez, 2014). Also, participants found it important to discuss both healthy and unhealthy relationships in the classroom. This is a more comprehensive approach than merely teaching abstinence and pregnancy prevention. Selecting topics that address the needs of LGBTQ youth is essential to creating an inclusive program, which is well described by Gowen and Winges-Yanez (2014):

> The suggestion to focus prevention discussions around STIs rather than pregnancy diminishes the heterocentric perspective of the curriculum. It also can open the door to conversations around types of sexual behavior beyond vaginal intercourse, which cannot cause pregnancy but possibly can transmit STIs. However, participants noted that while addressing STI transmission is important, this should not be done in a way that pathologizes LGBTQ persons specifically. Participants shared experiences in which the only instances in which persons of different sexual orientations (usually gay men) were mentioned in the sexuality education classroom were during discussions of HIV/AIDS and other STIs. This association of LGBTQ persons with disease can serve to increase stigmatization toward these populations. Devoting more time to discussing healthy relationships and communication also can be more inclusive of all youth regardless of their sexual and/or gender identity. Similarly, lessons on anatomy are arguably not as dependent on sexual orientation to be relevant to all students. Discussions of anatomy should be more inclusive of, and discuss changes that may occur in, transgender individuals who choose to undergo hormonal treatments (p. 797).

Supporting an inclusive sexual education for LGBTQ students requires additional strategies. Elia and Eliason (2010) discuss a continuum of models of sexuality education. They describe how often sexual education is referenced as either abstinence-only or comprehensive sexuality education, yet there is a broader classification for sexual education programs. Specifically, they posit that there are five points along a continuum for sexual education, including (1) no sexuality education, (2) abstinence-only-until-marriage sexuality education,

(3) abstinence-based sexuality education, (4) comprehensive sexuality education, and (5) antioppressive, inclusive sexuality education.

Elia and Eliason provide 10 principles to establish an ideal framework for sexuality education for LGBTQ youth.

1 Be broadened to include anti-oppressive or social justice education: The audience is much broader than just students who identify as LGBTQ, but also includes youth who have same-sex attractions, behaviors, and/or identities without adopting a label.
2 Be democratic: Students are equal participants in determining what they learn and when.
3 Be inclusive: Diversity in all of its forms is considered and multiple viewpoints are discussed.
4 Focus on social justice: The curriculum includes examination of power dynamics, forms of oppression, and offers skills in critical thinking to examine social justice.
5 Attends to intersectionality of oppressions: how do race, class, ability, gender, sexuality, and other sources of oppression intersect?
6 Makes values transparent: No educational program can be value-free.
7 Offers a balanced approach that considers concepts such as pleasure/danger, risk/protection, and coercion/mutuality, as continua rather than as dichotomous points.
8 Promotes health in the broadest sense following the World Health Organization's conceptualization of sexual health developed in 2002.
9 Recognizes both resilience and risk factors regarding LGBTQ youth.
10 Developmental sequencing is balanced with teachable moments.

(2010, pp. 41–44)

Furthermore, the CDC (2014b) recommends school-based strategies for addressing HIV among young men who have sex with men, but these strategies can be used for all students.

1 Collect and use health risk behavior data.
   The CDC describes how many school districts use the YRBS data to track health risk behaviors and outcomes among sexual orientation and gender diverse students. Beginning in 2015, the YRBS questionnaire will include questions about sexual identity and gender of sexual contacts. These data can help address the health needs of sexual orientation and gender diverse students in schools, inform intervention practices, and monitor outcomes. More information is available at www.cdc.gov/yrbs.
2 Establish safe and supportive school environments.
   The CDC also describes how HIV prevention activities are more likely to be effective if they address the challenges young men who have sex with

men face at school, such as bullying related to their sexual orientation. For LGBT students, having a safe and supportive school environment has been associated with "decreases in depression, suicidal feelings, substance use, and unexcused absences" (CDC, 2014b, p. 3). To help establish supportive school environments, educators should address bullying and sexual harassment. This will help LGBTQ youth feel safer in school.

3 Provide key sexual health services.

Connecting young gay men as well as other youth to HIV testing and treatment is key to preventing the spread of HIV/AIDS. Schools can help "youth access key preventive sexual health services such as HIV and STI testing, counseling, and referral, either by providing these services as schools or connecting students with community providers" (CDC, 2014b, p. 3).

4 Implement exemplary sexual health education.

Sexual health education programs often ignore issues of young gay men and other orientation and gender diverse students. Educators should ensure that health education curricula include evidence-based prevention information relevant to this population. Sexual health education programs should be medically accurate and tailored to students' needs. Professional development training can help educators understand the health needs of LGTBQ youth.

Additionally, counseling interventions targeting risky sexual behaviors to prevent STIs are also beneficial. O'Connor, Lin, Burda, Henderson, Walsh, and Whitlock (2014) found that high-intensity interventions were likely to reduce the rate of STIs in both adults and sexually active adolescents. Condom use also increased after high-intensity interventions. Some moderate- and low-intensity interventions were also beneficial but were less likely to decrease risky behaviors.

O'Connor et al. (2014) also found that successful interventions generally provided most or all of the following topics: "information about STIs, such as prevalence, transmission, and details on how to reduce the risk for transmission; help in identifying personal risk for STIs; training in common behavior change processes, such as problem solving, decision making, and goal-setting; training in communication surrounding condom use and safe sex; and hands-on practice with condoms. Many successful interventions were also specifically tailored to the gender and race/ethnicity of the participants" ("Results" section, para. 2). Goodenow et al. (2008) also found that "AIDS education in school appeared to exert protective effects on several HIV/AIDS-related risk behaviors. Adolescents receiving AIDS education were less than half as likely to have multiple lifetime or recent sexual partners and one third less likely to report illegal injection drug use or STD diagnosis" ("Discussion" section, para. 7).

In addition, Reisner et al. (2010) suggest that safer sexual education materials are needed to address the needs of transgender people. This includes distinguishing by (1) partner genders, like male, female, transgender men, and transgender women; (2) type of relationship, such as casual, anonymous, or monogamous; and

(3) sexual behaviors, such as vaginal/anal sex, oral sex, or body contact with exchange of body fluids (Reisner et al., 2010). Authors also suggest more broad sexual health topics, including information about pregnancy and how to navigate pregnancy-related healthcare services as a transgender man. Additionally, the Internet held an important role for many transgender men who have sex with men. It helped facilitate sexual partnerships with nontransgender men as well as reduced the risk of violence or rejection from potential sexual partners. Lastly, it allowed sexual safety to be discussed prior to engaging in sexual activity. Sexual educators should consider including discussions of the Internet and how to screen potential sex partners and to reduce risky practices.

All students should receive education about healthy relationships as a part of health education. These lessons should include understanding and identifying healthy and unhealthy relationship patterns, effective ways to communicate relationship needs and manage conflict, and strategies to avoid or end an unhealthy relationship (FoSE, 2014). "Interventions targeting perpetration and victimization of intimate partner violence among adolescents can be effective. Those interventions are more likely to be based in multiple settings, and focus on key people in the adolescents' environment" ("Results" section, para. 1, DeKoker, Matthews, Zuch, Bastien, & Mason-Jones, 2013). Additionally, because physical violence often arises during conflict, interventions that target youth experiencing physical dating violence should address communication and conflict resolution skills within relationships (Haynie, Farhat, Brooks-Russell, Wang, Barbieri, & Iannotti, 2013).

Lastly, Jeltova and Fish (2005) discuss the importance of gay-straight alliances. Forming alliances between LGBTQ students and families and straight students and families has been shown to be successful in stopping and preventing harassment and in establishing a welcoming environment in the school. Other important strategies for promoting responsive school environments are (1) to arrange the physical environment to signal diversity is welcomed and promoted; (2) to take a proactive approach in preventing harassment and intervening when discrimination occurs; (3) to promote inclusive language, both verbal and print, throughout school policies and programs; and (4) to create a safe zone or safe person in the school to support the LGBTQ. These strategies promote a more inclusive environment for LGBTQ youth.

CASE STUDY

A moderately sized Midwestern high school serves approximately 1,500 students in grades 9–12. Recently, there have been increasing reports of bullying of students identified or perceived as LGBT. Additionally, the recent passing of marriage equality in the high school's state has prompted administrators

(Continued)

(Continued)

to review their sexual education curriculum in terms of LGBTQ topics. The school currently has no programs focusing on LGBTQ youth, and administrators have instructed the student support services faculty to develop programs appropriate for their school. We will describe the steps the school community took to support and address LGBTQ youth.

1   The student support services faculty, including a school psychologist and a school counselor, as well as a health teacher and a social studies teacher met to create a plan. They decided to use the MTSS approach and first conducted a needs assessment to determine appropriate strategies and programing. They administered the CDC's YRBS to all students and found that 7% of the student population was engaging in same-sex behaviors. Additionally, among those who were sexually active, 60% were not using contraception consistently. Lastly, 4% of students identified as LGB, with 2% as gay men, 1% as lesbian, and 1% as bisexual.

2   The health teacher reviewed the sexual education curriculum with other faculty and indicated that it was an abstinence-based program. After reviewing data about lack of contraception use among students and the percent of students engaging in same-sex behaviors, the faculty concluded that the abstinence-based program was not effective for all students. The faculty needed to provide a new curriculum that focused more on effective contraception and healthy relationships, which would not only address risky sexual behaviors but also the bullying that was increasing. They selected the NSES (FoSE, 2014) as their foundation for the curriculum. The faculty would supplement additional topics on LGB sexual health needs as this is reflected in their student population. There were no students who identified as transgender, so the faculty decided not to include specific strategies for this population at this time. Lastly, the faculty collected and provided community resources to students, such as places for HIV and STI testing and treatment.

3   The team decided to provide professional development to all staff regarding LGBT topics. They discussed how to be culturally competent as well as strategies to support students in the classroom, such as including discussions of LGBT events within classwork. The school's Tier 1 supports included both professional development and new sexual education curriculum.

4   After obtaining parental consent, school psychologist and school counselor decided to provide Tier 2 services to address risky sexual behaviors by having group counseling for those interested in attending. These groups would focus discussing safer sex in detail and specific strategies for the specific behaviors in which students were engaging.

Tier 3 supports would be individual counseling and outside referrals determined on a case-by-case basis.

5   To determine efficacy, the faculty decided to conduct the YRBS annually and determine if there were improvements in use of contraception. The faculty would also collect bullying data twice a year to see if incidences related to LGBT youth had decreased. If bullying has not decreased, the faculty would then either refresh their current antibullying program or select a new one.

This fictional case study provides one example of how a school can begin to address the needs of their LGTBQ population. Each district and school will have their own central issues to address, and being current on research will help to provide the most evidence-based strategies. LGBTQ youth benefit from support at school as well as support from family and friends. Without proper support and education, LGBTQ youth can experience negative school experiences and negative sexual health outcomes. More data collection about LGBTQ youth needs, such as through YRBS, can help educators provide better support.

References

American Psychological Association and National Association of School Psychologists. (2014). *Resolution on gender and sexual orientation diversity in children and adolescents in schools.* Retrieved from http://www.apa.org/about/policy/orientation-diversity.aspx

Baeten, J. M., Donnell, D., Ndase, P., Mugo, M. R., Campbell, J. D., Wangisi, J., et al. (2012). Antiretroviral prophylaxis for HIV prevention in heterosexual men and women. *New England Journal of Medicine, 367*(5), 399–410.

Bailey, J. V., Farquhar, C., & Owen, C. (2004). Bacterial vaginosis in lesbians and bisexual women. *Sexually Transmitted Diseases, 31*(11), 691–694.

Blake, S. M., Ledsky, R., Lehman, T., Goodenow, C., Sawyer, R., & Hack, T. (2001). Preventing sexual risk behaviors among gay, lesbian, and bisexual adolescents: The benefits of gay-sensitive HIV instruction in schools. *American Journal of Public Health, 91*, 940–946.

Bockting, W., Miner, M., & Rosser, B. R. (2007). Latino men's sexual behavior with transgender persons. *Archives of Sexual Behavior, 36*(6), 778–786.

Bockting, W. O., Rosser, B. R., & Scheltema, K. (1999). Transgender HIV prevention: Implementation and evaluation of a workshop. *Health Education Research, 14*(2), 177–183.

Bridges, E. (2007). *The impact of homophobia and racism on GLBTQ youth of color.* Retrieved from http://www.advocatesforyouth.org/storage/advfy/documents/fsglbtq_yoc.pdf

Case, K., & Meier, C. (2014). Developing allies to transgender and gender non-conforming youth: Training for counselors and educators. *Journal of LGBT Youth, 11*(1), 62–82.

CDC. (2011). *HIV infection among transgender people.* Retrieved from http://www.cdc.gov/hiv/transgender/pdf/transgender.pdf

CDC. (2012). *HIV surveillance in men who have sex with men (MSM).* Retrieved from http://www.cdc.gov/hiv/library/slideSets/index.html

CDC. (2014a). *HIV among youth.* Retrieved from http://www.cdc.gov/hiv/risk/age/youth

CDC. (2014b). *HIV and young men who have sex with men.* Retrieved from http://www.cdc.gov/HealthyYouth/sexualbehaviors/pdf/hiv_factsheet_ymsm.pdf

Chin, H. B., Sipe, T. A., Elder, R., Mercer, S. L., Chattopadhyay, S. K., Jacob, V., et al. (2012). The effectiveness of group-based comprehensive risk-reduction and abstinence education interventions to prevent or reduce the risk of adolescent pregnancy, human immuno-deficiency virus, and sexually transmitted infections. *American Journal of Preventive Medicine, 42*(3), 272–294.

Coker, A. L. (2007). Does physical intimate partner violence affect sexual health? A systematic review. *Trauma, Violence & Abuse, 8*(2), 149–177.

Dank, M., Lachman, P., Zweig, J. M., & Yahner, J. (2014). Dating violence experiences of lesbian, gay, bisexual, and transgender youth. *Journal of Youth and Adolescence.* Retrieved from http://www.urban.org/UploadedPDF/412892-Dating-Violence-Experiences-of-Lesbian-Gay-Bisexual-and-Transgender-Youth.pdf

DeKoker, P., Matthews, C., Zuch, M., Bastien, S., & Mason-Jones, A. J. (2013). A systematic review of interventions for preventing adolescent intimate partner violence. *Journal of Adolescent Health, 54*(1), 3–13.

Dobinson, C. (2007). *Top ten bisexual health issues.* In M. Miller, A. André, J. Ebin, & L. Bessonova (Eds.), *Bisexual health: An introduction and model practices for HIV/STI prevention programming.* New York, NY: National Gay and Lesbian Task Force Policy Institute, the Fenway Institute at Fenway Community Health, and BiNet USA.

Dragowski, E. A. (2014). Let's talk about gender. *NASP Communiqué, 43*(3), 1, 21–22.

Dworkin, S. H. (2006). Aging bisexual: The invisible of the invisible minority. In D. Kimmel, T. Rose, & S. David (Eds.), *Lesbian, gay, bisexual, and transgender aging: Research and clinical perspectives* (pp. 36–52). New York, NY: Columbia University Press.

Eaton, D. K., Kann, L., Kinchen, S., Shanklin, S., Flint, K. H., Hawkins, J., et al. (2012). Youth risk behavior surveillance – United States, 2011. *Morbidity and Mortality Surveillance Weekly Report Surveillance Summaries, 61*(4), 1–162.

Elia, J. P., & Eliason, M. (2010). Discourses of exclusion: Sexuality education's silencing of sexual others. *Journal of LGBT Youth, 7,* 29–48.

Fethers, K., Marks, C., Mindel, A., & Estcourt, C. S. (2000). Sexually transmitted infections and risk behaviours in women who have sex with women. *Sexually Transmitted Infections, 76,* 345–349.

Foshee, V. A., Bauman, K. E., Arriaga, X. B., Helms, R. W., Koch, G. G., & Linder, G. F. (1998). An evaluation of safe dates, an adolescent dating violence prevention program. *American Journal of Public Health, 88,* 45–50.

Freedner, N., Freed, L. H., Yang, Y. W., & Austin, S. B. (2002). Dating violence among gay, lesbian, and bisexual adolescents: results from a community survey. *Journal of Adolescent Health, 31*(6), 469–474.

FoSE. (2014). *National Sexuality Education Standards: Core Content and Skills K-12.* Retrieved from http://www.futureofsexed.org/documents/josh-fose-standards-web.pdf

Garofalo, R., Deleon, J., Osmer, E., Doll, M., & Harper, G. W. (2006). Overlooked, misunderstood and at-risk: Exploring the lives and HIV risk of ethnic minority male-to-female transgender youth. *Journal of Adolescent Health, 38*(3), 230–236.

Gates, G. J. (2011). *How many people are lesbian, gay, bisexual and transgender? UCLA: The Williams Institute.* Retrieved from http://williamsinstitute.law.ucla.edu/wp-content/uploads/Gates-How-Many-People-LGBT-Apr-2011.pdf

Gay, Lesbian, and Straight Education Network (GLSEN). (2011). *Teaching respect: LGBT-inclusive curriculum and school climate* (Research Brief). New York, NY: Gay, Lesbian, and Straight Education Network.

Goodenow, C., Szalacha, L. A., Robin, L. E., & Westheimer, K. (2008). Dimensions of sexual orientation and HIV-related risk among adolescent females: Evidence from a statewide survey. *American Journal of Public Health, 98,* 1051–1058.

Gowen, L. K., & Winges-Yanez, N. (2014). Lesbian, gay, bisexual, transgender, queer, and questioning youths' perspectives of inclusive school-based sexuality education. *Journal of Sex Research, 51*(7), 788–800.

Grant, R. M., Lama, J. R., Anderson, P. L., McMahan, V., Liu, A. Y., Vargas, L., et al. (2010). Preexposure chemoprophylaxis for HIV prevention in men who have sex with men. *New England Journal of Medicine, 363*(27), 2587–2599.

Green, E., & Peterson, E. N. (2006). *LGBTTSQI terminology.* Retrieved from http://www. trans-academics.org/lgbttsqiterminology.pdf

Greytak, E. A., Kosciw, J. G., & Diaz, E. M. (2009). *Harsh realities: The experiences of transgender youth in our nation's schools.* New York, NY: Gay, Lesbian, and Straight Education Network.

Hatzenbuehler, M., Phelan, J., & Link, B. G. (2013). Stigma as a fundamental cause of population health inequalities. *American Journal of Public Health, 103*(5), 813–821.

Haynie, D. L., Farhat, T., Brooks-Russell, A., Wang, J., Barbieri, B., & Iannotti, R. J. (2013). Dating violence perpetration and victimization among U.S. adolescents: Prevalence, patterns, and associations with health complaints and substance use. *Journal of Adolescent Health, 53*(2), 194–201.

Ibanez, G. E., Purcell, D. W., Stall, R., Parsons, J. T., & Gomes, C. T. (2005). Sexual risk, substance use, and psychological distress in HIV-positive gay and bisexual men who also inject drugs. *AIDS, 19*(Suppl. 1), S49–S55.

Intersex Society of North America. (n.d.). *What is intersex?* Retrieved from http://www. isna.org/faq/what_is_intersex

Jeltova, I., & Fish, M. C. (2005). Creating school environments responsive to gay, lesbian, bisexual, and transgender families: Traditional and systemic approaches for consultation. *Journal of Educational and Psychological Consultation, 16*(1–2), 17–33.

Kellock, D., & O'Mahony, C. P. (1996). Sexually acquired metronidazole-resistant trichomoniasis in a lesbian couple. *Genitourin Medicine, 72*, 60–61.

Kenagy, G., & Bostwick, W. (2005). Health and social service needs of transgender people in Chicago. *International Journal of Transgenderism, 8*(2/3), 57–66.

Kenagy, G., & Hsieh, C. M. (2005). The risk less known: Female-to-male transgender persons' vulnerability to HIV infection. *AIDS Care, 17*(2), 195–207.

Koester, K., Amico, K. R., Liu, A., McMahon, V., Hosek, S., Mayer, K., et al. (2014). *Sex on PrEP: Qualitative findings from the iPrEX Open Label Extension (OLE) in the US.* Programs and Abstracts of the 20th International AIDS Conference, Melbourne, Australia, 20–25 July. Abstract TUAC0102.

Koh, A. S., Gomez, C. A., Shade, S., & Rowley, E. (2005). Sexual risk factors among self-identified lesbians, bisexual women, and heterosexual women accessing primary care settings. *Sexually Transmitted Disease, 32*(9), 563–569.

Kosciw, J. G., Greytak, E. A., Bartkiewicz, M. J., Boesen, M. J., & Palmer, N. A. (2012). *The 2011 National School Climate Survey: The experiences of lesbian, gay, bisexual, and transgender youth in our nation's school.* New York, NY: Gay, Lesbian, and Straight Education Network.

Kubicek, K. (2010). In the dark: Young men's stories of sexual initiation in the absence of relevant sexual health information. *Health Education Behavior, 37*(2), 243–263.

Kwakwa, H. A., & Ghobrial, M. W. (2003). Female-to-female transmission of human immunodeficiency virus. *Clinical Infectious Disease, 36*(3), e40–e41.

Markham, C., Tortolero, S., Escobar-Chaves, S., Parcel, G., Harrist, R., & Addy, R. (2003). Family connectedness and sexual risk-taking among urban youth attending alternative high schools. *Perspectives on Sexual and Reproductive Health, 35*(4), 174–179.

Marrazzo, J. M., Koutsky, L. A., Eschenbach, D. A., Agnew, K., Stine, K., & Hillier, S. H. (2002). Characterization of vaginal flora and bacterial vaginosis in women who have sex with women. *Journal of Infectious Diseases, 185*, 1307–1313.

Marrazzo, J. M., Stine, K., & Wald, A. (2003). Prevalence and risk factors for infection with herpes simplex virus type-1 and -2 among lesbians. *Sexually Transmitted Disease, 30*, 890–895.

McGuire, J. K., Anderson, C. R., Toomey, R. B., & Russell, S. T. (2010). School climate for transgender youth: A mixed method investigation of student experiences and school responses. *Journal of Youth and Adolescence, 39*, 1175–1188.

McNair, R. (2005). Risks and prevention of sexually transmissible infections among women who have sex with women. *Sexual Health, 2*(4), 209–217.

Meyer, I. H. (2003). Prejudice, social stress, and mental health in lesbian, gay and bisexual populations: Conceptual issues and research evidence. *Psychological Bulletin, 129,* 674–697.

Miller, M., André, A., Ebin, J., & Bessonova, L. (2007). *Bisexual health: An introduction and model practices for HIV/STI prevention programming.* New York, NY: National Gay and Lesbian Task Force Policy Institute, the Fenway Institute at Fenway Community Health, and BiNet USA.

Miller, E., Jordan, B., Levenson, R., & Silverman, J. G. (2010). Reproductive coercion: Connecting the dots between partner violence and unintended pregnancy. *Contraception, 81*(6), 457–459.

National Association of School Psychologists (NASP). (2011). *Lesbian, gay, bisexual, transgender, and questioning (LGBTQ) youth (Position Statement).* Bethesda, MD: NASP.

Nuttbrock, L., Hwahng, S., Bockting, W., Rosenblum, A., Mason, M., Macri, M., et al. (2009). Lifetime risk factors for HIV/sexually transmitted infections among male-to-female transgender persons. *Journal of Acquired Immune Deficiency Syndromes, 52*(3), 417–421.

O'Connor, E. A., Lin, J. S., Burda, B. B., Henderson, J. T., Walsh, E. S., & Whitlock, E. P. (2014). Behavioral sexual risk-reduction counseling in primary care to prevent sexually transmitted infections: A systematic review for the US preventive services task force. *Annals of Internal Medicine, 161*(12), 874–883.

Ott, M., & Santelli, J. (2007). Abstinence and abstinence-only education. *Current Opinion in Obstetrics & Gynecology, 19*(5), 446–452.

Palmer, N. A., Kosciw, J. G., & Bartkiewicz, M. J. (2012). *Strengths and silences: The experiences of lesbian, gay, bisexual and transgender students in rural and small town schools.* New York, NY: Gay, Lesbian, and Straight Education Network.

Phelan, J., Link, B. G., & Tehranifar, P. (2010). Social conditions as fundamental causes of health inequalities: Theory, evidence, and policy implications. *Journal of Health and Social Behavior, 51*, S28–S40.

Reisner, S., Perkovich, B., & Mimiaga, M. J. (2010). A mixed methods study of the sexual health needs of New England transmen who have sex with nontransgender men. *AIDS Patient Care and STDS, 24*(8), 501–513.

Rodríquez-Madera, S., & Toro-Alfonso, J. (2005). Gender as an obstacle in HIV/AIDS prevention: Considerations for the development of HIV/AIDS prevention efforts for male-to-female transgenders. *International Journal of Transgenderism, 8*(2/3), 113–122.

Russell, S. T., Ryan, C., Toomey, R. B., Diaz, R. M., & Sanchez, J. (2011). Lesbian, gay, bisexual, and transgender adolescent school victimization: Implications for young adult health and adjustment. *Journal of School Health, 81*(5), 223–230.

Ryan, C., Russell, S. T., Huebner, D., Diaz, R., & Sanchez, J. (2010). Family acceptance in adolescence and the health of LGBT young adults. *Journal of Child and Adolescent Psychiatric Nursing, 23*, 205–213.

Saewyc, E. M., Poon, C., Homma, Y., & Skay, C. L. (2008). Stigma management? The links between enacted stigma and teen pregnancy trends among gay, lesbian, and bisexual students in British Columbia. *Canadian Journal of Human Sexuality, 17*(3), 123–139.

Santelli, J., Ott, M., Lyon, M., Roger, J., Summer, D., & Schleifer, R. (2006). Abstinence and abstinence-only education: A review of US policies and programs. *Journal of Adolescent Health, 38*(1), 72–81.

Sausa, L. A. (2005). Translating research into practice: Trans youth recommendations for improving school systems. *Journal of Gay and Lesbian Issues in Education, 3*, 15–28.

Sevelius, J. (2009). There's no pamphlet for the kind of sex I have: HIV-related risk factors and protective behaviors among transgender men who have sex with non-transgender men. *Journal of the Association of Nurses in AIDS Care, 20*(5), 398–410.

Smith, D. K., Herbst, J. H., Zhang, X., & Rose, C. E. (2014). Condom effectiveness for HIV prevention by consistency of use among men who have sex with men (MSM) in the U.S. *Journal of Acquired Immune Deficiency Syndromes, 68*(3), 337–344.

Tider, D. S., Parsons, J. T., & Bimbi, D. S. (2005). Knowledge of human papillomavirus and effects on sexual behavior of gay/bisexual men: A brief report. *International Journal of STD & AIDS, 16*, 707–708.

University of Michigan. (2014). *LGBT terms and definitions.* Retrieved from http://internationalspectrum.umich.edu/life/definitions

Ward, B. W., Dahlhamer, J. M., Galinksy, A. M., & Joestl, S. S. (2014). Sexual orientation and health among U.S. adults: National health interview survey, 2013. *National Health Statistics Reports, 77*, 1–10.

Yakush, J. H. (2007). *Legalized discrimination: The rise of the marriage-promotion industry and how federally funded programs discriminate against lesbian, gay, bisexual, and transgender youth and families.* Washington, DC: Sexuality Information and Education Council of the United States (SIECUS). Retrieved from http://www.siecus.org/_data/global/images/Legalized-Discrimination.pdf

7
PROMOTING THE SEXUAL HEALTH OF CHILDREN AND ADOLESCENTS AT HOME

The purpose of this chapter is two-fold: (1) to outline evidence-based strategies that parents, caretakers, guardians, and adult family members can engage in to promote the sexual health of children and adolescents; and (2) to describe ways in which preventionists/interventionists such as healthcare providers (e.g., physicians, nurses), health instructors, and mental health professionals (e.g., school and clinical psychologists, social workers, counselors, therapists) can facilitate sexual health of youth through consultation efforts and coordination of supports across home, community, and school settings. We focus on two risk/protective factors identified by Kirby and Lepore (2007) that parents and adult caregivers can address in the home environment, which contribute to children and adolescents making healthy sexual behavior choices. Specifically, we consider the ways in which effective family and adolescent communication and parental monitoring can be facilitated in home settings as a way of preventing sexual risk behaviors and promoting healthy sexuality responses. We identify some strategies that preventionists/interventions can engage in to facilitate effective communication and supervision of teens during these critical years. Further, we provide a case study example related to facilitating effective parental communication and engaging in parental/adult caregiver monitoring of sexual risk behaviors.

Prevalence of Sexual Behaviors among Youth

Parents and their extended families often play a role where they would like not to think that their children or adolescents are thinking of or are already sexually active. However, recently gathered national survey data—the YRBS, collected by the CDC (2013) and described more thoroughly in Chapter 2—indicate that almost half (46.8%) of high school students reported having had sexual intercourse at least once. Nationally, 34% of adolescents are sexually active, defined as having had sexual intercourse in the 3 months prior to the completion of the survey.

Sexually active youth are at particularly high risk for STIs, as nearly two-thirds of those who have STIs are under the age of 25 (Institute of Medicine, Committee on Prevention and Control of Sexually Transmitted Diseases, 1997, cited in Hops et al., 2011).

These statistics are compelling evidence that a significant percentage of adolescents and a sizable minority of children are engaging in sexual activity and are making risky sexual decisions. Although abstinence is the only definite way in which unwanted teen pregnancies and STIs can be avoided, it is clear that, for the many years in which these data have been collected, teens have been engaging in sexual activity and not always doing so in the safest manner possible. At times, youth may be victimized through forced sexual activity or dating violence. Although parents may want to avoid the topic and assume that their child or adolescent is not involved in sexual activity, these data suggest that this is not the case for nearly half of the high school population and many who make choices that contribute to high-risk sexual activity leading to unwanted pregnancy, STIs, and HIV/AIDS. Parents or adult caretakers may further believe that if their children or adolescents are sexually active or engaged in high-risk sexual behaviors, they will not influence their children's decision making, feel no control over the situation, and avoid the topic altogether. However, specific risk and protective factors that can be influenced by education, support, and subsequent actions of parents and caregivers have been identified from among the totality of influences on sexual behaviors of children and adolescents (Kirby & Lepore, 2007). We describe *effective parental communication* and *monitoring of children and adolescent behaviors* identified by Kirby and Lepore as two protective factors that can be "altered" by parental and adult caregiver actions and supported by preventionists/interventionists through education and support. Unlike personal stable characteristics (e.g., one's gender), parental communication strategies and monitoring of adolescent behaviors are changeable through education and support by health professionals (e.g., nurses, physicians), health educators in schools, and mental health professionals (e.g., school psychologists, school social workers, school counselors). The timing of support and education related to effective parental communication and monitoring could happen prior to and during the difficult developmental time frame of adolescence (CDC, 2012). Parents may have the desire to engage in what they perceive as difficult conversations about sexual activity with their teens, but may not have had such conversations with their own parents during their own adolescence and thus lack role models (Rouvier, Campero, Walker, & Caballero, 2011). In addition, parents may simply lack factual information about a topic (e.g., contraception) or feel a sense of stigma or shame when discussing sexual behaviors with their children (Rouvier et al., 2011).

However, despite these challenges, parental behaviors, actions, and beliefs conveyed to children are variables that can be altered in facilitating sexual health of adolescents (CDC, 2012). Alterable variables, defined in other research such as school dropout, are those that can be modified through interventions, such as those implemented in school settings (Sinclair, Christenson, & Thurlow, 2005). For example, Sinclair et al. addressed the alterable variable of school engagement when implementing a school-based intervention with children at risk for dropping out. The idea of focusing on alterable variables can be applied to incorporating parents in efforts to addressing sexual risk behaviors. By focusing on activities like communication and monitoring that parents and adult caretakers have control over to impact change (e.g., "alter"), there is a higher probability of adult impact on adolescent choices that ultimately influence decisions that adolescents make, which in turn impact important outcomes such as teenage pregnancy, child-bearing, and STIs.

What Research Says about Parental Communication about Sexual Behaviors

Although research findings are inconsistent with respect to the impact of parental communication on whether adolescents engage in sexual risk behaviors (Eisenberg, Sieving, Bearinger, Swain, & Resnick, 2006; Jaccard & Dittus, 1993, as cited in Whitaker & Miller, 2000; Whitaker & Miller, 2000), parental communication about sexual behaviors has been identified as a protective factor that parents have control over (Kirby & Lepore, 2007). Further, most would argue that parents need to have a prominent role in the sexual education of their children and youth (Eisenberg et al., 2006). Research conducted in multiple contexts supports the role of effective parental communication that is comprised of open and clear dialogue in influencing healthy choices among children and adolescents, particularly the use of condoms and other forms of birth control when teens are sexually active. For example, higher rates of communication about sexual risk behaviors between mothers and sexually experienced daughters were associated with fewer self-reported incidents of sexual intercourse at a 3-month follow-up among adolescent females attending an inner-city clinic (Hutchinson, J. Jemmott, L. Jemmott, Braverman, & Fong, 2003). The researchers defined sexual risk communication as discussion about sexual intercourse, AIDS, birth control, STIs, and condom use. Hutchinson et al. also found that the higher levels of parental risk communication were associated with higher reported efficacy among adolescents for effective condom use, but not in attitudes toward condoms. Condom use was directly related to reports of having unprotected intercourse at a 3-month follow-up. Therefore, the authors concluded that condom efficacy was a "mediator" for the relationship between parental communication and unprotected sexual activity.

Whitaker and Miller (2000) specifically examined the relationship of parental communication specific to the sexual risk behaviors of sexual debut and condom use, adolescents' perceptions of peer norms for these behaviors, and high-risk sexual behaviors. They also examined the relationship between parental discussion about two specific sexual behaviors of initiating sex and condom use, adolescents' perception of peer norms about sexual activity (e.g., peer level of sexual activity), peer norms about condom use (e.g., peer perceptions and use of condoms), and reported sexual activity among African American and Hispanic youth drawn from high schools in Alabama, New York, and Puerto Rico. Their findings were that parental communication with adolescents about sexual activity was significantly, though marginally, related to having later age of onset for sexual activity and fewer partners. Peer norms related to sexual behaviors were related to adolescents' sexual behavior outcomes of having sex, having an earlier age of sexual onset, and an increased number of partners. However, of particular note was that parental communication about sexual behaviors moderated the relationship between perceptions of peer norms for sexual behaviors and adolescent-reported sexual behaviors. Adolescents who had discussed sexual behaviors with their parents did not show as strong of a relationship for peer norms influencing their sexual behavior choices. With respect to condom use, adolescent discussion with their parents about condom use was associated with greater condom use at the most recent sexual intercourse, as well as greater lifetime and more consistent condom use. In terms of peer influences related to condoms, peers' use of condoms and not liking them influenced adolescents' personal decisions to use condoms. Similar to sexual risk behaviors described above, parental communication about condom use moderated the strength of the relationship between perceptions of peer norms for condom use and the adolescents' reported use of condoms. Therefore, these findings are illustrative that parents' direct discussion about specific sexual risk behaviors (e.g., sexual activity and condom use) may play a role in the degree to which peers influence one another about sexual practices.

Eisenberg et al. (2006) examined the timing in which parents communicate with their children and adolescents about sexual activity by conducting phone interviews with over 1,000 parents of adolescents between the ages of 13 and 17 living in Minnesota and Wisconsin. Of the sexual topics on the phone survey, parents were most likely to discuss the negative consequences of pregnancy and negative outcomes of STIs and least likely to discuss where to get condoms and other methods of birth control. Parents of younger children in the study (ages 13–15) were more likely to discuss where to get condoms and birth control relative to older children in the study (ages 16–17). Overall, parents were more likely to have these discussions when they believed that their son/daughter was in a romantic relationship. Recommendations made by the authors of the study were that conversations and communication with parents are most effective when they occur prior to the initiation of a romantic relationship.

Although clearly more research is needed to better understand the role of parental communication in preventing and addressing high-risk sexual activity among children and adolescents, Whitaker and Miller (2000) articulate that one of the concerns about the research to date may be how parental communication is defined. Whitaker and Miller (2000) state that some of the research defines parental communication about sexual activity as simply whether a general discussion about the topic occurred or did not (e.g., was sex in general discussed) versus communication quality (e.g., breadth, parent responsiveness). Therefore, inconsistency in the literature may be due, in part, to the lack of consistency by which parental communication is measured in the literature (Whitaker & Miller, 2000).

Recommendations for Parental Communication Based on Research

Although more research is clearly needed in relation to the role of parental communication in addressing sexual risk behaviors among children and adolescents, there appears to be ample evidence that effective parental communication either directly impacts or mitigates youth behaviors and decisions around sexual activity. Further, the quality of communication is important. Parent and caregiver communication with children and adolescents that is open, frequent across multiple occasions, and spontaneous—rather than the one "big talk" about sexuality—may be a preferred approach (Eisenberg et al., 2006; Hutchinson et al., 2003). In addition, early timing of parental communication prior to children engaging in sexual activity or becoming involved in romantic relationships is preferred from a prevention-oriented standpoint (Eisenberg et al., 2006).

The National Campaign to Prevent Teen and Unplanned Pregnancy (National Campaign, 2014) offers practical suggestions to parents when having important and meaningful dialogues with their teens about engaging in sexual activity and sexual risk behaviors (e.g., unprotected sex). Based on data collected and interviews conducted with teens by the National Campaign, parents have significant influence on adolescents' choices to engage in sexual activity. Teens interviewed by this organization have specific suggestions for having meaningful conversations with parents and other adults in their lives. They would like clear messages about the value of delaying sexual activity (e.g., abstinence) but also an understanding of the dangers associated with unprotected sexual activity. In other words, specific communication about the preference for delaying sexual activity, as well as information about contraception, is important from teens' perspectives. Based on the interviews conducted by the National Campaign, teens report that rather than being told just "don't have sex," they want parents to provide a rationale and an explanation. They want to be listened to and to have their opinions heard and valued, as stressed in Chapter 3 about the importance of hearing all youth perspectives, even those that might be marginalized or out of the society mainstream. There are excellent resources for parents and families on the National Campaign to Prevent Teen and Unplanned Pregnancy (2014) website, including a link to a PowerPoint that parents can download for presentation to others on the topic of sexual health in their communities.

Another excellent resource and practical advice for parents in having ongoing conversations with teens about sexual activity is through the U.S. Department of Health and Human Services/Office of Adolescent Health, a federally funded resource center designated specifically for topics and support related to a range of adolescent health issues. Specific to parent and youth communication, a resource titled "Talking with Teens" is particularly germane to having important yet often challenging dialogue related to sexual health and risk behaviors (U.S. Department of Health and Human Services/Office of Adolescent Health, 2014). Practical tips, as well as a sample script for use with teens in talking about sexual behaviors, are posted on the website for parents to access when thinking about ways to raise the topic with their children. Specific strategies on the website include selecting everyday spontaneous situations for raising conversations about teen sexuality (e.g., when watching a movie or hearing a song on the radio depicting teen relationships or teenage pregnancy) in a natural manner and having frequent, short, and spontaneous conversations rather than a prescheduled meeting. An analogy to the preference for frequent, brief conversations rather than sole, larger conversations might be akin to sensitizing the teen to conversations they as well as their parents may perceive as embarrassing. As the Office of Adolescent Health website describes, parents need to stay calm and nonjudgmental when these conversations occur. Further, although technology has clearly advanced at a point well beyond where most parents were exposed themselves as youth or may be comfortable, the importance of texting as a tool was stressed given the reliance of teens on this form of communication. However, in order to communicate with youth, parents and adult caregivers need to be conversant in the common means by which their children and adolescents communicate with one another. Perhaps the readers saw the movie scene in "American Pie" during the mid-1990s in which a father attempted to have "the one big talk" about sexual activity with his son. The actor portraying the father clearly was embarrassed about this conversation, as many of us who are currently parenting or have parented teenagers have experienced. However, in order for teens to have healthy relationships, we all must embark on this journey and are fortunate to have increased resources available through federal websites for doing so.

Recommendations for Preventionists/Interventions to Support Effective Parental Communication

Preventionists/interventions can play an important role in not only encouraging communication between parents and children/adolescents about sexual behaviors but also promoting healthy and effective communication that begins early and prior to youth engaging in sexual behaviors or beginning a romantic relationship. One example of a strategy may be the use of consultation with parents/guardians and families to teach effective communication between families and children that follows the recommendations of the prior research cited, as well as the recommendations of the National Campaign (2014) and the U.S. Department of Health and Human Services/Office of Adolescent Health (2014). These strategies include open dialogue and frequent and unplanned conversations that invite future conversations, perhaps at a time when a teen may be contemplating sexual activity or wants to know of strategies to avoid peer pressure or seek contraception. Having honest and factual conversations about sexual risk for STIs and HIV in the absence of condom use among sexually active teens is very important, and preventionists/interventions can support these critical experiences, which are often intimidating for parents without proper knowledge, resources, and support (U.S. Department of Health and Human Services/Office of Adolescent Health, 2014). Preventionists/ interventionists can avail themselves to parents and caregivers in preparing for difficult conversations that parents may want to have and feel are necessary, but may not be clear where to turn for assistance. For example, if parents can have support when they have concerns about the sexual activity of their adolescents or simply want support to engage in early conversations about the topic, having accessible and knowledgeable preventionists/interventionists, such as healthcare providers and mental health clinicians, is very important. Such professionals can serve as agents to have such important conversations or refer to local healthcare settings where additional support may be necessary and available. Preventionists and interventionists can also teach parents basic counseling skills, such as reflecting feelings, summarizing, and providing clear information about their beliefs and attitudes concerning initiation of sexual activity and engaging in unprotected sexual intercourse.

Another strategy may be the coordination, explanation, and delivery of services and resources between home, school, and community. For example, health professionals and preventionists/interventionists may act as valuable resources for families in accessing and understanding the sexuality education resources available to them at school and in the community and similarly act as a liaison between schools, communities, and families. Most states require some type of health education in their schools and the curriculum varies to some degree by region of the country and the specific values of the community/locale (see Chapter 4 related to legal issues). Having parents reinforce the curriculum the students are being exposed to, such as making healthy relationship choices, delaying sexual intercourse, and using contraception when sexual intercourse occurs, would be useful. Further, having an overview of the curriculum that students receive would be helpful in parents initiating conversations with their children and adolescents about what is being covered, which could increase the frequency of reflective conversations that are recommended in the literature. In essence, having communication and support among the multiple agencies that impact adolescents, including home, schools, leisure and sport settings, and healthcare environments, can provide a continuum of supports that range from prevention (universal supports), followed by supplemental supports for students who are at risk (secondary supports), with more intensive individualized supports for individual students who have a diagnosed issue related to sexual activity (e.g., engaging in high-risk sexual behaviors or having an STI), akin to the public health model (CDC, 2010), the MTSS/RTI systems of support (Burns & Gibbons, 2008), and population-based mental health models (Doll & Cummings, 2008) described throughout this book (e.g., see Chapters 3 and 8). We suggest these system-wide approaches be adapted for sexual health instruction provided along a continuum, beginning with system-wide applications (universal; Tier 1) to supplemental/group (secondary; Tier 2) and more individualized approaches (tertiary; Tier 3) (Burns & Gibbons, 2008).

It is also important that preventionists/interventionists consider cultural and linguistic factors of families when providing support and consultation for effective family communication. A broader discussion of cultural factors related to the overall sexual health of children and adolescents is the focus of Chapter 5. Cultural beliefs about sexual communication may impact the degree to which families discuss issues of sexuality with their children and adolescents (Rouvier et al., 2011). Rouvier et al. completed a qualitative study in Mexico that focused on an examination of parents' and adolescents' perceptions of family communication about sexual behaviors. They interviewed 18 parents and 15 first-year students in five public high schools within rural and urban centers. Although the adolescents interviewed preferred to discuss sexual issues with their parents compared to other sources such as peers, conversations with parents were very rare. When conversations between parents and children did occur, they tended to be nonspecific (e.g., messages such as "be careful"). When prevention messages were conveyed, the focus was on abstinence, rather than on condom use or day-after emergency contraception. Parents reported a lack of knowledge about condom use and perceived that their children were at low risk for initiating sexual activity. Some also believed that having a discussion about sexual activity would promote initiation of it among their children. The results were interpreted in light of the social and cultural values based on the primarily Catholic population that considered sexual activity as a moral issue that should be delayed until marriage. In the one instance in which clear messages and direct explicit instruction about condoms was provided, the profession of the participant (a nurse) likely influenced the decision to have candid conversations. The authors pointed to the need for respecting the cultural beliefs of the families, yet also finding avenues to provide updated information to parents about prevention and sexual health through prevention workshops and integration of families into sexual health curriculum at the school level. Guzman, Golub, Caal, Hickman, and Ramos (2013) conducted a similar study focused on prevention of teenage pregnancy in a Mid-Atlantic region. Using a qualitative methodology similar to Rouvier et al.'s (2011), the researchers conducted focus groups with 44 Latino adolescents (ages 15–17) and 19 interviews with Latino parents, primarily mothers who immigrated to the United States. Most of the adolescents were born in the United States. The findings of the study were that both parents and adolescents believed that communicating with one another about sexual activity was important, but awkward. Several parents reported that they would speak to their children if necessary, but they believed that their children were not sexually active. Teenagers reported getting somewhat mixed messages when conversations occurred—primarily to delay having sex until later in life or when married, but to use a condom if sexual intercourse did happen. All adolescents received the message to avoid pregnancy because of the limitations in future opportunities and the significant responsibilities of parenting prior to being ready for it. In general, explicit instructions about birth control were very uncommon, and several parents believed that students were receiving this information elsewhere, such as at school. Parents reported that their native countries and family of origin avoided the topic of sexual activity with children and adolescents, but there were also several reports among parents that they wanted to have more open dialogue with their own children compared to what occurred during their own upbringings. Females tended to receive different messages than males, based on both parent and adolescent reports. In many cases, females were expected to have chastity and be responsible for consequences of pregnancy, such as raising children. Males were sometimes given the message that they needed to have sexual prowess.

Open dialogue among children and adolescents was facilitated by capitalizing on real-world situations that spontaneously occurred (e.g., seeing a young girl with a baby) and having a generally open and trusting parent–adolescent relationship about other topics. The researchers made several recommendations, including the need for parental support in practicing messages with adolescents and utilizing Latino parents to recruit adolescents into groups to allay fears and potential stigma associated with participation.

International work has also increased the knowledge base about the importance of cultural issues as related to parent–adolescent communication about sexual behaviors. A recent study conducted by Ayalew, Mengistie, and Semahegn (2014) in eastern Ethiopia collected quantitative survey data with 695 high school students (grades 9–12) and focus group qualitative interview data with parents about knowledge related to STIs and HIV/AIDS. Approximately 75% of students knew about STIs and HIV/AIDS, the vast majority (over 80%) knew at least one contraceptive method, and about 6 in 10 reported having discussed these topics with their parents. The adolescents preferred discussing sexual health issues with peers relative to other supports (e.g., parents). Most parents were not comfortable discussing sexual topics with their son or daughter, but most adolescents reported that parental communication about the issue was important. The findings were interpreted in light of a cultural taboo in parent and adolescent discussion about sexual health.

CASE STUDY EXAMPLE: SUPPORTING PARENTS IN HEALTHY COMMUNICATION AND MONITORING OF TEENS

The purpose of this hypothetical case study is to illustrate how some of the recommendations made in the literature and from our clinical experiences can be applied to facilitate effective family communication. Effective family communication can, in turn, facilitate sexual health among children and adolescents. We also consider some cultural issues that need to be considered among preventionists/interventions in effectively working with families. We additionally conceptualize ways in which preventionists/interventionists such as school counselors, school psychologists, or school social workers might handle similar situations in day-to-day practice.

Trina, a Hispanic female, is a 15-year-old high school freshman who just transitioned to a large public high school of 3,600 students from her smaller Catholic middle school. The public high school is relatively diverse and includes a mixture of White (50%), Latino (30%), African American (15%), and students of Middle Eastern and Asian backgrounds (5%). Trina lives with her father (Marcus) and mother (Maria) and her 10-year-old younger brother (Isaac) in a northeastern mid-size city. Isaac is in fifth grade at the same Catholic school Trina attended. Trina's family emigrated from Mexico when she was a baby and is very close and tight-knit. Maria is a stay-at-home mom, while Marcus is a manager at a local car dealership and is a mechanic by training, but his hours have recently been cut back, and some financial challenges have ensued.

Trina's family is part of a larger extended family that lives in the same town comprised of aunts, uncles, and cousins who comprise the primary group with which Trina's family interacts. Both sets of grandparents still reside in Mexico. Maria and Marcus send money back to Mexico to financially support their parents. Spanish is spoken in the home, but Trina and Isaac have been instructed in English and are more comfortable with English. Marcus is also comfortable in English, but Maria is more comfortable speaking Spanish. The other social and community group the family interacts with are members of the local Catholic parish. For instance, the family is very involved in church events and activities. They attend church regularly. Trina's mother goes to mass daily. Trina's parents wanted her to attend a Catholic high school but were concerned about the financial implications of the tuition and are working hard to set money away for college tuition.

As Trina transitioned to high school, she has made many new friends on the high school soccer team and in her classes. Recently, she has met an

(Continued)

(Continued)

older boy in his junior year on the soccer team. He has asked her to the fall Homecoming dance and would like to "hang out" with her at his house one day when his parents are at work. At this point, Trina has received no formal instruction in school about sexual risk behaviors, STIs/HIV, pregnancy prevention, or contraception, as health class is provided during the sophomore year and she did not receive instruction in sexual health while in the Catholic school. Trina approaches her school psychologist and begins asking questions about how one can avoid pregnancy. Although she does not think that her relationship will result in sexual activity or intercourse, she feels wholly unprepared to enter the world of dating and being in new social situations that involve dating and the presence of males. She wants to "hang out" with this boy, but she is afraid of being in an uncomfortable situation. She knows that she is not ready for sexual activity but also does not know where to turn for answers about questions. When she started menstruation a couple of years ago, her mother explained some things about her body and how her monthly cycle worked, but she felt that the conversation was awkward (Guzman et al., 2013). Her mother also told her that she needed to "be careful" and "safe," and Trina believed that her mother was cautioning her to avoid sexual advances from boys, but she was nervous about asking more specific questions as to how she might actually do this. Trina mentioned to her mother that she would like to go to the fall Homecoming dance, and her mother consented and left it at that, focusing more on questions about what she should wear, how she will be transported there, and in general what needs to be done to prepare for the event because this was not a custom in Mexico. Maria felt that the discussion about Homecoming might have been a good opportunity to talk more about sexual activity, the risks for pregnancy and STIs, and contraception, but then dismissed this thought as she believed the conversation would be premature and perhaps give her daughter unspoken permission that sexual activity is okay (Rouvier et al., 2011). Trina approached the school psychologist for some assistance in how she can talk with her mom about her feelings and learn more about how to say "no" to sexual advances if such a situation would occur. Trina was very sure that she was not ready for sexual activity, but also felt that she did not have nearly the information that other peers had who have been exposed to health instruction in a public middle school. She was considering turning to her peers for advice, but also felt that her mom has always been supportive of her, and she is close to her mom. Trina also felt close to her dad, but from her perspective, she felt that her mom is the one to approach for "girl things" like this.

If you were the school psychologist or have a role as a preventionist/ interventionist, how would you handle the situation in an effective and culturally responsive way? Following are some perceptions that each character might have that the school psychologist might use to conceptualize the issues:

1 Trina was very conflicted about her situation. She felt a lack of knowledge and wanted more information and was nervous about raising the issue with her mom. On a positive note, despite feeling nervous, Trina desired communication with her mom and Maria's perspective was important and valued by her (U.S. Department of Health and Human Services/Office of Adolescent Health, 2014). Trina has a close relationship with her family, particularly her mother, and openness and trust can be a facilitator of healthy conversations about sexual risk behaviors (Guzman et al., 2013). She has received general messages about "being safe" but has not received factual and clear information about sexual risk behaviors, pregnancy prevention, STIs/HIV and AIDs, or healthy relationship tips. As reported by other adolescents, Trina was concerned that approaching her mother about sexual topics may result in Maria's belief that Trina was already sexually active or planning to become so very soon, which might be reinforced by Maria's perception that discussions about sex would promote adolescent curiosity and desire to become sexually active (CDC, 2012; Guzman et al., 2013).

2 Maria's worldview was one that focused priority on family "Familismo" (Carteret, 2011). The teachings of the Catholic church strongly guided her worldview and child-rearing practices. Although she had what might be considered traditional values in some circles, she also had a priority for her children to delay childbearing and attend college, as was documented in the Guzman et al. (2013) findings. She also considered the need for more in-depth and focused conversations with her daughter, but had dismissed them as premature.

3 The school psychologist was conflicted between a priority of helping this young lady by providing more detailed and accurate information and also being respectful of the cultural and social beliefs of the family (Rouvier et al., 2011). This is a sensitive issue, and one way to approach it might be to assist Trina with effectively communicating to her mother that she desires more detailed information about sexual topics and to share her perceptions in a respectful manner. This conversation could happen in the school psychologist's office. Specific talking points similar to the script developed for parents (U.S. Department of Health and Human Services/Office of Adolescent Health, 2014) could be developed, modeled, and practiced in the office with Trina. The script could contain specific talking points that Trina would like to convey, such as "I am not planning on becoming sexually active in the near future and I am not asking you these questions because I plan on becoming sexually active in the near future" (U.S. Department of Health and Human Services/Office of Adolescent Resources, 2014). Another point might be "I don't feel that I have the same information that other kids in my grade do and I think that it is important for me to know about pregnancy prevention and important information about sexually transmitted infections."

(Continued)

(Continued)

The school psychologist could also have a separate discussion with Maria so that factual information about these topics can be shared, as Maria may not have an awareness of how to use contraception or other relevant information as documented in the literature (Rouvier et al., 2011). Also, Maria might need to consult with her husband about what to do with this information and how much to share with her daughter throughout this process if the family dynamics adhere to "machismo," the notion that the father is the decision maker and head of household despite Maria being responsible for domestic matters (Galanti, 2003). Another tactic that the school psychologist could take is to form a parental group (Guzman et al., 2013) that focuses on open dialogue about issues related to adolescence, with an incorporation of literature related to WHO (2014) recommendations related to adolescent health, including the right of adolescents' access to reliable and accurate information and services related to contraception. As Guzman et al. recommend, having Hispanic/Latino families recruit members from their own culture into groups that promote healthy family communication around sexual topics and having a safe space for such dialogue are important. Although these issues are complex, and there are no clear-cut definitive solutions, considering the perspectives of Trina and her family and remaining sensitive to their cultural and social beliefs, even if not aligned with those of the preventionist/interventionist, is very important. If thought through carefully, there is a way to balance and honor the family beliefs on adolescent sexuality with Trina's need for information and her desire to maintain her adolescent health, inclusive of that related to sexuality.

What Research Says about Parental Active Supervision and Monitoring of Children and Adolescents

Adolescence is a developmental period wherein an individualization process occurs through an emerging understanding of one's self-identify separate from others, including family members (Aquilino, 1997). This process is one that often simultaneously occurs with being placed for the first time in adult and potentially life-altering situations, which include what sometimes may be split-second decisions such as whether to engage in sexual activity and whether to do so without contraception. Parents and caregivers find themselves in the often-conflicting position where they would like to provide such autonomy for their adolescents to gain self-sufficiency, yet also understand that their youth may not have the capacity or the forethought to live with the potentially long-term decisions they may make. Therefore, parents and other caregivers are in desperate need for guidelines that assist them with the degree and type of monitoring they should engage in with respect to the sexual health of their children and adolescents. Parents are often left with the question regarding the degree of independence they should be giving their adolescents versus direct supervision. Huebner and Howell (2003) examined the impact of parental monitoring, parental communication, and parenting style on the sexual risk behaviors (defined as number of lifetime sexual partners and condom use during last sexual intercourse) in a sample of over 1,100 seventh–twelfth graders who reported ever having sex. The study was conducted in six rural and ethnically diverse high schools in the southeast. Twenty-three percent of the sample was placed in the "high-risk group," while 77% were in the "low-risk group." The adolescents completed surveys about their perceptions of parental monitoring (e.g., parental knowledge of whereabouts), parental communication (e.g., frequency of communication), and parenting styles (e.g., authoritarian, permissive, or authoritative styles). Logistic regression analyses using results from the survey and demographic information (e.g., gender, ethnicity) were conducted.

The findings were that parental monitoring was directly related to risk-taking, as adolescents closely monitored by their parents were less likely to engage in sexual risk behaviors, defined as having had only one sexual partner and using a condom during last sexual intercourse. There was no direct relationship in this study for parental communication, parenting style, or the demographic characteristics of gender, age, or race. Some interaction effects for parental communication and monitoring, as well as by parental communication and race/ethnicity (being a minority), were found. Borawski, Ievers-Landis, Lovegreen, and Trapl (2003) surveyed close to 700 ninth- and tenth-grade students enrolled in health education courses within urban schools about their sexual risk behaviors, which included self-reported sexual risk behaviors and substance use. Students were asked about their perceptions related to parental monitoring, defined similarly to Huebner and Howell (2003) (e.g., parents knowing their whereabouts), negotiated unsupervised time (e.g., being given opportunities for unsupervised time), and parental trust (e.g., adolescents' belief that parents trusted them). The results were examined with respect to the following sexual behaviors/sexual risk behaviors: having engaged in sexual behaviors ever, having engaged in sexual behaviors within the last 3 months, having intentions to engage in sexual activity, or having engaged in high-risk sexual behaviors (e.g., multiple sexual partners, having an STI). The authors also assessed "proactive preventive methods" (e.g., carrying a condom, not having sex). The overall sample reported high levels of parental monitoring and trust, with relatively lower scores for negotiated unsupervised time. Females and older students had higher and lower rates of parental monitoring, respectively. In terms of ethnicity, negotiated unsupervised time was higher for White students compared to African American and Hispanic students. Students in households with higher median income, but not in lower socioeconomic settings, reported higher rates of negotiated unsupervised time. Parental monitoring was higher in two-parent households (whether a mother/father, grandparent, or foster parent situation) compared to single-parent household settings (mother or father only). When examining the relationships between student survey responses and outcomes, high levels of perceived parental monitoring were associated with less sexual activity at any point or in recent months, low intentions to have sex in the future, and higher rates of consistent condom use. Further, higher reported perceptions of unsupervised negotiated time were associated with more sexual activity, yet there was no association with this variable for initiating sex early, intending to have sex, having unprotected sex, or reporting having an STI. What is perhaps a unique finding was associated with protective behaviors of carrying a condom and not having sex because of not having a condom. Perhaps this finding is novel in contrast to other studies on the topic because prevention and protective behaviors are not studied to the degree that sexual risk behaviors are examined in the literature. Students who reported a higher rate of parental trust were less likely to report engaging in sexual activity in recent months or ever, less likely to report STIs and intentions to have sexual intercourse. The authors also reported findings with respect to alcohol, tobacco, and marijuana use that will not be described here, but the readers should consult Borawski et al. (2003) for these findings. Some gender differences were found, as males with high reported rates of parental monitoring were less likely to engage in recent sexual activity (barely significant) and higher rates of consistent condom use. Males with high levels of unsupervised time were more likely to be sexually active, but also more likely to report carrying and using condoms. Females revealed a slightly different pattern than males, as there was no impact of parental monitoring. However, similar to males, females with high levels of unsupervised time were also more likely to be sexually active, but also to use condoms and decide not have sex when no condom was available. In contrast to males, females who reported high rates of parental trust were much less likely to engage in sexual activity, but there was no impact of trust on protective behaviors.

Another study about the relationship between parental monitoring and teenagers' subsequent sexual initiation was completed with a population of adolescent visitors to a San Francisco clinic. Participants were described by the researchers as "sexually inexperienced" and were interviewed about their intentionality to have sex within the next 6 months and their perceptions of parental monitoring. The participants were subsequently contacted 6 months later to assess whether they had engaged in sexual intercourse within that time period. If they did not engage in sexual activity, they were interviewed and contacted once again in 6 months. The findings of the study were that successful parental monitoring, assessed by parents truly knowing their adolescents' location and what activities they were engaged in, was associated with adolescents who had not experienced sexual activity and had fewer intentions of initiating sex relative to those who reported less successful parental monitoring. However, the only significant predictor of whether adolescents ultimately reported engaging in sexual activity was their own reported intentions to do so. The researchers explained the findings in terms of a cognitive behavioral model and pointed to the need for future research about the pathways leading from intention to have sexual activity, measured through adolescent-reported beliefs and attitudes versus actually engaging in sexual behaviors.

International research completed by Kerr and Stattin (2000) has focused efforts of researchers away from a conceptualization of parental monitoring as one of surveillance and tracking to a broader focus on parental monitoring. In their research with 14-year-olds in a Swedish urban city, Kerr and Stattin examined monitoring in ways that have been commonly examined in other studies. In addition, they added measures of the sources in which such knowledge was gained—through child disclosure, parental solicitation, or parental control. Further, measures of delinquency, school problems, failure expectations, depressed mood, low self-esteem, deviant friends, and whether poor relationships existed with teachers or parents were collected. Parents, teachers, and adolescents served as informants. As has been found in other studies reported here, monitoring was associated with better youth adjustment, although the outcomes measured were not specific to high-risk sexual behaviors. What is a unique finding with implications for parental monitoring in the arena of sexual risk behaviors is the relative strength of each source of parental knowledge about sexual risk behaviors. Child disclosure is more strongly linked to most adjustment variables measured compared to parent solicitation and parental control. In addition, child reports of being controlled were negatively and independently associated with all outcome measures, as one might hypothesize. The researchers interpreted the findings as having important implications for the parental monitoring literature, describing the importance of children/adolescent disclosure as information sources and as agents in effective parental monitoring of adolescent behaviors versus one of surveillance and parent-directed solicitation. In addition, maintaining close family connections was also important as part of effective parental monitoring. Although we certainly would not discount the importance of knowing the whereabouts of children and adolescents and verifying what our youth tell us, these findings support having a perspective that integrates dialogue and self-disclosure of adolescents within a trusting relationship as a viable means of contributing to healthy sexual decisions and choices. It is highly improbable that parents and caregivers will be present in every high-risk situation an adolescent may face, be it one of sexual decision making or another risk behavior. Therefore, building a trusting relationship that offers the opportunity for disclosure in a safe environment appears to be supported by the research literature (Kerr & Stattin, 2000).

Parental knowledge of the peer groups that children and adolescents associate merits special attention in a discussion of parental monitoring. As children enter late childhood and adolescence, the peer groups they closely identify with exert increased influence on many decisions they make, including whether to engage in a range of sexual risk behaviors. For example, Kapadia, Frye, Bonner, Emmanuel, Samples, and Latka (2012) examined whether perceptions of partner and peer beliefs about the importance of safe sex impacted the sexual risk behaviors of having multiple partners and using condoms. A sample of Latino(a) adolescents aged 16–19 participating in a larger-scale study of HIV prevention was recruited for the project. The study participants were already sexually active, reported smoking marijuana or drinking alcohol in the last 3 months, and were HIV-negative. The findings of the study were that peer norms for engaging in safer sexual practices (e.g., carrying a condom before dates) were associated with safer sexual practices of condom use and having few sexual partners. Kotchick, Shaffer, Forehand, and Miller (2001), as part of their recommended multisystemic approach to addressing sexual behaviors among adolescents, conducted an extensive literature on the topic. The "extrafamilial system" was identified in their literature review as a systemic factor, which incorporated research on the impact of peers on the sexual behavior choices made by adolescents. Within the extrafamilial dimension, Kotchick et al. cited research that outlined the role that sexual behaviors of peers, particularly behaviors critical for adolescent sexual health such as condom use, have on the choices that adolescents make with respect to their sexuality (Miller, Forehand, & Kotchick, 2000, cited in Kotchick et al., 2001). Further, the Kotchik et al. literature review included research documenting that associating with a deviant peer group that engages in delinquent or substance use increases the probability of adolescent sexual risk behaviors (Gillmore, Lewis, Lohr, Spencer, & White, 1997, as cited in Kotchik et al., 2001). Other research has demonstrated that having an older romantic partner increases the likelihood of initiating sexual intercourse at a younger age (Marin, Kirby, Hudes, Coyle, & Gomez, 2006). Therefore, based on these findings, parental monitoring should include knowledge and oversight of the peers their children are associating with, particularly romantic partners, and the attitudes and behaviors of such youth.

Recommendations for Parental Active Monitoring and Supervision Based on Research

Similar to the findings related to parental communication, the literature on parental monitoring needs continual development and refinement. Conclusions that can be drawn speak to the importance of conveying to children and adolescents a desire and concern for their safety and having a true sense of their whereabouts and the activities they are engaged in. The focus of such monitoring and supervision is ideally one of trust and a situation where the youth are able to confide and approach the parent or adult caretaker in situations in which sexual risk behaviors are being contemplated or have already been made. Although parents and other central adults in an adolescent's life want to allow for more autonomy, it is important for responsible adults to have information about where their child/adolescent is, what activities he/she is engaged in, and what other peer groups are on the scene. The CDC (2012) created a fact sheet that outlines many of the variables that were significant in the research reviewed within this chapter. The CDC recommendations include having knowledge not only of the adolescent's whereabouts but whether an adult is present in the home and getting to know the peer group and the boyfriend or girlfriend. Parents can set limits that require meeting anyone their adolescent is dating and the parents of the youth. Sometimes adolescents circulate in a mixed group that often results in "pairing off." In these situations, it is important to know who everyone is in the group and when adolescents move locations; this needs to be reported to the parents or privileges could be lost. It is important for these expectations to be communicated to the adolescent ahead of time. Although parents may hear that "they are the only one setting these limits" on knowing their adolescent's whereabouts, this is highly unlikely. If it is true, it is likely that other parents are appreciative of this limit setting. An additional recommendation from the CDC is having check-ins with adolescents via cell phone, texting, etc. We have entered an age of electronics in which adolescents may have superior technology skills than parents and other adult caregivers. Monitoring text messages as well as social media communications that youth have with others, inclusive of peer groups (e.g., Pinterest, Facebook, Skype, FaceTime) is very important in this technology era, given that these mediums are the most frequent method by which adolescents communicate with one another, which includes those they are dating and having intimate relationships with. Adolescents may make unwise sexual decisions as they relate to technology, such as posting sexually explicit content and cyberbullying. In working with legal advocates and colleagues, the authors have anecdotal information that "sexting" cases are among the most common cases that attorneys see with youth who have made very poor impulsive decisions that have resulted in harm to victims and targets of such actions, as well as legal and long-term consequences for the perpetrators of such actions. Adolescents need to understand the permanency and quick dissemination of information they post on social media for not only themselves but also others around them. Communicating the potential for long-term negative implications of short-term actions can be challenging with adolescents who may lack forethought given their developmental stage. Parents and families need support in having such conversations with them. Parents will benefit from strategies that help them to explain to their adolescents that some technology decisions may have social, legal, reputation, and hurtful implications not only for the adolescents themselves but for others as well. Parents can cite legal cases aired in the media to help explain their case and also seek input and dialogue with their youth so as not to seem like they are lecturing. Although parents are often not as adept in technology, it is within the purview of a legal guardian to monitor and supervise decisions their youth are making with respect to social media. Parents are often the ones purchasing cell phones, computers, etc., for their youth and such privileges can be contained through time limits and review of texts, etc., that adolescents produce. Parents need an awareness of who their adolescents are interacting with on social media (e.g., who their friends are on social media) and to have open and ongoing dialogue about the importance of decisions about friend requests and the dangers inherent in befriending individuals who may not be accurately and honestly representing themselves. Therefore, parents need to have login details and monitor social media of their adolescents for not only sexually related material but other high-risk behaviors and situations their adolescents may enter, such as being groomed by child predators.

The U.S. Department of Health and Human Services/Office of Adolescent Health (2014) additionally stress the importance of being aware of what television shows children and adolescents are watching and understanding how texting is the preferred method of communication among most teens. Adolescents also spend a great deal of time on their computers and have access to videos, etc., that parents may not be watching at the same time. Therefore, requiring a central location for the computer (if even a laptop) might be a consideration. Teenagers need to often do homework on computers, laptops, but this can be done in a structured location where parents have access.

Recommendations for Preventionists/Interventionists to Support Parental Active Monitoring and Supervision

Preventionists/interventionists can take a very significant role in supporting parents in children and adolescent monitoring and supervision activities. One of these strategies can be to offer support and educational groups at school and within the community about effective and reasonable limit setting. Parents can benefit not only from professional expertise on the topic (Stanton et al., 2000) but from the experiences and shared concerns of other parents who are in the same situation and may feel very alone in navigating new adolescent parenting responsibilities. Parents and other caregivers will benefit from taking an active communication role and helping parents of other adolescents in the community to solve problems and issues that arise in the daily raising of adolescents. Shared dialogue, parents knowing one another, and taking collective responsibility for the well-being of all adolescents in the community can be very helpful. Parents can also share information with one another, as well as assume responsibility for monitoring behaviors of youth while in their homes. Parents who have positive relationships with one another and communicate openly and effectively may be more likely to express concerns earlier prior to escalating problematic behaviors. For example, families who have a relationship with one another might be more likely to disclose a situation to the parent of an adolescent they witnessed or had heard might have engaged in a high-risk behavior or is showing a problem or issue that parents need to be aware of so that steps can be taken to address it. Preventionists/interventionists can facilitate the formation and maintenance of these important relationships.

Further, preventionists/interventionists can facilitate connections and partnerships of parents with other important community representatives who are responsible for youth. For example, in situations of technology and "sexting" that is prevalent in some communities, making connections to local law enforcement officers, probation officers, technology specialists, and youth service workers can be helpful for information dissemination through consultation activities and the delivery of workshops in community centers and schools. Parents need information in this rapidly changing world of technology and ways in which youth communicate with one another through social media (e.g., posting on Facebook, Twitter, etc.). Parents are often much further behind their children and adolescents with respect to technology skills because they did not grow up in an era of technology. In contrast, this generation of youth has been exposed to technology almost since birth. With knowledge and information, parents can be better informed and can also convey concerns and dangers to their children about the permanency and legality of split-second technology decisions, not only in terms of sexual risk behaviors but other health risk behaviors as well. For example, in the community where one of the authors lives, the school district in collaboration with local Parent Teachers Association organized an event in which local law enforcement detectives provided a workshop to parents about the technology that youth are accessing as well as demonstrating through a live demonstration how prevalent child sexual predators are online and how they have easy access to children and adolescents through social media, such as chat rooms and Skype. Recommendations for monitoring the technology that children and adolescents can access, inclusive of software that can be used to facilitate this monitoring, were shared during the workshop. Further, the behaviors of youth for parents to watch as part of a partnership to prevent and stop child predators were discussed. The school can serve as a critical resource, along with community agencies, in helping parents to gain understanding of processes and procedures to effectively supervise children and adolescents online and elsewhere. This information was very practical and useful for families, and schools can take the lead in sponsoring such important events. We believe that the more parents and families can be informed about sexual risk behaviors, particularly as it relates to technology, the more likely they will prevent and seek help when encountering potentially tragic events.

Finally, preventionists/interventionists can engage in individual, group, and family therapy for adolescents and their families with a focus on setting appropriate boundaries, limits, and encouraging trust and child-initiated disclosure of activities they are engaged in (Kerr & Stattin, 2000). Often, two parents may have different perspectives from each other on limit setting and standards for unsupervised time and other boundaries, which adolescents have a tendency to pick up on and then approach the more lenient parent. Parental counseling and/or family therapy may be of assistance in negotiating these limits so that adolescents receive clear and consistent messages in the family. Individual therapy with adolescents, siblings, or other family members may also be helpful as adolescents begin to work toward their developmental milestones of autonomy, but yet maintain trusting parental relationships that support a comfort level and safety in disclosing information to family about the activities they engage in outside of the home setting and concerns that may arise related to sexual risk behaviors and other health concerns that are common during the adolescent developmental period (e.g., depression, physical changes, peer pressure to engage in substance use).

CASE STUDY RELATED TO PARENTAL MONITORING OF ADOLESCENT BEHAVIORS

The following case study illustrates some strategies that parents and adult caregivers can engage in to effectively supervise and monitor adolescent behaviors as a method of preventing high-risk sexual activity. The role of the parent and adult caregivers in the scenario and the role of the preventionist/interventionist in facilitating work on the adult supervision process will be reviewed.

Alex is a White male who is a junior at a large suburban high school located outside of a major Midwestern city. The school is in a middle-class neighborhood, and the expectation is that all students will graduate and attend a university. There is some racial and ethnic diversity, with approximately 60% of the 3,550 students in the building being White, approximately 25% are African American, 10% are Hispanic, and approximately 5% are Asian/Pacific Islander. Alex is being raised by single mother, Lisa, as his father passed away when Alex was in elementary school. Lisa's mother, Alex's maternal grandmother (Jodi), and grandfather (Rex) are very involved in Alex and Lisa's life and live right down the block. They have helped supervise Alex and his older sister, Jamie, who is 23 and recently graduated from college. Lisa works as an accountant at a large public accounting firm. She frequently travels, at which time Alex's grandparents supervise him. Up until this past year, Alex's grandparents would stay at Lisa's house, but now that Alex has his driver's license, they have allowed him to stay overnight on his own. Alex was always a strong student and very athletic. He is the captain of the varsity Lacrosse team and runs track in the spring. Recently, Lisa and her parents have noticed that Alex is not as consistent in checking in with them, particularly on the weekends when Lisa is out of town. Alex does not consistently respond to texts and phone calls from his adult caregivers for many hours. He has also taken the family car without permission, and when his grandparents checked on him later at night on the weekends, they found him alone in the house with his girlfriend. Alex has always been a very social child and a good student. He is close to his Lacrosse and track teams and his coaches. Alex has always been close to coaches over the years and has often been drawn to male coaches. He has also been very close to his maternal grandfather. Although Alex appears to be doing well with his grades at school, his mother and grandparents are concerned about the supervision that he has been receiving. There was also an incident at school in which Alex was nearly kicked off his sports team indefinitely. Alex, along with several teammates on the Lacrosse team, was caught drinking alcohol at a party hosted by another teammate when his parents were out of town. The police came and broke up the party after neighbors called the police. The school has a policy whereby suspensions are reduced if those caught confess to violating the athletic code of conduct prohibiting drinking. Alex, along with several other teammates, approached his Lacrosse coach and came forward about the incident. As a result, Alex was given a short-term suspension from the team and 5-day suspension from school, which was reduced to 2 days because he agreed to participate in a school-based alcohol and drug awareness program co-led by a community-based counselor and school psychologist. There is a family component that comprises three of the eight sessions, in which parents and caregivers are taught communication skills. Lisa was consulted for participation and asked that her parents be included in the sessions as well. During the sessions, the issue of adult supervision arose as well as Alex's perception that he does not have easy access to speak with someone about sexual issues and choices. Alex feels that he is in his first serious relationship with his girlfriend and misses the opportunity to have these discussions with his dad. Although he feels that his mom and grandparents are approachable and have always taken care of him, he is not sure how to begin the conversation. As a preventionist/interventionist, following are some factors that might be considered as the case is conceptualized and strategies are implemented to help Alex and his family.

1   Consistent adult monitoring and supervision of Alex would be an important priority. Given that multiple caregivers (e.g., Lisa, Jodi, and Rex) are involved in Alex's life and provide supervision for him, having clear and predictable expectations for monitoring his behavior would be helpful. These expectations could be clearly laid out for Alex as part of a parental monitoring program that is inclusive of the parental role that the grandparents take. For example, establishing ground rules such as who can be at the house when an adult is absent and routines for checking in with adults could be established and then communicated to Alex with a "united front." Such limit setting discussion could take place in the context of family therapy (Kerr & Stattin, 2000) or in a group that focuses on parenting teens offered through the school or in a community mental health setting. It is likely that such a group would not only be useful for Alex's family but for other families who may not be in the exact situation but could use support with limit setting and establishing/maintaining healthy relationships with teens. In Alex's case, given that Lisa travels for work and the grandparents assume a supervisory role, setting reasonable limits is important. It is perhaps not ideal that a 16-year-old is left overnight, so alternative supervision arrangements could potentially be made. Alex could be required to stay with his grandparents or one or both of his grandparents can stay at his house, particularly since Alex has been beginning to show high-risk behaviors such as alcohol use,

(Continued)

(Continued)

associating with teammates who are drinking, and being alone with his girlfriend. Another possibility is for the school counselor, school psychologist, or school social worker to coordinate supports in the community, such as wraparound planning and processes (Bruns, 2010). In the wraparound process, priorities as described by the family are honored and established. The needs identified by the family are met through a team approach that involves multiple stakeholders, including those who are naturally present with the family rather than professionals typically identified such as mental health clinicians who might not have a relationship with the family (e.g., see Bruns et al., 2004). The National Wraparound Initiative has a comprehensive website (http://www.nwi.pdx.edu/index.shtml) that contains resources and publications that provide a lot of details about the origins and current status of the wraparound process.

2   Once ground rules are established, having communication methods that all involved are comfortable with will be important. For example, according to the CDC (2012), teens text much more frequently than they make phone calls. This might be a familiar method of communication for Alex and perhaps his mother, but given that his grandparents are one generation removed, they may need to weigh in on the communication methods and receive some assistance in using texting. Although this point may seem trivial, having common communication methods that all are comfortable with is important for getting everyone on the same page.

3   Given that Alex lost his father at a young age, he may not have adequately dealt with issues of grief, followed by his mother's absence when traveling for work. Therefore, family therapy and counseling, as well as individual counseling for Alex, could address these potentially unresolved issues. Alex has felt a close bond with his grandfather and male coaches in his life, and perhaps building on these connections could be a goal for Alex as he enters the unchartered territory of later adolescence and young adulthood. Adolescence may have brought up unresolved issues of grief and loss as Alex begins to face more adult lifestyle decisions, including those related to sexual activity and use of alcohol. These decisions could clearly have a significant impact on not only his future but also that of others around him, including his girlfriend and peers. Having an adult role model during this important developmental period will be important.

4   Alex has many questions about his adolescence and seems open to talking about sexual activity. Explicit instruction about prevention (WHO, 2014) that involves pregnancy prevention and information about STI/HIV/AIDS, including contraception methods, will be very important. Alex's family support network can be instructed in these methods, but

there might be an additional role for a trusted adult in Alex's life, such as a classroom teacher or coach that he trusts. Alex should also receive information about the potential relationship between alcohol use and high-risk sexual activity, such as not using a condom and having multiple sex partners (Schantz, 2012). Building trusting relationships among the multiple adult role models in Alex's life will be important and potentially lead to the protective factor of higher rates of adolescent disclosure that is associated with higher overall adjustment (Kerr & Stattin, 2000).

Overall, this is a situation with multiple components that go beyond the issue of sexual activity. However, it is our perception that this case is a realistic one from the standpoint that adolescents and families are multifaceted and often require comprehensive supports that address other adolescent health behaviors that are often intertwined with sexual risk behaviors. Concerns about sexual activity are one of many possible issues that might arise in the complex lives of adolescents and the parents and extended family members who support them. We also think that this case illustrates family structures that are common in the communities and schools where many of us work, whereby there is not a "traditional" two-parent family but a family that is comprised of extended family members, such as grandparents, who play a key role in children and adolescents' lives. Their viewpoints need to be honored and considered. We articulate that by providing support to all families, which more likely than not does not comprise the traditional nuclear family, we will place adolescents in a much more likely situation to make an effective transition to young adulthood. We see the role of the family, defined by the family members themselves in terms of composition, as critical in facilitating important developmental transitions among today's youth.

Overall Summary and Future Directions in Establishing Home Supports for Healthy Adolescent Sexual Behaviors

Adolescence and emerging sexual activity of youth is often met with a range of emotions among the adolescents themselves and their family members. If we are a parent, we may not want to believe that our children are at the stage of becoming sexually active, and although abstinence is the only way in which teenage pregnancy and other sexual risk behaviors can be avoided, sexual activity is part of the human experience, and statistics document that, on the average, by around age 19, most youth have engaged in sexual intercourse (Schantz, 2012). Parents and other adult caregivers and extended family may have anticipated this developmental stage with anxiety, fear, and uncertainty. Coupled with such concerns is the lack of knowledge and confidence that parents may have in providing accurate and factual information about prevention of pregnancy, STIs, and HIV/AIDS, and use of condoms (Rouvier et al., 2011). Although these concerns of parents may not be unique to this generation, the gap in technology skills between parents and youth creates a novel situation whereby parents may always be playing "catch up" in knowing who their children and adolescents are communicating with, the content of their messages, and which social media they are selecting as a medium. Parents may feel that they have limited influence on the decisions that their adolescents are making, but the research is consistently counter to this perception, as adolescents want to hear what their parents think and their input does influence their sexual risk behaviors, even in this age of technology whereby society is bombarded with information, some of it factual and some of it not (CDC, 2012).

In this chapter, we focused our review of the research on two major areas that families can have an impact on: parental communication and parental monitoring related to the prevention and response to sexual risk behaviors. We have considered the implications of these two areas for parents, families, as well as preventionists/interventionists (e.g., school psychologists, school social workers, school counselors, therapists) who work with adolescents and their families during this critical developmental period. There is certainly much more work that needs to be done and knowledge to gain, but recently developed resources through the U.S. Department of Health and Human Services/Office of Adolescent Health (2014) are excellent practical documents that can help not only families but preventionists and interventionists who support them to initiate healthy conversations with adolescents about a range of health topics, including sexual risk behaviors. Consistent and skilled support of families will hopefully advance adolescent health through facilitating open dialogue and knowledge about healthy sexual choices, as well as valuable information about limit setting and effective monitoring of adolescent behaviors. If we are to collectively raise healthy responsible adolescents who are sexually healthy, parents and family members need to be supported in the critical role they have on decisions of youth to engage in sexual risk behaviors or to make healthy choices that support not only their current sexual health but also their future aspirations to live a productive adult life.

References

Aquilino, W. S. (1997). From adolescent to young adult: A prospective study of parent-child relations during the transition to adulthood. *Journal of Marriage and Family, 59*(3), 670–686.

Ayalew, M., Mengistie, B., & Semahegn, A. (2014). Adolescent-parent communication on sexual and reproductive health issues among high school students in Dire Dawa, Eastern Ethiopia: A cross sectional study. *Reproductive Health, 11*(1), 77. Retrieved from http://www.reproductive-health-journal.com/content/11/1/77

Borawski, E. A., Ievers-Landis, C., Lovegreen, L. D., & Trapl, E. S. (2003). Parental monitoring, negotiated unsupervised time and parental trust: The role of perceived parenting practices in adolescent health risk behaviors. *Journal of Adolescent Health, 33*, 60–70.

Bruns, E. J. (2010). *The wraparound evidence base: April 2010 update*. Portland, OR: National Wraparound Initiative, Portland State University.

Bruns, E. J., Walker, J. S., Adams, J., Miles, P., Osher, T. W., Rast, J., et al. (2004). *Ten principles of the wraparound process*. Portland, OR: National Wraparound Initiative, Research and Training Center on Family Support and Children's Mental Health, Portland State University.

Burns, M. K., & Gibbons, K. (2008). *Implementing response-to-intervention in elementary and secondary schools: Procedures to assure scientific-based practice* (2nd ed.). New York, NY: Routledge.

Carteret, M. (2011). *Cultural values of Latino patients and families*. Retrieved from http://www.dimensionsofculture.com/2011/03/cultural-values-of-latino-patients-and-families

CDC. (2010). *A public health approach for advancing sexual health in the United States: Rationale and options for implementation* (Meeting Report of an External Consultation). Atlanta, GA: Centers for Disease Control and Prevention.

CDC. (2012). *Monitoring your teen's activities: What parents and families should know*. Retrieved from http://www.cdc.gov/healthyyouth/protective/pdf/parental_monitoring_factsheet.pdf

CDC. (2013). Youth risk behavior surveillance—United States 2013. *CDC Morbidity and Mortality Weekly Report, 63*(4), 1–168.

Doll, B. A., & Cummings, J. A. (2008). *Transforming school mental health services: Population based approaches to promoting the competency and wellness of children*. Thousand Oaks, CA: Corwin Press/NASP.

Eisenberg, M. E., Sieving, R. E., Bearinger, L. H., Swain, C., & Resnick, M. D. (2006). Parents' communication with adolescents about sexual behavior: A missed opportunity for prevention? *Journal of Youth and Adolescence, 35*(6), 893–902.

Galanti, G. (2003). The Hispanic family and male-female relationships: An overview. *Journal of Transcultural Nursing, 14*(3), 180–185. doi:10.1177/1043659603253548

Gillmore, M. R., Lewis, S. M., Lohr, M. J., Spencer, M. S., & White, R. D. (1997). Repeated pregnancies among adolescent mothers. *Journal of Marriage and the Family, 59*, 536–550.

Guzman, L., Golub, E., Caal, S., Hickman, S., & Ramos, M. (2013, November). *Let's (not) talk about sex: Communication and teen pregnancy prevention within Hispanic families*. Retrieved from http://www.childtrends.org/wp-content/uploads/2013/11/2013-50LetsNotTalkAboutSex.pdf

Hops, H., Ozechowski, T. J., Waldron, H. B., Davis, B., Turner, C. W., Brody, J. L., et al. (2011). Adolescent health-risk sexual behaviors: Effects of a drug abuse intervention. *AIDS Behavior, 15*(8), 1664–1676. doi:10.1007/510461-011-0019-7

Huebner, A. J., & Howell, L. W. (2003). Examining the relationship between adolescent sexual risk taking and perceptions of monitoring, communication and parenting styles. *Journal of Adolescent Health, 33*(2), 71–78.

Hutchinson, M. K., Jemmott, J. B., Jemmott, L. S., Braverman, P., & Fong, G. T. (2003). The role of mother-daughter sexual risk communication in reducing sexual risk behavior among urban adolescent females: A prospective study. *Journal of Adolescent Health, 33*(2), 98–107. doi:10.1016/S1054.139X(03) 00183-6

Institute of Medicine, Committee on Prevention and Control of Sexually Transmitted Diseases. (1997). *The hidden epidemic: Confronting sexually transmitted diseases*. Washington, DC: National Academy Press.

Jaccard, J., & Dittus, P. J. (1993). Parent-adolescent communication about premarital pregnancy. *Families in Society, 74*, 329–343.

Kapadia, F., Frye, V., Bonner, S., Emmanuel, P. J., Samples, C. L., & Latka, M. H. (2012). Perceived peer safer sex norms and sexual risk behaviors among substance-abusing Latino adolescents. *AIDS Education Prevention, 24*(1), 27–40. doi:10/1521/aeap.2012.24.1.27

Kerr, M., & Stattin, H. (2000). What parents know, how they know it, and several forms of adolescent adjustment: Further support for a reinterpretation of monitoring. *Developmental Psychology, 36*(3), 366–380. doi:10.1037/0012-1649.36.3.366

Kirby, D., & Lepore, G. (2007). *Sexual risk and protective factors: Factors affecting teen sexual behavior, pregnancy, childbearing, and sexually transmitted disease: Which are important? Which can you change?* Washington, DC: National Campaign to Prevent Teen and Unplanned Pregnancy.

Kotchick, B. A., Shaffer, A., Forehand, R., & Miller, K. S. (2001). Adolescent sexual risk behavior: A multisystem perspective. *Clinical Psychology Review, 21*(4), 493–519.

Marin, B. V., Kirby, D. B., Hudes, E. S., Coyle, K. K., & Gomez, C. A. (2006). Boyfriends, girlfriends, and teenagers' risk of sexual involvement. *Perspectives on Sexual and Reproductive Health, 38*(2), 76–83.

Miller, K. S., Forehand, R., & Kotchick, B. A. (2000). Adolescent sexual behavior in two ethnic minority samples: A multi-system perspective. *Adolescence, 35*, 313–333.

National Campaign to Prevent Teen and Unplanned Pregnancy. (2014). *Advice for parents from teens.* Retrieved from http://thenationalcampaign.org/sites/default/files/resource-supporting-download/how_parents_can_help_prevent_teen_pregnancy.pdf

Rouvier, M., Campero, L., Walker, D., & Caballero, M. (2011). Factors that influence communication about sexuality between parents and adolescents in the cultural context of Mexican families. *Sex Education, 11*(2), 175–191. doi:10.1080/14681811.2011.558425

Schantz, K. (2012). *Substance use and sexual risk taking in adolescence.* ACT for Youth Center of Excellent at Cornell University. Retrieved from http://www.actforyouth.net/resources/rf/rf_substance_0712.pdf

Sinclair, M. F., Christenson, S. L., & Thurlow, M. L. (2005). Promoting school completion of urban secondary youth with emotional and behavioral disabilities. *Exceptional Children, 71*(4), 465–482.

Stanton, B. F., Li, X., Galbraith, J., Cornick, G., Feigelman, S., Kaljee, L., et al. (2000). Parental underestimates of adolescent risk behavior: A randomized control trial of a parental monitoring intervention. *Journal of Adolescent Health, 26*(1), 18–26. doi:10.1016/51054-139X(99) 00022-1

U.S. Department of Health and Human Services/Office of Adolescent Health. (2014). *Talking with teens.* Retrieved from http://www.hhs.gov/ash/oah/resources-and-publications/info/parents/conversation-tools

Whitaker, D. J., & Miller, K. S. (2000). Parent-adolescent discussions about sex and condoms: Impact on peer influences of sexual risk behaviors. *Journal of Adolescent Research, 15*(2), 251–273.

WHO. (2014). *Adolescents: Health risks and solutions fact sheet.* Retrieved from http://www.who.int/mediacentre/factsheets/fs345/en

8

PROMOTING THE SEXUAL HEALTH OF CHILDREN AND ADOLESCENTS AT SCHOOL

Schools play a prominent role in the lives of children and adolescents. They are the most likely institutions in which formal instruction in promoting sexual health practices will be delivered to adolescents, as has been articulated by noted scholars, policy makers, and agencies that have devoted significant energy to addressing the sexual health of youth (e.g., see Kirby & Lepore, 2007). Schools are critical locations not only to support academic but health needs of children as well (CDC, 2010). The ASCD/CDC (2014) disseminated a document that calls for an integrated approach to sexual wellness of youth across health and school environments to collaborate and coordinate the delivery of health services. We support the argument of prominent scholars in the field that the most likely venue for the delivery of education in sexual health is within and linked to schools in collaboration with other professionals, as professional educators can deliver health supports in an integrated fashion with other health curriculum that youth receive.

Youth need support to address sexual health concerns, as consistent evidence documents that a relatively high proportion of youth are not abstaining from sexual activity and high-risk sexual behaviors that put them at risk for significant health concerns. A reasonably high proportion of youth are not abstaining from sex, and when they do, they may not use contraception to prevent pregnancy, STIs, and HIV/AIDS (Kirby & Lepore, 2007). Recently collected data through Child Trends Data Bank (2014) document that about one-third of teens reported being sexually active, defined as having sex in the last 3 months, which has not markedly changed from 1991 through 2013, with the most recent 2013 prevalence rates for sexually active teens at 34%. Recent CDC findings document that nearly half of high school students reported having had sexual intercourse at least once (CDC, 2013). Young people are also at heightened risk for sexual risk outcomes, as two-thirds of those under the age of 25 comprise the percentage within the population that have contracted STIs (Institute of Medicine, Committee on Prevention and Control of Sexually Transmitted Diseases, 1997). These statistics, also reviewed in Chapter 7 related to home supports, underscore the need for sexuality education for youth.

Recent statistics also document that many schools are not necessarily realizing their potential in providing prevention of sexual risk behaviors. For instance, not all states require that schools provide sexuality education or HIV/AIDS information. With respect to support and intervention, an even smaller percentage of schools provide for the identification, treatment, and referral of STIs. Findings from a 2012 CDC-sponsored national survey, the School Health Policies and Practices Study, were that only 15.2% of districts formalized a policy that their schools were to provide identification, treatment, or referral for STIs, while 36.7% had approved a policy for their schools to provide STI prevention in one-on-one or small group intervention (CDC, 2012a).

The field is currently at an ideal time for all schools in every state across the country to take on the role of providing sexual health supports for students in collaboration and cooperation with healthcare agencies that will impact children, adolescents, and their families (ASCD/CDC, 2014). Major health organizations stress that an evidence-based curriculum includes instruction in the prevention of high-risk behaviors, which includes "medically accurate" and "age-appropriate" (PL 111–117: Consolidated Appropriations Act, 2010, cited in Solomon-Fears, 2015) information about pregnancy prevention, as well as information related to HIV/AIDS and STI prevention (CDC, 2010) and contraception (PL 111–148: Patient Protection and Affordable Care Act [ACA], 2010; WHO, 2014).

There are two federal resources that can guide more states to support schools and districts in serving as a principal institution, in collaboration with healthcare settings, to provide evidence-based, prevention-oriented instruction and accurate information about pregnancy prevention and effective contraception to prevent STIs and HIV/AIDS (WHO, 2014). As described in more detail throughout Chapter 4, NSES was developed for use in schools that provide specific curricular goals and content to prevent high-risk sexual behaviors, such as not using a condom and engaging in early sexual debut (FoSE, 2014). A second resource produced by the CDC is a curricular tool aligned with the NSES to use when analyzing local and national sexual health curriculum in planning evidence-based instruction to meet the developmental needs of children and adolescents. This resource is titled "Health Education Curriculum Analysis Tool (HECAT)" (CDC, 2012b). These resources are available to facilitate effective instruction in sexual health for youth within schools. We assert that it is unlikely that a structured sexual health curriculum will be delivered unless it happens in a school setting and in collaboration with community healthcare providers, as articulated by major agencies that support healthy development of youth (ACSD/CDC, 2014). We certainly do not discount the importance of parents and community members in providing instruction and support in sexual health, as articulated in

Chapter 7 on home supports, and in partnering with schools and community agencies to provide the most optimal support not only for the child and adolescent but also for the family as well during important developmental milestones. At the same time, schools in collaboration with health agencies are uniquely positioned to provide structured support not only with respect to classroom instruction but in providing additional resources and consultation to adolescents and families who may be at higher risk than those in the general population due to issues of poverty, community disorganization, family concerns, or individual risk factors such as behavioral inhibition, social-emotional, mental health, academic or substance abuse concerns—all potential risk and protective factors described in more detail within Chapter 3. Further, schools have additional personnel beyond teachers, such as school psychologists, school social workers, school counselors, and school nurses who provide additional supports as part of a school-based team and in partnership with healthcare teams in the community comprised of community mental health professionals, physicians, nurses, and other agencies that work with youth. Although it is our position that all schools are uniquely qualified to provide sexual health education and supports, each school will vary in its capacity to do so. Some factors that may either facilitate or inhibit whether schools in partnership with healthcare organizations have the capacity to provide evidence-based sexual health supports are described below.

External School Factors Related to Sexual Health Promotion

Systemic factors external to schools and districts include the degree to which federal and state funding is available to support schools in the adoption and delivery of a sexual health curriculum. Federal legislators tied to their constituents' viewpoints on whether to focus on an "abstinence-only" versus more comprehensive teaching including information about contraceptive use in the prevention of STIs and HIV/AIDS have driven the types of curriculum that are funded and greatly impact what is subsequently taught (SIECUS, 2010). Federal funding has shifted over many years from teaching "abstinence-only" versus a more comprehensive approach that not only emphasizes abstinence and delaying sexual activity but also covers contraception use and providing accurate medical information about STIs/HIV/AIDS, as well as teaching adolescents effective problem solving, negotiation, and communication skills when confronted with adult-like situations (Santelli, Ott, Lyon, Rogers, Summers, & Schleifer, 2006, cited in Advocates for Youth, 2006).

The SIECUS (2010) completed a comprehensive historical overview of federal funding opportunities for sexual health curriculum, which has had a direct impact on whether schools/districts implement sexual health and, if so, what is covered in the curriculum. Although there are certainly political, personal, and value beliefs about what to include in a sexuality curriculum, scientific evidence favors the application of more comprehensive teachings rather than an "abstinence-only" message (Advocates for Youth, 2006; Stranger-Hall & Hall, 2011). A historical overview of federal funding produced by SIECUS (2010) chronicles the changing shift from a focus on abstinence-only to more comprehensive practices inclusive of STI/HIV prevention, contraception use, and instruction in problem solving. See SIECUS (2010) for this detailed summary and analysis. As articulated by SIECUS (2010), federal funding during the 1970s and 1980s was through the CDC for teen pregnancy prevention, with HIV/STI prevention as an "add on" not necessarily tied to the sexual health curriculum in schools (SIECUS, 2010). In the years following, federal tax dollars continued to focus on "abstinence-only" programs until some major changes happened around 2010. The passage of the Consolidated Appropriations Act, 2010, also known as the Teen Pregnancy Prevention (TPP) program, provided $110 million in 2010 in the form of grants to public and private agencies that provided "medically accurate" and "age-appropriate" sexual education (Advocates for Youth, 2006; SIECUS, 2010; Solomon-Fears, 2015). A pivotal health reform event related to sexual health around the same time frame was the creation of the Office of Adolescent Health through the U.S. Department of Health and Human Services (SIECUS, 2010). The Office of Adolescent Health, with continued but tenuous funding since 2010, offers very comprehensive resources on its website (http://www.hhs.gov/ash/oah/oah-initiatives/teen_pregnancy/db). For example, there are posted statistics by state related to teen birth rates, reported use of contraception at last sexual intercourse, education with respect to HIV/AIDS, as well as other risk behaviors such as early sexual debut and having multiple partners (Office of Adolescent Health, 2014a). Further, the Office of Adolescent Health website contains extensive information about a range of adolescent health concerns, including mental and physical health issues in addition to sexual health. Specific to sexual health, a listing of evidence-based programs through the TPP Evidence Review was completed, with a focus on evidence-based programs implemented with a range of diverse populations with outcomes and scope not only related to teen pregnancy but sexual risk behaviors as well, including STIs (Office of Adolescent Health, 2014b).

Perhaps the federal healthcare program with the potential to have the most far-reaching national implications for impact on adolescent sexual health is the recent passage of the ACA. Specific to sexual health, the ACA contains the Personal Responsibility Education Program (PREP), which mandates age-appropriate sexual health education not only focused on pregnancy prevention but also requires instruction in HIV/AIDS and STIs (CDC, 2010; SIECUS, 2010; Solomon-Fears, 2015). In addition, the provisions of PREP call for instruction and programing in "life skills" that afford youth the skills to make healthy choices (CDC, 2010; SIECUS, 2010; Solomon-Fears, 2015). One only has to watch the media and varied responses as the tenets of the ACA have unfolded to see that this legislation is potentially tenuous and could change with varied elections and federal administrations. Given the relatively new status of the ACA, how each state provides for the mandates is relatively new to the nation.

Overall, there have been significant changes in scope and focus of federal funding for sexual health, with the inclusion of instruction related to not only delaying sexual activity through abstinence but contraception and accurate information about STIs and HIV/AIDS. We support the current, more comprehensive federal funding focus and the efforts of the Office of Adolescent Health with its concentrated focus on adolescent health concerns, including an emphasis on funding and disseminating evidence-based programs that are inclusive of diverse populations, including underserved and high-risk populations, in concert with national policy makers and professionals who have devoted significant systematic efforts to improving support and outcomes related to the sexual health of youth (Stanger-Hall & Hall, 2011).

Community Beliefs and Support

Federal funding, as described above, has a profound impact on what states do with respect to directing and supporting sexual health at the local community level. At the same time, the values and beliefs of each state and community impact the degree to which state-funded efforts are implemented. For example, a 2011–2017 evaluation of the federally funded PREP program, underway by Mathematica Policy Research, documents that although most states have taken this funding for more comprehensive instruction in sexual heath, a few have not. In 2010, during the first year of funding, 42 states, the District of Columbia, and other U.S. territories (e.g., Puerto Rico, Virgin Islands, and Federated States of Micronesia) took the funding and were joined by three more the following year (U.S. Administration for Children and Families/Office of Planning Research and Evaluation, 2014). As of 2011, a few states did not take the funding, including Florida, Indiana, North Dakota, Virginia, Palau, Texas, and territories including Guam, American Samoa, Marshall Islands, and Northern Mariana Islands (U.S. Administration for Children and Families/Office of Planning Research and Evaluation, 2014).

In addition to state decisions about acceptance of federal funding and the accompanying mandates for what is included in the curriculum and subsequently delivered in the classroom, the local control of school boards can often greatly influence the ways in which curriculum is ultimately delivered and taught within the latitude that the states allow for educational practices to be implemented on a daily basis. Local school boards make specific curricular and policy decisions within the parameters of state requirements for graduation and have latitude within legal limits as far as who is hired and retained. In the city where the authors reside, the local school council, comprised of community members, has the sole authority to hire and terminate the principal, so the council has a great deal of power and influence over decisions that are made.

A challenging task for professionals who work to address the sexual health needs of youth is balancing what is currently considered best practices in the field while still respecting the values and viewpoints of the families and communities served within the local community and school environment. Context matters with respect to beliefs among community members and constituents as to what should be taught and emphasized with regard to the sexual health of adolescents. Contextual factors may be defined in multiple ways, based on one's religious convictions, personal values and cultural heritage, and geographic region of the country. Olsho, Cohen, Walker, Johnson, and Locke (2009) conducted a survey for the U.S. Department of Health and Human Services/U.S. Administration for Children and Families. Their findings, based on a survey with the parent identified as "most knowledgeable" and the adolescents themselves, were that approximately 70% of parents surveyed did not approve of premarital sex overall or for their adolescents, but reported more permissive beliefs when asked about males versus females. Beliefs about maintaining abstinence until marriage were held most strongly by those who were more religious or had lower reported incomes and among non-Hispanic Blacks (Olsho et al., 2009). The adolescents themselves also favored abstinence, but not to the level of their parents. Older adolescents were more permissive than younger respondents, and male adolescents were more permissive about sexual intercourse compared to females. The Olsho et al. study is an example of the importance of context in any discussion about stakeholder perspectives about what should be taught in the classroom about sexual health. Although the Olsho et al. study found that parents do not approve of their adolescents engaged in premarital sex, other research has found that parents favor a comprehensive educational approach to sexual health in the schools that not only includes information about abstinence but accurate information about contraception and STIs (Constantine, Jerman, & Huang, 2007; Eisenberg, Bermat, Bearinger, & Resnick, 2008). Statewide studies are also available, such as a California phone survey that found that over 89% of parents surveyed favored comprehensive sexual education that included information about abstinence and protection (Constantine et al., 2007). Their sample included approximately 46% Hispanic families and 38% White families sampled across the state of California.

The findings of the current research related to family perceptions of sexual health may vary depending on the types of questions asked (e.g., approval of premarital sex versus whether contraception should be included in a comprehensive analysis of sexual education). We would argue that family and other key stakeholders need to have a voice in the sexual health of youth and also need to have clear information about the current evidence-based research related to sexual health. If parents are familiar with the research and the recommendations of the major federal agencies and organizations that focus on sexual health (e.g., CDC, Office of Adolescent Health, WHO), they will be more likely to be knowledgeable and buy in to evidence-based sexual health curriculum.

Internal School Factors Related to Sexual Health Promotion

Another important factor to consider is the structure by which the sexual health curricula will be delivered as part of the overall school academic offerings, whether at the elementary, middle, or high school level. Each school grade level has particular constraints and parameters that include not only state requirements for sexual health curricula but a myriad of other state curricular requirements that must be fit within the constraints of the school day. For example, at all levels of education, mandated assessments and content across all academic areas must be delivered. For example, graduation requirements tend to drive what students take, although some states have more flexibility than others, which impacts school districts in the choices that youth have and ultimately what is taught. Relatedly, a majority of states have adopted the Common Core Standards (National Governors Association Center for Best Practices & Council of Chief State School Officers 2010), which require content converge across a variety of curriculum areas that lays a foundation for the structure of the curriculum. In order to ensure that all requirements are met, school districts have a variety of approaches that impact the way in which the sexual health curriculum is delivered and integrated into the school day. Schools that have adopted the NSES (FoSE, 2014) or are among the school settings that currently serve as a community site through which states have secured federal PREP dollars (U.S. Administration for Children and Families/ Office of Planning Research and Evaluation, 2014) offer a sexual curriculum that includes abstinence as well as factual and developmentally appropriate information about STIs/HIV/AIDS and contraception. However, the mechanism by which the curriculum is being offered, such as whether it is a stand-alone curriculum or integrated into other health-related content or physical education/wellness, is going to vary by school district. It is our experience and observation that decisions made by schools as to where to place the sexual health curriculum is connected to other decisions about mandated content that must be covered and the philosophy of the district as well as parental and community practices. In one setting one of the authors is familiar with, the middle school students received sexual health information related to basic reproductive and developmental information about puberty and emerging adolescence in a wellness class that was a unit tied to physical education. Parents were instructed about the content via a letter and could have their adolescent "opt out" of the instruction. At a high school one of the authors is familiar with, students are required to take an entire course in health education that provides information about contraception, HIV/AIDS, STIs, benefits of abstinence, as well as the psychological aspects of being in a relationship. Each district will make such decisions based on state mandates, local district and school board input, and the other content that is required for students.

The Division of Adolescent and School Health, under the CDC, conducts the School Health Policies and Practices Study (SHPPS) and collects data every 2 years from states and a national representative sample of school districts about policies related to the content of health curriculum and how it is delivered across grade levels from elementary to high schools. Specifically, the SHPPS assesses district and state policies related to the coverage of 15 health education topics, the types of support given to districts by states, training, credentials and professional development opportunities of health educators, and the types of collaborations that occur in schools related to health (CDC, 2012c). Of the 15 health topics studied, several relate to sexual health, including HIV and other STI prevention, pregnancy prevention, and human sexuality (Kann, Telljohann, H. Hunt, P. Hunt, & Haller, 2012).

A few of the key findings from the SHPPS will be reported here. The reader is directed to the full report for the comprehensive findings. More than half of the states provided professional development to districts on HIV prevention, human sexuality, other STI prevention, and pregnancy prevention (the sexual health topics that were among the 15 topics assessed—with more than 96% of states providing professional development on at least one of the 15 health topics assessed, and close to 71% of states provided professional development on at least 8 of 15 topics) (Kann et al., 2012). Further, more than half the states provided professional development on the alignment of health standards to curriculum and assessment of students in health education. With respect to training, about 35% of states had a policy that required newly hired health educators at the elementary level have certification, licensure, or credentials to teach health, which increased at the middle school level (61.6% of states) and the high school level (over 79%). In terms of professional development, about 35% of districts in the national sample reported that they required those who teach health education to obtain continuing education on health-related topics or instruction. Finally, only 43% of districts reported that health staff collaborated or worked with mental health/social service professionals.

Based on these findings, although many states and districts are working very hard to coordinate health education efforts and increase support and collaboration, we believe that more can be done. We would recommend that health educators in all states receive ongoing professional development and support specific to topics related to sexual health. We would further recommend that health educators across all districts have the opportunity to collaborate with school- and community-based health professionals including school psychologists, school social workers, counselors, and community therapists. These mental health and social service professionals can assist health educators when there are specific concerns that may arise with a group of students or on an individual basis. For example, as briefly alluded to in Chapter 3 related to adolescent sexual risk factors, a discussion of sexual health may bring up issues of sexual abuse or dating violence, as well as other related health concerns, like youth who have tested positive for STIs or have mental health concerns, such as having experienced trauma. In such a situation, school- and community-based mental health professionals and healthcare providers, such as nursing staff, should be available to assist classroom-based health educators to recognize warning signs of concerns, such as a change in a child or adolescent's behavior (e.g., withdrawal, acting out, lack of attendance, slipping grades) or if the student reports a concern. It would be ideal for an inter-connected team of professionals to be on hand to assist and support the health educator, the youth, as well as the family and extended caregivers. As another example, if a health educator is working with a particularly high-risk population, such as youth exposed to community violence and with a higher likelihood of experiencing dating violence or at risk for engaging in substance abuse, or having been involved in the juvenile justice system (risk factors and related issues identi-fied in Chapter 3), then mental health and health educators could teach or co-teach segments of the course and provide resources to the youth and their fami-lies for other needed community supports. Sometimes, an entire population within a school might be at risk and could benefit from specialized health pro-graming. A nurse who worked with one of the authors provided a health cur-riculum to a group of female adolescents who had been removed from their homes due to abuse and had lived in a residential treatment. As a result, there were major gaps in their health education because they had been relocated numerous times due to several school changes tied to frequent moves. Because of the trauma histories of the girls, they were considered a high-risk population for early preg-nancy and STIs. The school nurse received funding to teach the adolescents a specialized health curriculum that related directly to the curriculum they had missed due to their situations. These examples are a few of the many that illustrate the need for a collaborative approach among health educators and specialists in the arena of mental and physical health.

In addition to the importance of interdisciplinary collaboration, school-based health curriculum and health educators function within a larger school that can foster a positive school climate and school connectedness. School connectedness was identified in Chapter 3 as a protective factor for adolescents making healthy sexual choices (CDC, 2009; McNeely, Nonnemaker, & Blum, 2002). Building a positive school climate that is built with the entire school population in mind can foster school connectedness. Schools with positive school connectedness among youth have a positive approach to classroom management and encourage youth to participate in a range of extracurricular activities, so they identify with and believe that they are valued members of the school community (McNeely et al., 2002). Further, youth who feel a sense of school connectedness tend to attend smaller schools with less punitive discipline policies (McNeely et al., 2002). The CDC (2009) disseminated a report solely focused on strategies that schools can adopt to build school connectedness.

School-Based Sexuality Education Programs

In addition to the system variables above, another variable to consider when promoting youth's sexual health in schools is the identification and implementa-tion of sexuality education programing. Ruiz, Oster, and Sacks (2015) present a framework we believe may be beneficial to schools in guiding the process of selecting an evidence-based program, and they suggest the selection process may be facilitated via four phases: getting ready, identifying options, examining programs, and assessing fit.

To get ready, assessing needs and resources and developing a logic model are first steps schools can take as they consider ways to meet the specific needs of its student population. To begin, schools may find it beneficial to create a workgroup specifically tasked with collecting and analyzing data around the students' needs to inform the development of a logic model that will comprehensively capture the school's inputs, activities, outputs, and outcomes and guide the program selection process.

Next, in identifying program options, the U.S. Department of Health and Human Services' TPP Evidence Review is one current and active source of data for schools seeking to provide sexuality education (U.S. Department of Health and Human Services, 2015). The systematic evidence review, led by the U.S. Department of Health and Human Services' Office of the Assistant Secretary for Planning and Evaluation and conducted by Mathematica Policy Research and Child Trends, was first conducted in 2009, is regularly updated, and was last updated in February 2015 to include a review of programs from April 2013 through July 2014. Through an extensive review process, the review team assesses studies of programs designed to reduce teen pregnancy, STIs, and associated sexual risk behaviors (U.S. Department of Health and Human Services, 2015). The review process includes the following steps delineated in a regularly revised review protocol: (a) searching for studies, (b) screening and selecting studies, (c) assessing individual studies, and (d) analyzing evidence for individual programs. The search for studies includes a broad literature search of published and unpublished studies and periodic public calls for studies. Identified studies are then screened, and studies that measure the program's impact on pregnancy, STIs, or associated sexual risk behaviors and are conducted in the United States with a sample of youth 19 years of age or younger are retained. The research designs of retained studies are then assessed and assigned a quality rating of low, moderate, or high. Of note, the review team does not assess the extent to which reviewed programs are medically or scientifically accurate or designed to support diverse populations, so meeting criteria do not indicate U.S. Department of Health and Human Services endorsement of the program. As such, schools will want to carefully review the content of program options, as well as fit with target populations. Finally, program models of studies that receive a moderate or high quality rating are then analyzed to assess effectiveness.

To date, over 200 studies have been reviewed, 113 studies have received a quality rating of moderate or high based on research design, and 37 program models have met effectiveness criteria (indicating a positive, statistically significant impact on sexual activity such as sexual initiation or abstinence, recent sexual activity, number of sexual partners, or frequency of sexual activity; contraceptive use; STIs or HIV; or pregnancy/birth). Interested readers may locate reviewed studies via a searchable database (http://tppevidencereview.aspe.hhs.gov) and may also view and review the 37 programs, along with their quality ratings (http://tppevidencereview. aspe.hhs.gov/EvidencePrograms.aspx). Specifically, within the searchable database, programs can be filtered by program type, setting, program length, age, race/ethnicity, outcomes affected, and/or study rating. Further, the 37 program models, along with their evaluation settings, are also presented in a user-friendly listing on the TPP website (http://www.hhs.gov/ash/oah/oah-initiatives/teen_pregnancy/db). On this list, schools may quickly identify programs that have been evaluated in elementary schools, middle schools, high schools, and after-school programs. Finally, interested researchers may submit a study for review (http://tppevidencereview.aspe.hhs.gov).

Although most programs have only been evaluated one time, efforts to evaluate these programs when implemented more broadly and in diverse settings or populations continue. The review team is staying abreast of this work and is developing methods to compare and synthesize studies. In addition, one of three grant programs funded through the TPP program (an initiative of the Office of Adolescent Health (OAH)) is the TPP Replication of Evidence-Based Programs— a program designed to support efforts to replicate programs from the U.S. Department of Health and Human Services' TPP Evidence Review. The additional TPP grant programs are the TPP Research and Demonstration Programs and TPP Communitywide Initiative (see Chapter 9).

Once program options are identified, schools may examine program options closely by studying detailed reports of each program's components and implementation requirements and guidance, including implementation fidelity. Finally, considering the systems variables outlined earlier in this chapter, along with the needs of the school's target population, it will be critical to assess the program's fit. In addition to the work of Ruiz et al. (2015), the interested reader may also wish to review the OAH's e-learning module on selecting evidence-based TPP programs (http://www.hhs.gov/ash/oah/resources-and-publications/learning/tpp-evidence-based/index.html). Further, the TPP Resource Center (OAH, 2014b) offers additional resources to support sites in efforts such as building collaborations, choosing an evidence-based program and curriculum, developing cultural competence, engaging select populations, evaluation, implementation, and sustainability.

Public Health Models Adapted to Effective Delivery of School-Based Sexual Health Supports

Throughout this chapter, we have stressed the importance of building a positive school climate and considering system-level internal and external school factors, such as curriculum delivery methods, training of health educators, and support from mental health and health service providers (e.g., school nurses). We also consider effective models and programs that relate to effective delivery of sexual health support to children and adolescents along a continuum. We advocate for the application of multitiered system of support models, aligned with response to intervention (Burns & Gibbons, 2012) and population-based school mental health services perspective (Doll & Cummings, 2008).

MTSS/RTI and population-based mental health models share the common underlying framework of the public health model. In Chapter 3, we provided an outline of the MTSS/RTI population-based health model as it applies to risk and protective factors that either increase or decrease the likelihood of sexual risk behaviors, as well as a more detailed analysis of the MTSS/RTI (Burns & Gibbons, 2012) and the population-based mental health model (Doll & Cummings, 2008). The focus of the proposed model applied to sexual health is on evidence-based, developmentally appropriate sexuality education for all adolescents in a particular population (equivalent to "Tier 1"), followed by additional supplemental supports beyond "Tier 1" delivered through more intensive services to all students in high-risk settings (Doll & Cummings, 2008) or with subgroups of students identified as needing additional support (equivalent to "Tier 2") provided to a smaller proportion of students who are not successful solely with Tier 1 curriculum (Burns & Gibbons, 2012). Beyond Tier 2, for individual students with the most intensive needs, intensive supports (equivalent to "Tier 3") that may include wraparound supports that provide a coordination of care (National Wraparound Initiative, 2014) are delivered.

We advocate for an alignment with delivery of Tier 1 at the universal level (core curriculum) to all students in a school population that is aligned with the NSES (FoSE, 2014) and ACA's PREP. Both national efforts advocate for comprehensive age-appropriate sexual health education that includes pregnancy prevention, as well as accurate information about HIV/AIDS and STIs (CDC, 2010; SIECUS, 2010; Solomon-Fears, 2015). We also strongly advocate for a curriculum that is inclusive of LGBTQ youth (SIECUS, 2010). Similar to the delivery of a core academic curriculum that is federally mandated to be scientifically supported, such as in the area of reading in legislation in the Individuals with Disabilities Education Act, 2004, we argue that a core curriculum delivered in a developmentally appropriate manner and with accurate information is critical as a foundation for supporting sexual health among youth. The stakes are too high in terms of serious and life-altering outcomes that include not only early pregnancy but STIs, inclusive of HIV/AIDS. Therefore, at the system level, all students in a school population should receive accurate and scientifically supported instruction in sexual health. Further, at the system or universal core level, similar to the approach taken by population-based approaches to mental health, a school system may determine based on its school population or needs of most that additional curricular instruction be added to the "core" curriculum. For example, if the school setting services youth who are exposed to community violence on a continual basis or are living in poverty with high rates of substance abuse in the community, then additional content related to making healthy choices, factual information about substance abuse, and the risk factors for engaging in alcohol or drug use could be infused in the core curriculum and delivered to the entire school population based on the time frame in which they are in the most optimal developmental stage to receive the instruction.

Once the school healthcare team works to put an evidence-based sexual health curriculum that is delivered to all on a universal basis, the supplemental supports can be delivered to groups of students who continue to demonstrate need, which is an approach adapted for sexual health instruction and supports from multitiered systems of supports for academic, behavioral, and social-emotional supports (Burns & Gibbons, 2012; Sugai & Horner, 2009). Based on data collected about outcomes related to sexual health, such as data from a screening tool that assesses rates of sexual risk behavior, substance abuse, violence at home school or community (e.g., YRBS), the impact of the sexual health program can be evaluated and programing developed or modified as a response. At this Tier 2, if data indicate a subset of students could benefit from groups related to dating violence, substance abuse, or communication with parents, for example, then these supports could be delivered to a subset of students identified either through screening tools, from teacher or parent referral, or from the adolescents themselves.

At Tier 3, for individual students identified as having the most significant health and mental health needs, intensive and coordinated supports can be provided. For example, if students are identified as having significant mental health issues as a result of sexual trauma, they could receive an individualized mental health assessment, and supports could be coordinated not only within the school but through collaboration and connection with other supports in the youth's life or through community-based mental health supports, akin to wraparound services (National Wraparound Initiative, 2014).

Multitiered systems of supports are often depicted via a triangle to depict the various tiers when providing information about how academic, behavioral, and social-emotional supports are provided. As aligned with multitiered systems of supports, we provide the tiers of the graphic in such a manner that movement across them is fluid. A student can easily move back and forth between tiers based on data collected to determine progress and need for additional support and is not "set" in any one tier indefinitely. Parents should be consulted and provide consent for their child or adolescent to participate in programing related to sexual health in accordance with federal, state, and school district policies tied to the age of the student and based on the ethical and legal considerations of each situation. We illustrate how a multitiered system of supports could be applied to sexual health of adolescents using the following brief case scenario and provide a graphic representation in Figure 8.1.

Moore High School is a relatively large urban high school in a major metropolitan city in the southwest. There are roughly 2,500 students in the school, which is comprised primarily of students from Latino (65%), White (25%), and Asian/Pacific Islander (10%) backgrounds. Families in the community are primarily working class, with a high percentage of students that qualify for free and reduced lunch (85%). There are some concerns in the community such as gang-related issues, higher unemployment due to closures of some industry, and alcohol and substance abuse, as well as an increasing dropout rate, particularly among the Latino students. The school staff is dedicated, and many are veteran teachers who have worked with the district for many years. Mental health supports are provided on a group and individual basis. Ongoing psycho-educational groups are offered on adolescent topics, such as divorce, peer relationships, and substance use, through the school-based health center. In addition, there are a number of specialty clubs in the school, some formed through student recommendations and voice, such as a group specific to the Latino population and a Gay-Straight Alliance. The school has the support of a school psychologist, school social worker, three school counselors, and a school nurse. The school houses a health clinic that is staffed by a full-time nurse clinician, clinical social worker, and part-time physician. There are many varied cases seen in the clinic, but the main issues seen are adolescent depression, substance abuse issues, and sexual health issues that include teenage pregnancy and STIs. The clinic staff has noted that a disproportionate number of cases related to sexual health are occurring among the Latina females. The types of cases seen by the school-based mental health staff are similar to the health clinic with referrals for depression, anxiety, and academic-related concerns, such as not being on track to graduate and inconsistent attendance. The school-based health center staff decides to form a team comprised of the health center staff; the school-based mental health professionals including the school psychologist, school social worker, and two school counselors; as well as representative grade-level teachers, two teachers who teach health education, and the school administrator.

First, the high school students and their families complete a needs assessment about mental health, behavioral, academic, and social-emotional concerns. The YRBS (CDC, 2013) and a social-emotional screening tool are used as part of the screening assessment. The findings of the data collection are consistent with the clinical experiences of the school and clinic staff. There are reported concerns about internalizing issues that include anxiety and depression across all subgroups. Students who rate above a clinically significant range on the screening measure receive additional follow-up in the form of subsequent more in-depth assessment that includes a clinical interview completed by the school- or clinic-based mental health staff. In addition, the findings of the YRBS screening are that about 45% of the school population have tried alcohol, 35% have tried marijuana, and 15% have used harder drugs. About 20% of the high school population uses some type of substance at least once per week. In addition, around 30% of the school population have had sexual intercourse in the last 3 months, 25% report having unprotected sex in the same time period, with the rates for unprotected sex highest among Latino males in the upper grades. Further, about 40% of students and roughly the same percentage of parents (45%) report wanting to have conversations about sexual health. The students also report wanting more authentic conversations about contraception, but fear doing so.

As a result of these data, the school-based health team meets. They decide to consider how to provide supports to students along a multitiered continuum that is depicted as a triangle commonly used to illustrate supports under the RTI/MTSS model (Figure 8.1), described below by tier of support as a starting point for an evidence-based approach that would be modified in practice based on ongoing review of data, such as pregnancy rates, dropout due to pregnancy, anonymous rates of STI, students and parents' perceptions of the quality of health education, etc.

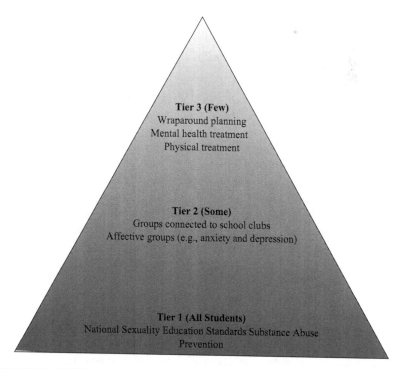

Tier 3 (Few)
Wraparound planning
Mental health treatment
Physical treatment

Tier 2 (Some)
Groups connected to school clubs
Affective groups (e.g., anxiety and depression)

Tier 1 (All Students)
National Sexuality Education Standards Substance Abuse
Prevention

FIGURE 8.1 MTSS supports proposed at Moore High School.

Tier 1 (all students): At Tier 1, the team recommends that the students receive the content recommended in the NSES (FoSE, 2014) for students in grades 9–12, preferably beginning in the freshman year, so they can receive developmentally appropriate and evidence-based instruction as early as possible within the high school years. The NSES is outlined in detail within Chapter 4. For the purposes here, we would recommend that students receive medically accurate information about the prevention of STIs and HIV/AIDS, effective contraception, and ways to navigate healthy relationships—inclusive of information about dating violence and effective communication skills with peers, parents, and other key individuals in the youth's lives. Given the scenario described above, we would also advocate that all students in the population receive accurate information about substance use using components of an evidence-based program, such as those provided in the National Registry of Effective Programs, given the high rates of substance use reported in the data collected by the team and aligned with adaptations for high-risk environments using a population-based mental health approach to providing supports (Doll & Cummings, 2008).

Tier 2 (some students): At this level of support, the team would offer supplemental groups to those who have some identified risk factors (substance abuse, poverty environment, exposure to violence or are part of a population that has historically been underserved in the health arena, and thus may not currently be having their needs served—e.g., youth in the LGBTQ community). The team decides to build upon some existing groups in the school by infusing offerings and discussions related to sexual health and to incorporate the expertise and involvement of the health clinic staff to co-lead groups. For example, students associated with the Gay-Straight Alliance work together with the school team to develop some workshops on sexual health specific to this population, as well as compile community resources to disseminate, such as health centers and community agencies that are sensitive to the needs of the LGBTQ population. Through the Latino club, a parent and adolescent group is organized that is focused on building family communication skills, an inclusion of effective ways to have meaningful conversations about adolescent sexual health topics. Another group is formed that addresses affective issues, using a cognitive behavioral approach to address issues of anxiety and depression. Finally, the counseling team surveys and informally converses with students about other groups that might be useful in the school and health clinic to address their needs.

Tier 3 (few students): At the most intensive needs of supports, students who require individual support are identified through multiple mechanisms, which include the results of needs assessment and referrals from teachers, families, and the students themselves. These supports would be provided to students who have already identified health needs, including those related to sexual health (e.g., having an STI), substance abuse, and physical concerns that would be seen in the clinic as well as mental health issues, both internalizing (e.g., depression, anxiety, suicidal ideation) and externalizing (ADHD, conduct disorder). In addition, supports could be provided to students who have experienced trauma, such as sexual, physical, and emotional abuse and may meet the criteria for posttraumatic stress disorder. The team decides to work on an integrated team approach that capitalizes on the experiences of the clinic and school staff to provide a continuum of care that may include wraparound services (National Wraparound Initiative, 2014). Wraparound services take a family strength approach whereby the family and the student direct the treatment and prioritize goals for outcomes. The family identifies key individuals in their lives who provide ongoing support and are part of the wraparound planning and supports.

Figure 8.1 provides a graphical representation aligned with MTSS that displays the supports that could be provided through the joint collaboration of the health and mental health service providers in the school and clinic settings. This case scenario provides a possible approach that a school and health team can take in addressing the sexual health and related needs in a high school through which supports are provided along a continuum aligned with the perspective of MTSS and population-based mental health. Each school can collaborate to determine the types of supports needed in their particular building tied to data collection as well as the resources that are available.

The purpose of this chapter was to provide an overview of considerations for promoting the sexual health of children and adolescents at school using evidence-based practices. Given the nature of schools, we first presented contextual variables schools wishing to adopt sexual health programing will want to consider. Following it, we offered a framework for selecting school-based sexuality education programs, emphasizing the current and active U.S. Department of Health and Human Services' TPP Evidence Review as an essential resource for school teams. Finally, we proposed an adaptation of public health models that can be adopted in the delivery of school-based sexual health supports and presented a case scenario to illustrate the proposed framework.

References

Advocates for Youth. (2006). *Effective sex education*. Retrieved from http://www.advocatesforyouth.org/storage/advfy/documents/fssexcur.pdf

ASCD/CDC. (2014). *Whole school, whole community, whole child: A collaborative approach to learning and health*. Retrieved from http://www.ascd.org/ASCD/pdf/siteASCD/publications/wholechild/wscc-a-collaborative-approach.pdf

Burns, M. K., & Gibbons, K. (2012). *Implementing response-to-intervention in elementary and secondary schools: Procedures to assure scientific-based practice* (2nd ed.). New York, NY: Routledge.

Centers for Disease Control and Prevention (CDC). (2009). *School connectedness: Strategies for increasing protective factors among youth*. Atlanta, GA: U.S. Department of Health and Human Services.

CDC. (2010). *Effective HIV/STD prevention program for youth: A summary of scientific evidence*. CDC Division of Adolescent and School Health. Retrieved from http://www.cdc.gov/healthyyouth/sexualbehaviors/pdf/effective_hiv.pdf

CDC. (2012a). *School health policies and practices study: Results from the school health policies and practices study*. Retrieved from http://www.cdc.gov/healthyyouth/shpps/2012/pdf/shpps-results_2012.pdf

CDC. (2012b). *Health education curriculum analysis tool (HECAT)*. Retrieved from http:// www.cdc.gov/healthyyouth/HECAT

CDC. (2012c). *Results from the school health policies and practices study*. Retrieved from http:// www.cdc.gov/healthyyouth/shpps/2012/pdf/shpps-results_2012.pdf#page=27

CDC. (2013). Youth risk behavior surveillance—United States 2013. *CDC Morbidity and Mortality Weekly Report, 63*(4), 1–168.

Child Trends Data Bank. (2014, July). *Sexually active teens: Indicators on children and youth*. Bethesda, MD: Child Trends Data Bank.

Consolidated Appropriations Act of 2010, Pub. L. No. 111-117, 123 Stat. 3034 (2009).

Constantine, N. A., Jerman, P., & Huang, A. X. (2007). California parents' preferences and beliefs regarding school-based sex education policy. *Perspectives on Sexual and Reproductive Health, 39*(3), 167–175.

Doll, B. A., & Cummings, J. A. (2008). *Transforming school mental health services: Population based approaches to promoting the competency and wellness of children*. Thousand Oaks, CA: Corwin Press/NASP.

Eisenberg, M. E., Bermat, D. H., Bearinger, L. H., & Resnick, M. D. (2008). Support for comprehensive sexuality education: Perspectives from parents of school-age youth. *Journal of Adolescent Health, 42*(4), 352–359.

FoSE. (2014). *National Sexuality Education Standards: Core Content and Skills K-12*. Retrieved from http://www.futureofsexed.org/documents/josh-fose-standards-web.pdf

Institute of Medicine, Committee on Prevention and Control of Sexually Transmitted Diseases. (1997). *The hidden epidemic: Confronting sexually transmitted diseases*. Washington, DC: National Academy Press.

Kann, L., Telljohann, S., Hunt, H., Hunt, P., & Haller, E. (2012). *Health education: Results from the school health policies and practices study*. Retrieved from http://www.cdc.gov/ healthyyouth/shpps/2012/pdf/shpps-results_2012.pdf#page=27

Kirby, D., & Lepore, G. (2007). *Sexual risk and protective factors: Factors affecting teen sexual behavior, pregnancy, childbearing, and sexually transmitted disease: Which are important? Which can you change?* Washington, DC: The National Campaign to Prevent Teen and Unplanned Pregnancy.

McNeely, C. A., Nonnemaker, J. M., & Blum, R. W. (2002). Promoting school connectedness: Evidence from the National Longitudinal Study of Adolescent Health. *Journal of School Health, 72*(4), 138–146.

National Governors Association Center for Best Practices & Council of Chief State School Officers. (2010). *Common Core State Standards*. Washington, DC: NGA/CCSSO.

National Wraparound Initiative. (2014). *National wraparound basics*. Retrieved from http:// www.nwi.pdx.edu/wraparoundbasics.shtml

Office of Adolescent Health. (2014a). *Adolescent reproductive health facts*. Retrieved from http:// www.hhs.gov/ash/oah/adolescent-health-topics/reproductive-health/fact-sheets/

Office of Adolescent Health. (2014b). *TPP resource center: Evidence-based programs*. Retrieved from http://www.hhs.gov/ash/oah/oah-initiatives/teen_pregnancy/db/

Olsho, L., Cohen, J., Walker, K. D., Johnson, A., & Locke, G. (2009). *National survey of adolescents and their parents: Attitudes and opinions about sex and abstinence* (Project No. 60005). Cambridge, MA: Abt Associates Inc.

Patient Protection and Affordable Care Act of 2010, Pub. L. No. 111–148, 124 Stat. 119 (2010).

Ruiz, J., Oster, M., & Sacks, V. (2015). *How to select an evidence-based teen pregnancy prevention program that works for you!* Retrieved from http://www.hhs.gov/ash/oah/snippets/508%20 documents/february5thwebinar_slides.pdf

Santelli, J., Ott, M. A., Lyon, M., Rogers, J., Summers, D., & Schleifer, R. (2006). Abstinence and abstinence-only education: A review of U.S. policies and programs. *Journal of Adolescent Health, 38*(1):72–81.

SIECUS. (2010). *A brief history of federal funding for sex education and related programs*. Retrieved from http://www.siecus.org/index.cfm?fuseaction=page.viewpage&pageid=1341&nodeid=1

Solomon-Fears, C. (2015). *Teenage pregnancy prevention: Statistics and programs.* Washington, DC: Congressional Research Service. Retrieved from https://www.fas.org/sgp/crs/misc/RS20301.pdf

Stanger-Hall, K. F., & Hall, D. W. (2011). Abstinence-only education and teen pregnancy rates: Why we need comprehensive sex education in the U.S. *PLoS One, 6*(10), e24658. doi:10.1371/journal.pone.00246658

Sugai, G., & Horner, R. H. (2009). Responsiveness to intervention and school-wide positive behavior supports: Integration of multi-tiered system of approaches. *Exceptionality, 17*(4), 223–237.

U.S. Administration for Children and Families/Office of Planning Research and Evaluation. (2014, April). *Personal responsibility education program (PREP) evaluation.* Retrieved from http://www.acf.hhs.gov/sites/default/files/opre/prep_dis_brief_032814_edited.pdf

U.S. Department of Health and Human Services. (2015). *Teen pregnancy prevention evidence review.* Retrieved from http://tppevidencereview.aspe.hhs.gov/Default.aspx

World Health Organization (WHO). (2014). *Adolescents: Health risks and solutions fact sheet.* Retrieved from http://www.who.int/mediacentre/factsheets/fs345/en/

9

PROMOTING THE SEXUAL HEALTH OF CHILDREN AND ADOLESCENTS IN THE COMMUNITY

In previous chapters, we addressed ways to promote the sexual health of children and adolescents at home and at school. In this chapter, we will extend our discussion to the community's role in promoting sexual health of youth. Although communities are certainly inclusive of homes and schools, the focus of this chapter is on broader community efforts, particularly those of community-based organizations (CBOs), healthcare providers, and faith-based organizations.

Promoting sexual health of youth in communities can be facilitated through the development of community coalitions. ACT (Assets Coming Together) for Youth Center of Excellence (2015), a partnership among Cornell University, the Center for School Safety, and the University of Rochester that focuses on the promotion of positive youth development and adolescent sexual health, posits that a successful community coalition will include the following nine components: (1) engage community partners across sectors, (2) engage youth in the coalition, (3) understand the core principles of positive youth development, (4) conduct a comprehensive community assessment, (5) address community collaboration with intentionality, (6) plan for evidence-based programing, (7) initiate a community conversation to question local norms regarding adolescent sexual health, (8) assess and enhance community readiness for change, and (9) address inequities in the community.

In engaging community partners across sectors, ACT for Youth (2015) emphasizes the importance of collaborating with partners across the multiple community sectors in which youth engage. For example, depending on the particular needs of the community, community coalitions may find it beneficial to enlist the support of youth, local businesses, faith communities, families, healthcare providers, and policy makers. By coordinating efforts with multiple community partners, community coalitions' initiatives to promote sexual health among youth are not only supported proximally but also distally, as support and involvement from and between multiple agencies is more likely to maintain and generalize impact. To enhance collaboration among partners, ACT for Youth (2015) shares the asset-based community development model (ABCD), a model developed by the Asset-Based Community Development Institute of Northwestern University (ABCD Institute, 2009) to effectively link multiple assets across partners to the community's identified needs. ACT for Youth (2015) also provides resources to guide identification of assets including an individual assets worksheet and organizational assets worksheet. The interested reader may wish to access additional information about the ABCD model and the Institute at the ACT for Youth (2015) and ABCD Institute (2009) websites.

Youth engagement is also a critical component of a successful community coalition (ACT for Youth, 2015). As such, it is essential that community coalitions certainly involve youth in initiatives that impact them (e.g., sexual health promotion of youth) and also in initiatives that impact the broader community. By including youth in all phases of community initiatives, especially initial planning, community coalitions can ensure youth voices, interests, and needs remain central to conversations surrounding sexual health promotion. Developmentally, structured youth–adult partnerships can also work toward fostering the development of mutually beneficial relationships that, in turn, enhance learning. For the interested reader, the ACT for Youth website offers a valuable resource describing youth participation in communities developed by Zeldin, Petrokubi, Collura, Camino, and Skolaski (2009) from the Center for Nonprofits at the University of Wisconsin-Madison, as well as guidance in preparing and supporting youth evaluators.

Successful community coalitions also understand the core principles of positive youth development including a focus on strengths and positive outcomes, youth voice and engagements, strategies that involve all youth, community involvement and collaboration, and long-term commitment (ACT for Youth, 2015). That is, community coalitions recognize and build youths' strengths, partner with all youth, and support youth for over the first 20 years of their lives. The ACT for Youth website offers exemplary resources to promote understanding of positive youth development, including a manual authored by Jutta Dotterweich of Cornell University (2014), a narrated presentation (2015) designed to provide an introduction to youth development, a chapter outlining the principles of youth development (S. Hamilton, M. Hamilton, & Pittman, 2004), and an overview of the key features of the positive youth development framework (Whitlock, 2004).

To conduct a comprehensive community assessment, community coalitions will also want to gather data to describe both the prevalence of sexual risk behaviors (and safer sexual behaviors) as well as the populations impacted by the behaviors (ACT for Youth, 2015). Depending on the community, data regarding sexual behaviors of youth in the community may already be readily available (e.g., YRBS) or may be collected via surveys such as the YRBS (Kann et al., 2014). An additional component of conducting a community assessment includes the identification of risk and protective factors for youth in the community. Examples of risk and protective factors were identified in Chapter 3 and may exist in multiple domains of youths' lives including community, home, and social networks, as well as unique individual factors. Because data regarding risk and protective factors may be less accessible than the prevalence of youth sexual behaviors, community coalitions may wish to collect these data through surveys and interviews. To guide the data collection process, ACT for Youth (2015) offers a data collection planning tool that assists community coalitions in collaboratively determining assessment questions and how the data for each question will be collected. Finally, as part of a comprehensive community assessment, community coalitions will want to identify community resources to support the promotion of sexual health among youth in the community, and the ACT for Youth (2015) provides exemplary resources to guide this portion of the assessment process.

In addressing community collaboration with intentionality, ACT for Youth (2015) suggests that the success of collaborative efforts can be impacted by time, turf, and trust and further conceptualizes five levels of collaboration on a continuum of increasing commitment and complexity: networking (sharing information), coordinating (changing services), cooperating (sharing resources), collaborating (cross-training), and integrating (merging structure). For example, less time and lower levels of trust are necessary when potential collaborators simply network to share information. As well, at this level, although issues of turf may exist, less emphasis is placed on the need to resolve them. Further on the continuum, however, as the time commitment and complexity of partnerships increases (when collaborators consider merging structures, for example), greater levels of trust and an ability to effectively work toward common goals, despite turf issues, are essential. In addition to these considerations and to collaborate with intentionality, ACT for Youth (2015) offers the following key strategies for effective collaboration: recognize the power of time-turf-trust; clarify purpose and goals; establish a common ground/framework; identify roles and responsibilities; establish clear communication paths; use and open structure and processes (e.g., decision making, conflict resolution); encourage participatory leadership; and reflect, recognize, and celebrate. Additional resources to facilitate collaboration within communities are available at the Office of Adolescent Health (2015).

The U.S. Department of Health and Human Services' TPP Evidence Review (2015) described in Chapter 8 is a resource community coalitions may use to inform their selection of evidence-based programing to promote sexual health among youth. A useful framework for communities to plan for evidence-based programing, and to perhaps use in conjunction with the evidence review, is Promoting Science-Based Approaches Using Getting to Outcomes (PSBA-GTO)—a framework that provides strategies communities can use from conducting a community needs assessment to implementing, evaluating, and sustaining evidence-based programing to prevent adolescent pregnancy, STIs, and HIV infection. The PSBA-GTO is a 10-step, comprehensive framework that has been implemented by the CDC, ETR Associates, and Healthy Teen Network, as well as states across the nation. It guides community coalitions through conducting a community needs assessment, beginning a logic model and developing goals, identifying evidence-based programs (communities may wish to access and review community programs in the U.S. Department of Health and Human Services' TPP Evidence Review), assessing program fit with the community context or adapting programs to enhance fit, examining organizational capacities to implement the selected program (such as personnel, fiscal, leadership, evaluation, and community partnerships and support), developing a plan to implement the program, conducting a process evaluation, conducting an outcome evaluation, continuing quality improvement strategies, and developing a sustainability plan (Dotterweich, 2010). Further, the ACT for Youth (2015) website offers additional resources on its website for community coalitions wishing to carefully adapt evidence-based programs using best practices to enhance fit with their communities. Finally, successful community coalitions also initiate community conversations to question local norms regarding adolescent sexual health, assess and enhance readiness for change, and work toward addressing inequities in the community (ACT for Youth, 2015).

With regard to readiness for change, community coalitions may wish to use the community readiness model, developed at the Tri-Ethnic Center (2015) of Colorado State University, to assess a community's readiness for change. The low-cost and user-friendly model has been used across multiple communities to determine communities' readiness to address various issues from health risk behaviors to environmental issues. Through a process of identifying the issue, defining the community, conducting key respondent interviews, scoring to determine the readiness levels, and developing strategies consistent with those readiness levels, the model facilitates assessment of readiness across key dimensions of efforts, community knowledge of efforts, leadership, community climate, community knowledge of the issue, and resources. Stages of readiness include no awareness, denial/resistance, vague awareness, preplanning, preparation, initiation, stabilization, confirmation/expansion, and high level of community ownership. The Tri-Ethnic Center offers community readiness services for a fee, as well as a one-day community readiness training and free online resources including a community readiness assessment handbook.

Community-Based Organizations

CBOs play an essential role in any community coalition, though unlike the roles of families and schools, the research around CBOs' roles in promoting the sexual health of children and adolescents, rather than adults, is still emerging (e.g., Fisher, Reece, Dodge, Wright, Sherwood-Laughlin, & Baldwin, 2010; Fisher, Reece, Wright, Dodge, Sherwood-Laughlin, & Baldwin, 2012). Nevertheless, the research that does exist suggests CBOs can and should be quite central in communities' support of youth sexual health.

For example, using a community-based participatory research approach, Fisher et al. (2012) conducted a study examining the role of CBOs in promoting sexual health of youth in Indiana. Participants for the study were recruited through multiple methods including emails sent to youth-oriented nonprofit organizations, an advertisement in a newsletter distributed to people who work with youth in CBOs, emails sent to professional contacts of persons involved in the study's development, and snowball sampling. Recruitment yielded 169 participants, primarily female (77.5%) and White (82.8%), with a mean age of 35 years. Most participants worked at nonprofit organizations serving primarily heterosexual youth in middle and high school, with a median budget of $347,000 (range $600–$16.3 million). Most CBOs with which the participants were affiliated were not faith-based organizations, although almost half had an affiliation with faith-based organizations.

Survey findings indicated youth generally ask participants questions about personal skills such as values, decision making, communication, assertiveness and negotiation, and looking for help (85.7%) and relationships (68.3%), rather than sexual behavior (33.5%) or sexual health (29.1%). Participants reported programing/services topics most frequently covered by CBOs, as well as resources offered to youth, to be relationship issues (58.0%), alcohol/drugs (56.8%), and communication/refusal skills (53.3%). Topics such as sexual decision making (42.6%), pregnancy (33.1%), HIV/AIDS (32.5%), condom use/safer sex (31.4%), STIs (30.2%), contraception (29.6%), and sexual orientation (29%) were also covered through CBOs, though at a lower frequency. It should be noted, however, that greater percentages of participants reported resources for the aforementioned topics being offered to youth. With regard to programing format, programing was generally led by a staff member or volunteer and offered most frequently through multi-session classes (44.4%) and least frequently through parent involvement (18.9%) or online resources (17.8%). In terms of the CBOs' philosophical approaches to sexual health, most participants (68.1%) expressed the belief their CBO "would support access for youth to sexual health and sexuality-related information and accurate answers to any questions on the topic" (p. 547), whereas 25.5% believed their CBO's approach would be aligned with abstinence-only until marriage, and 24.2% did not respond to the item. Finally, CBOs most frequently had referral protocols for sexual abuse issues (70.4%), domestic violence (62.7%), and psychological distress (58.6%) and least frequently for abortion (33.3%) or sexual orientation issues (37.3%).

Fisher et al. (2012) also compared their findings to a study conducted in Indiana schools by Tanner, Reece, Legocki, and Murray (2007). Unlike individuals working at CBOs, the questions the Tanner et al. (2007) sample received from students were usually focused on sexual behavior, pregnancy, and contraception. Like CBOs, relationship issues were reportedly addressed in school programing. Further, although participants in the Fisher et al. (2012) sample reported their CBOs offered formal programing addressing STIs and HIV/AIDS, findings from the Tanner et al. (2007) sample indicated teachers addressed these topics more frequently—41.7% and 48.7%, respectively. In contrast, schools addressed topics such as abortion and sexual orientation (8.1%) less frequently than CBOs.

Although research regarding the role of CBOs in the promotion of sexual health among youth is still emerging, the findings above indicate CBOs are already supporting youth's sexual health and underscore the importance of including them in community coalitions. In addition, the reported differences between the CBO sample (Fisher et al., 2012) and the school sample (Tanner et al., 2007) further illuminate the importance of collaborating across community agencies and partners, as neither is likely to meet the sexual health needs of youth alone but together may be better able to provide comprehensive coverage across a continuum of care.

For CBOs interested in providing sexual health education for youth, a document titled "Guiding Principles for Sexual Health Education for Young People: A Guide for Community-Based Organizations," developed by the New York State Department of Health's Adolescent Sexual Health Work Group (2010), provides a useful framework for developing sexual health education programing that addresses developmental tasks related to sexuality: accepting his/her body; gender identity and sexual orientation; communicating effectively with family, peers and partners; possessing accurate knowledge of human anatomy and physiology; understanding the risks, responsibilities, outcomes and impacts of sexual actions; possessing the skills needed to take action to reduce his/her risk; knowing how to use and access the healthcare system and other community institutions to seek information and services as needed; setting appropriate sexual boundaries; acting responsibly according to his/her personal values; and forming and maintaining meaningful, healthy relationships. To better support the development of sexually healthy youth, then, the guide offers strategies to realize the following guiding principles of effective sexual health education programs: youth-centered; strength-based; comprehensive; evidence-based; skills-driven; developmentally appropriate; culturally appropriate; supported by parents, families, and communities; facilitate access to health and support services; and measurable outcomes.

Consistent with ACT for Youth's (2015) support of youth engagement in successful community coalitions, the guide provides strategies for CBOs to implement in creating youth-centered programing. After first examining the organization's current structure and culture around youth involvement, CBOs may then work toward addressing any identified barriers through strategies such as scheduling meeting times and locations with youth convenience in mind; providing youth with food at meetings that are scheduled near meal times; and intentionally involving youth in all phases of development and implementation, seeking their input, and providing opportunities for them to engage in decision making around CBO sexual health initiatives.

Similarly, consistent with ACT for Youth's (2015) emphasis on positive youth development, the guide provides strategies for CBOs to adopt a strength-based approach to promoting sexual health among youth through the fostering of youth's assets. The guide suggests that in addition to applying youth development principles, CBOs may also use youth development tools to assess youth's strengths and inform program development. In addition, by focusing on a strength-based approach, CBOs can develop programing that further develops protective factors (see Chapter 3).

In addition to facilitating youth engagement and a strength-based approach to promoting sexual health, the guide provides strategies to inform CBOs' development of comprehensive, evidence-based, and skills-driven sexual health education, specifically stating, "sexual health education provides a full range of scientifically accurate information and options for sexual health and for reducing the negative outcomes of sexual behavior" (p. 4) and emphasizing the importance of adopting or adapting programing with demonstrated effectiveness among youth with which it will be implemented for sexual health outcomes relevant to the community, while facilitating opportunities for youth to not only acquire knowledge but also develop and apply related life skills to improve their own sexual health. Comprehensive programing involves not only broad coverage of topics related to sexual health but also collaboration among CBOs and community partners in the delivery of programing (ACT for Youth, 2015; Rogers, Augustine, & Alford, 2005). In addition to the creation of a community coalition, CBOs seeking to create comprehensive programing may wish to "invite staff members from sexual health organizations to meetings and conferences to provide presentations and share materials; cross-train staff in HIV, STD and pregnancy prevention; and develop integrated messages and materials that address common risk factors" (New York State Department of Health's Adolescent Sexual Health Work Group, 2010, p. 4). Further, consistent with our previous discussions of evidence-based programing and practices, the guide also offers CBOs with guidance in adopting and implementing evidence-based programing to promote sexual health among youth. Finally, the guide offers a useful resource that may assist CBOs in the identification of community-based evidence-based programing—the third edition of "Science and Success: Programs that Work to Prevent Teen Pregnancy, HIV and STIs in the U.S." (Advocates for Youth, 2012). Organized by program setting (i.e., school-based programs, community-based programs, and clinic-based programs), we believe CBOs can use this exceptional resource, along with the findings of the U.S. Department of Health and Human Services' TPP Evidence Review (2015) and the Community Guide (2015), to aid in their study and identification of evidence-based sexual health programing. Finally, the guide provides specific strategies for CBOs to consider as they plan programing that includes skill development. In particular, CBOs may plan programing that guides youth through decision-making and problem-solving exercises, incorporates role-play activities (e.g., initiating a conversation about STI prevention with a partner), provides in vivo opportunities to practice life skills (e.g., searching the internet for an STI testing site), and allows youth to practice skills in community settings.

We provided a comprehensive discussion of developmental and cultural considerations in Chapter 5. In addition, the guide offers the following developmentally appropriate strategies CBOs can use when communicating with youth:

- Use non-threatening questions that help adolescents define their identities;
- Listen without judgment so that adolescents know that you value their opinions;
- Ask open-ended questions to assist adolescents with thinking through their ideas;
- Avoid asking "why" questions, which may put adolescents on the defensive; and,
- Provide examples of how you or someone you know made a decision (e.g., how to handle a personal conflict).

(p. 7)

Further, the guide offers a resource from Advocates for Youth that supports youth leaders in building cultural competence (Messina, 1994).

In planning for sexual health programing, CBOs will also want to ensure programing is supported by parents, families, and the larger community by considering collaborative efforts such as those described by ACT for Youth (2015) and also strategies detailed by the guide (New York State Department of Health's Adolescent Sexual Health Work Group, 2010). For example, CBOs can effectively connect various community partners like schools, families, and other CBOs, plan and host initiatives and events to strengthen familial relationships, and also work with the community in conducting a comprehensive community assessment.

In addition to providing sexual health education programing, a key role CBOs can play in the promotion of youth sexual health is the facilitation of access to health and support services (New York State Department of Health's Adolescent Sexual Health Work Group, 2010). Given that CBOs do not generally provide direct healthcare services, CBOs can be central to youths' physical and mental health needs around sexual health by establishing referral networks with local healthcare providers, developing and providing youth-friendly service directories, and educating youth about access to healthcare services (e.g., requirements for parental consent).

A final guiding principle as CBOs establish sexual health programing is the careful identification and consistent evaluation of measurable outcomes (New York State Department of Health's Adolescent Sexual Health Work Group, 2010). The guide offers specific strategies CBOs can use to develop and measure meaningful outcomes including the use of active and specific verbs and a plan for measuring outcomes both quantitatively and qualitatively.

Healthcare Providers

In addition to CBOs, healthcare providers also play an essential role in a community's promotion of sexual health among youth. In fact, for some youth and their families, healthcare providers, particularly physicians, are the primary source of sexual health information. However, recent discussions and reviews of the literature suggest that although community members may seek this support from their physicians, physicians may not feel comfortable or be prepared to discuss sexual health with their patients, especially youth (Criniti, Andelloux, Woodland, Montgomery, & Hartmann, 2014; Shindel & Parish, 2013).

Given the sexual health needs of individuals, especially youth, it then becomes critical to address physicians' preparedness to address them, so recent conversations have turned to ways to enhance physicians' training (Coleman et al., 2013; Criniti et al., 2014; Shindel & Parish, 2013). For example, one recommendation from a 2013 summit addressing medical education in sexual health is mandatory training in sexual health across medical school and residency (Coleman et al., 2013). Criniti et al. (2014) further offer suggestions for a comprehensive standardized curriculum designed to meet the needs of diverse patients; support the development of physicians' skills in supporting patients' sexual health; and allow for reflective practices in which medical students and residents may develop awareness of, and examine, their own biases around sexuality, so they may better care for their patients in a supportive manner. Specifically, Criniti et al. (2014) recommend the following topics be included in a standardized curriculum for medical students and residents: "reproductive/sexual anatomy and physiology; normal sexual function (including pleasure) and sexual dysfunction; sexual response cycles; gender identity and sexual orientation; contraceptive methods and mechanisms; testing and management of STIs, including HIV; sexual risk reduction techniques; sexual side effects of common medications, treatments and illnesses; sexual abuse and assault (adult and children); health disparities of lesbian, gay, bisexual, and transgender patients and other marginalized populations; how and when to refer patients to sexuality specialists" (p. 73). In addition, to complement a standardized curriculum, Criniti et al. (2014) further recommend the implementation of a sexual wellness framework that shifts the focus to patients' sexual well-being, rather than dysfunction; incorporating different learning models from didactic lectures to applied skills-based learning opportunities; development of standards for curriculum assessment and evaluation; and the creation of national certification standards.

In addition to the above recommendations, school-based health centers (SBHCs) offer another means for youth to receive sexual health supports from healthcare providers (School-Based Health Alliance, 2015). In a recent survey, for example, education about sexual health was one of the top three reasons students reportedly visited the SBHC, following illnesses and vaccines (O'Leary et al., 2014). SBHCs, through a multidisciplinary approach, provide accessible and comprehensive healthcare services typically to school-aged children and adolescents, but also to community members. Recently, data were collected via a triennial national survey administered to school-based, school-linked, and mobile health centers (Lofink et al., 2013). At the time of the survey, 1,930 centers were identified, with 1,485 responding to the survey and data from 1,381 respondents used in the analyses. Findings indicated SBHCs are primarily located in urban areas (54.2%) but are also in rural (27.8%) and suburban (18.0%) areas. Most SBHCs are located in public schools (81.3%) and serve at least one grade of adolescents (82.7%). However, services are often not limited to students within the school in which the SBHCs are located, as SBHCs also serve students from other schools (50.7%), family of student users (37.4%), faculty/school personnel (37.1%), out-of-school youth (33.1%), and other people in the community (18.9%). Staffing models included primary care only (29.2%), primary care and mental health (33.4%), or primary care and mental health plus additional healthcare providers (37.4%) (e.g., health educator, oral health provider, social service case manager, and/or nutritionist).

It should also be noted that although SBHCs are typically housed in schools, they are also an illustrative example of collaboration among community organizations. For example, one of this book's authors works closely with two SBHCs in local high schools. At one of the high schools, the SBHC was established by the county. As such, although the location is within a school, the SBHC's promotion of sexual health actually occurs through strong partnerships with the county, the school, and a local CBO. Similarly, the second SBHC was established by a local university, and efforts to support the sexual health of youth are the result of a university–high school partnership. These types of sponsorships and partnerships are consistent with the findings from the national survey indicating that SBHCs are usually sponsored by community health centers (33.4%), hospitals (26.4%), or local health departments (13.3%), rather than the school system (Lofink et al., 2013). Further, a common characteristic of SBHCs is an advisory board composed of community representatives and organizations, parents, and youth (School-Based Health Alliance, 2015).

With regard to the promotion of sexual health, SBHCs reported offering supports around sexual orientation/gender identity differences (individual: 65.3%; small group: 20.2%; classroom/school-wide: 18.5%), sexual assault/rape prevention and counseling (individual: 76.2%; small group: 22.2%; classroom/school-wide: 20.2%), and intimate partner/teen dating violence prevention and counseling (individual: 75.8%; small group: 26.5%; classroom/school-wide: 22.7%) (Lofink et al., 2013). In addition, SBHCs reported providing direct reproductive health services such as abstinence counseling (82.1%), pregnancy testing (81.2%), STD diagnosis and treatment (69.2%), HIV testing (55.1%) and HIV/AIDS counseling (59.8%), counseling for contraceptive services (64.5%), or gynecological examinations (59.3%). Further, of the survey respondents, 49.8% of SBHCs reported they are prohibited from dispensing contraceptives, predominantly due to school district policy (76.3%) or school policy (54.4%), but also due to health center policy (34%), state law/regulation (27.1%), sponsor policy (23.9%), or state policy (22.6%).

Given the work of SBHCs nationwide, as well as their direct connection to the communities they serve, we believe they should certainly be considered partners in community coalitions. In their role as healthcare providers, they are well positioned to not only provide sexual health education to youth but also to provide direct healthcare services for youths' sexual health needs.

Faith-Based Organizations

In our experience, faith-based organizations may also be instrumental in supporting youths' sexual health. In this emerging area of study, faith-based organizations are navigating their roles in sexual health promotion among youth, and researchers have recently begun studying their roles more closely (Abara, Coleman, Fairchild, Gaddist, & White, 2015; Williams, Dodd, Campbell, Pichon, & Griffith, 2014). For example, in a study conducted in two African American churches and using a community-based participatory research model, Williams et al. (2014) "introduced the largely unexplored perspectives of adult and adolescent congregants to the discourse of involving churches in sexual health education" (p. 341). The churches were located in Flint, Michigan, of Genesee County. Not including the incarcerated population, Genesse County ranked seventh in state for the total number of people living with HIV/AIDS in 2009 (Michigan Department of Community Health, 2009). As such, interventions to support sexual health of youth in this community could be particularly salient. During the study, six focus groups were conducted with 30 adolescents and 19 adults, predominantly African American (84%) and female (67%). The average age for adolescent participants was 15 years, and the average age for adult participants was 47 years. Almost half of the youth participants reported having been sexually active during their lifetime. Findings indicated that they received messages about sexual health information from their churches (primarily the pastors, but sometimes from others within the church), with the primary message being to "wait until you're married." Participants also discussed the complexities of the "church family" and shared mixed views about the supports fellow congregants might offer to support youths' sexual health. Finally, participants shared ways in which they believed the churches could support sexual health such as "making sexual health brochures available, which could be picked up anonymously, posting information about local sexual health resources on the church's website, addressing the emotional aspects of sex, and having a question box where youth could anonymously ask questions related to sex, sexuality, and relationships" (p. 347), but emphasized the desire for opportunities to discuss sex. The findings of this study could provide a starting point for faith-based organizations and communities wishing to explore their role in promoting sexual health among youth. Further, replication of this study could provide faith-based organizations and communities with invaluable information about the needs of their youth and ways the church's youth population believes their specific church may support their sexual health.

Abara et al. (2015) also studied the role of faith-based organizations in promoting sexual health. Specifically, Abara et al. (2015) describe the project Fostering AIDS Initiatives That Heal (F.A.I.T.H.), "a faith-based model for successfully developing, implementing, and sustaining locally developed HIV/AIDS prevention interventions in African American churches in South Carolina" (p. 122). Through a partnership with South Carolina HIV/AIDS Council and local African American churches, across five years, multiple churches received funding to support their HIV/AIDS prevention efforts. Further, each funded church composed its own "care team" to receive comprehensive training across four modules (ICARE) to implement the prevention interventions at their church. The comprehensive training sequence included topics such as an introduction to HIV/AIDS; disparities in the African American community; the African American church and HIV/AIDS; testing; and prevention strategies. Abara et al. (2015) conclude the paper by providing a reflective description of lessons learned that communities may wish to consider useful as they partner with faith-based organizations in their formation of community coalitions. Although the focus of the project was not specifically on youth, it does provide an example of how faith-based organizations can partner in efforts to prevent HIV/AIDS.

School-Based STI Screening

We have reviewed components of successful community coalitions (ACT for Youth, 2015); strategies for CBOs to consider in their roles planning for, and providing, sexual health supports for youth; and considered the roles of healthcare providers and faith-based organizations in the promotion of youth sexual health. In this section, we present an example of a community initiative that illustrates one way various communities have promoted sexual health among youth. In particular, these initiatives, developed through partnering of schools with city governments, states, and/or community agencies to provide healthcare services, are designed to provide youth with education around STIs, screen youth for STIs (typically chlamydia and gonorrhea), and provide treatment or referrals for treatment. The first STI screenings in high schools took place in Louisiana in 1995 and have since been conducted within schools, including some middle schools, across multiple cities including Baltimore, Chicago, Los Angeles, Miami, New York City, Philadelphia, San Francisco, and Washington, D.C. (e.g., Asbel, Newbern, Salmon, Spain, & Goldberg, 2006; Bauer et al., 2004; Burstein, Waterfield, Joffe, Zenilman, Quinn, & Gaydos, 1998; Cohen et al., 1998; Cohen, Nsuami, Martin, & Farley, 1999; Cohen, 2009; Han, Rogers, Nurani, Rubin, & Blank, 2011; Kent, Branzuela, Fischer, Bascom, & Klausner, 2002; Low, Forster, Taylor, & Nsuami, 2013; Nsuami, Nsa, Brennan, Cammarata, Martin, & Taylor, 2013).

Although the process can vary depending on the specific partnership and contextual variables in the community and school, the general process involves notifying parents (and providing an opt-out option), providing an educational overview of STIs, screening, and follow-up or treatment. In Philadelphia, for example, the Philadelphia Department of Public Health partnered with the School District of Philadelphia to serve youth attending the city's public high schools through the Philadelphia High School STD Screening Program (PHSSSP) (Asbel et al., 2006). PHSSSP began in 2003 and serves approximately 30,000 students each year. Following parent notification, students attend an educational and screening session in groups of approximately 60. Disease intervention specialists and STD educators provide a 25-minute educational session, during which time students learn about the screening process and are encouraged to complete the screening if they have ever had sexual intercourse. During the screening process, students are provided a brown paper bag with "1) a form to be completed by the students that requested name, date of birth, address, phone number, racial identification (including Hispanic as a category), their preferred method for PDPH staff to contact them, and a self-selected secret code; 2) a urine collection cup; and 3) a card with a PDPH telephone number to call for test results" (p. 615). All students are then escorted to the restroom in small groups to provide a urine sample and then are instructed to return the brown paper bag with all contents. That is, even students who do not provide a urine sample return the brown bag. Samples are then tested at a lab, and students may call for their results. Students with positive results are then informed of the date staff will return to provide treatment and are also told treatment will be available for their partners who attend the same school. Students who are treated are also provided with referral information for community service providers to obtain care. Staff also actively follow up with students who have positive results but do not attend the treatment day.

Although school-based STI screening is not a comprehensive approach to promoting sexual health of youth in a community, it is certainly a critical component and an example of how partnerships within a larger community coalition can effectively meet specific needs of youth. Together, additional community efforts and supports such as comprehensive sexuality education can work in concert with initiatives such as school-based STI screening to fully support youths' sexual health needs.

The purpose of this chapter was to provide an overview of the role of the community in promoting sexual health among youth. To this end, we chose to highlight considerations we believe are particularly salient in sexual health promotion within communities such as the development of community coalitions (ACT for Youth, 2015) and the roles of CBOs, healthcare providers, and faith-based organizations in promoting sexual health. Finally, we presented an example of a community initiative that began 20 years ago and has since been implemented in multiple cities nationwide.

References

ABCD Institute. (2009). *The asset-based community development institute: School of Education and Social Policy, Northwestern University.* Retrieved from http://www.abcdinstitute.org

Abara, W., Coleman, J. D., Fairchild, A., Gaddist, B., & White, J. (2015). A faith-based community partnership to address HIV/AIDS in southern United States: Implementation, challenges, and lessons learned. *Journal of Religion and Health, 54,* 122–133.

ACT for Youth Center of Excellence. (2015). *Community approaches to adolescent sexual health.* Retrieved from http://www.actforyouth.net/sexual_health/community

Advocates for Youth. (2012). *Science and success: Programs that work to prevent teen pregnancy, HIV and STIs in the U.S.* (3rd ed.). Washington, DC: Advocates for Youth. Retrieved from http://www.advocatesforyouth.org/publications/367-science-and-success-2nd-ed-programs-that-work-to-prevent-teen-pregnancy-hiv-and-stis-in-the-us

Asbel, L. E., Newbern, E. C., Salmon, M., Spain, C.V., & Goldberg, M. (2006). School-based screening for chlamydia trachomatis and Neisseria gonnorrhoeae among Philadelphia public high school students. *Sexually Transmitted Diseases, 33*(10), 614–620.

Bauer, H. M., Chartier, M., Kessell, E., Packel, L., Brammeier, M., Little, M., et al. (2004). Chlamydia screening of youth and young adults in non-clinical settings throughout California. *Sexually Transmitted Diseases, 31,* 409–414.

Burstein, G. R., Waterfield, G., Joffe, A., Zenilman, J. M., Quinn, T. C., & Gaydos, C. A. (1998). Screening for gonorrhea and chlamydia by DNA amplification in adolescents attending middle school health centers: Opportunity for early intervention. *Sexually Transmitted Diseases, 25,* 395–402.

Cohen, D. A. (2009). School-based STD screening: What next? *Sexually Transmitted Infections, 85,* 160–162.

Cohen, D. A., Nsuami, M., Etame, R. B., Tropez-Sims, S., Abdalian, S., Farley, T. A., et al. (1998). A school-based chlamydia control program using DNA amplification technology. *Pediatrics, 101,* 1–5.

Cohen, D. A., Nsuami, M., Martin, D. H., & Farley, T. A. (1999). Repeated school-based screening for sexually transmitted diseases: A feasible strategy for reaching adolescents. *Pediatrics, 104,* 1281–1285.

Coleman, E., Elders, J., Satcher, D., Shindel, A., Parish, S., Kenagy, G., et al. (2013). Summit on medical school education in sexual health: Report of an expert consultation. *Journal of Sexual Medicine, 10,* 924–938.

Criniti, S., Andelloux, M., Woodland, M. B., Montgomery, O. C., & Hartmann, S. U. (2014). The state of sexual health education in U.S. medicine. *American Journal of Sexuality Education, 9,* 65–80.

Dotterweich, J. (2010). *Planning for evidence-based programming: Introducing the PSBA-GTO.* ACT for Youth Center of Excellence (in consultation with Healthy Teen Network) [narrated presentation]. Retrieved from http://www.actforyouth.net/resources/n/n_plan4ebp

Dotterweich, J. (2014). *Manual: Positive youth development 101.* ACT for Youth Center of Excellence. Retrieved from http://www.actforyouth.net/youth_development/professionals/manual.cfm

Dotterweich, J. (2015). *Positive youth development.* ACT for Youth Center of Excellence [narrated presentation]. Retrieved from http://www.actforyouth.net/resources/n/n_pyd

Fisher, C. M., Reece, M., Dodge, B., Wright, E., Sherwood-Laughlin, C., & Baldwin, K. (2010). Expanding our reach: The potential for youth development professionals in community-based organizations to provide sexuality information. *American Journal of Sexuality Education, 5,* 36–53.

Fisher, C. M., Reece, M., Wright, E., Dodge, B., Sherwood-Laughlin, C., Baldwin, K. (2012). The role of community-based organizations in adolescent sexual health promotion. *Health Promotion Practice, 13*(4), 544–552.

Hamilton, S. F., Hamilton, M. A., & Pittman, K. (2004). Principles for youth development. In S. F. Hamilton, & M. A. Hamilton (Eds.), *The youth development handbook: Coming of age in American communities* (pp. 3–22). Thousand Oaks, CA: Sage.

Han, J. S., Rogers, M. E., Nurani, S., Rubin, S., & Blank, S. (2011). Patterns of chlamydia/gonorrhea positivity among voluntarily screened New York City public high school students. *Journal of Adolescent Health, 49*, 252–257.

Kann, L., Kinchen, S., Shanklin, S. L., Flint, K. H., Hawkins, J., Harris, W. A., et al. (2014). Youth risk behavior surveillance – United States, 2013. *CDC Morbidity and Mortality Weekly Report, 63*(4), 1–168.

Kent, C. K., Branzuela, A., Fischer, L., Bascom, T., & Klausner, J. D. (2002). Chlamydia and gonorrhea screening in San Francisco high schools. *Sexually Transmitted Diseases, 29*, 373–375.

Lofink, H., Kuebler, J., Juszczak, L., Schlitt, J., Even, M., Rosenberg, J., et al. (2013). *2010–2011 school-based health alliance census report.* Washington, DC: School-Based Health Alliance.

Low, N., Forster, M., Taylor, S., & Nsuami, M. J. (2013). Repeat chlamydia screening among adolescents: Cohort study in a school-based programme in New Orleans. *Sexually Transmitted Infections, 89*(1), 20–24.

Messina, S. A. (1994). *A youth leader's guide to building cultural competence.* Washington, DC: Advocates for Youth.

Michigan Department of Community Health. (2009). *HIV/AIDS rates by race/ethnicity in 25 highest HIV prevalence counties in Michigan: Focus on Hispanics.* Retrieved from https://www.michigan.gov/documents/mdch/07_01_2009_HIVAIDS_Rates_by_Race_ethn_Counties_07.2009_286633_7.pdf

New York State Department of Health's Adolescent Sexual Health Work Group. (2010). *Guiding principles for sexual health education for young people: A guide for community-based organizations.* Retrieved from http://planaheadnewyork.com/publications/0206/index.htm

Nsuami, M. J., Nsa, M., Brennan, C., Cammarata, C. L., Martin, D. H., & Taylor, S. N. (2013). Chlamydia positivity in New Orleans public high schools, 1996–2005: Implications for clinical and public health practices. *Academic Pediatrics, 13*(4), 308–315.

Office of Adolescent Health. (2015). *Building collaborations.* Retrieved from http://www.hhs.gov/ash/oah/oah-initiatives/teen_pregnancy/training/building-collaborations.html#community

O'Leary, S. T., Lee, M., Federico, S., Barnard, J., Lockhart, S., Albright, K., et al. (2014). School-based health centers as patient-centered medical homes. *Pediatrics, 134*(5), 957–964.

Rogers, J., Augustine, J., & Alford, S. (2005). *Integrating efforts to prevent HIV, other STIs, and pregnancy among teens.* Washington, DC: Advocates for Youth.

School-Based Health Alliance. (2015). *School-based health alliance: Redefining health for kids and teens.* Retrieved from http://www.sbh4all.org

Shindel, A. W., & Parish, S. J. (2013). Sexuality education in North American medical schools: Current status and future directions. *Journal of Sexual Medicine, 10*, 3–18.

Tanner, A., Reece, M., Legocki, L., & Murray, M. (2007). Informal sexuality education in schools: Student's sexuality-related questions asked of public school personnel. *American Journal of Sexuality Education, 2*, 79–96.

The Community Guide. (2015). *Preventing HIV/AIDS, other STIs, and teen pregnancy: Interventions for adolescents.* Retrieved from http://www.thecommunityguide.org/hiv/adolescents.html

Tri-Ethnic Center. (2015). *Community readiness.* Retrieved from http://triethniccenter.colostate.edu/communityReadiness_home.htm

U.S. Department of Health and Human Services. (2015). *Teen pregnancy prevention evidence review.* Retrieved from http://tppevidencereview.aspe.hhs.gov/Default.aspx

Whitlock, J. (2004). *Understanding youth development principles and practices.* ACT for Youth Upstate Center of Excellence Research Facts and Findings. Retrieved from http://www.actforyouth.net/resources/rf/rf_understandyd_0904.pdf

Williams, T. T., Dodd, D., Campbell, B., Pichon, L. C., & Griffith, D. M. (2014). Discussing adolescent sexual health in African-American churches. *Journal of Religion and Health, 53,* 339–351.

Zeldin, S., Petrokubi, J., Collura, J., Camino, L., & Skolaski, J. (2009). *Strengthening communities through youth participation: Lessons learned from the ACT for youth initiative.* Ithaca, NY: ACT for Youth Center of Excellence. Retrieved from http://ecommons.library.cornell.edu/bitstream/1813/19326/2/Strengthen.pdf

10

CONCLUSION AND FUTURE DIRECTIONS

Our aim in writing this book was two-fold. First, we wanted to introduce the reader to the topic of sexual health, as it pertains to youth. We began by presenting the state of the field, sexual behaviors in which youth engage, sexual risk and protective factors, standards and professional guidelines for promoting sexual health of youth, developmental and cultural considerations, and a discussion of promoting sexual health of LGBTQIA youth. Then, in the remaining three chapters, we specifically addressed considerations in promoting sexual health of youth across settings—specifically at home, in schools, and in communities. As noted below, the field is ever growing and is in need of continued growth, across these areas.

First, in Chapter 2, a review of sexual behaviors among youth revealed adolescents are engaging in some protective sexual behaviors (Kann et al., 2014). Areas of note among youth who completed the high school 2013 YRBS include condom use during last intercourse, birth control pill use, and being tested for HIV. In particular, 59.1% of youth reported using a condom during last intercourse, with a prevalence of 65.8% among males and 73% among Black males. Further, 19% of youth reported they or their partner used a birth control pill, with a prevalence of 25.9% among White youth and an increase across grade levels. Finally, 12.9% of youth reported being tested for HIV, with a prevalence of 19.8% among Black youth and 20.9% among Black females. In addition to these behaviors, 85.3% of youth reported having been taught in school about AIDS or HIV infection.

The review of sexual behaviors among youth who completed the high school 2013 YRBS also revealed engagement in risky behaviors (Kann et al., 2014). Nationally, 46.8% of youth reported they had ever had sexual intercourse, with a prevalence of 30% among ninth graders and 68.4% among Black males. Nationally, 5.6% of youth reported having had sexual intercourse before the age of

13 years, with a greater prevalence among males within each grade level and racial group and a prevalence of 24% among Black males—the prevalence across other grade levels, racial groups, and gender was below 10%. Fifteen percent of youth reported having had sexual intercourse with four or more persons during their life, with the prevalence increasing across grade levels (23.4% in 12th grade) and a prevalence of 37.5% among Black males. Nationally, 34% of youth reported currently being sexually active (within the last 3 months), with a prevalence of 47% among Black males and 50.7% among females in 12th grade. With regard to pregnancy prevention, 13.7% of youth reported they did not use any method to prevent pregnancy during last intercourse, with a prevalence of 23.7% among Hispanic females and 18.1% among females in the ninth grade. Finally, 22.4% of youth reported they drank alcohol or used drugs before last intercourse. Further, although national data from the middle school YRBS are not available, data specific to states and cities, for example, indicate the youth in middle school are also engaging in sexual risk behaviors. YRBS data also indicated a greater percentage of youth who identified as gay, lesbian, or bisexual (rather than heterosexual or unsure) engaged in the measured sexual risk behaviors (Kann et al., 2011).

In addition, a review of risk and protective factors, particularly "alterable"/ modifiable risk and protective factors in Chapter 3 (Sinclair, Christenson, & Thurlow, 2005), illuminated the important contributions of community, school, family, and peer influences in promoting sexual health of youth. For example, although more research is certainly needed, youth involvement in the community, particularly faith communities, for example, may positively influence adolescents' engagement in sexual risk behaviors (Crosby, DiClemente, Wingood, Harrington, Davies, & Oh, 2002; Kirby & Lepore, 2007; Markham et al., 2010). Relatedly, school connectedness and teachers may also serve as protective factors for some sexual risk behaviors (McNeely & Falci, 2004; Paul, Fitzjohn, Herbison, & Dickson, 2000, as cited in Markham et al., 2010; Resnick et al., 1997, as cited in Markham et al., 2010). With regard to family and peers, parental communication (Jaccard & Dittus, 1993, as cited in Whitaker & Miller, 2000), parental monitoring (Huebner & Howell, 2003), parent–family connectedness (Resnick et al., 1997), and partner connectedness (e.g., see Ford, Sohn, & Lepkowski, 2001, cited in Markham et al., 2010; see Manlove, Ryan, & Franzetta, 2004, cited in Markham et al., 2010) were found to have a protective influence on sexual risk behaviors.

In addition to factors that may have a protective association with sexual risk behaviors of youth, we also reviewed risk factors. Within the community and school, for example, engagement in sexual risk behaviors was associated with factors such as living in a disorganized environment, defined as having high rates of community violence, substance abuse, and hunger, as well as a lack of school connectedness (Kirby & Lepore, 2007). Further, early sexual debut was associated with familial risk factors such as poor parental relationships, living in a nonintact family, and having parents with lower educational levels (Price & Hyde, 2009). Finally, having older friends, friends who engage in status offenses or nonstatus delinquent offenses, or older romantic partners was associated with adolescent sexual risk behaviors (Kirby & Lepore, 2007; Marin, Kirby, Hudes, Coyle, & Gomez, 2006; Morrison-Beedy, Xia, & Passmore, 2013).

We presented an overview of state laws and standards regarding sexual education in Chapter 4, noting that 22 states and the District of Columbia require public schools teach sexual education and 33 states and the District of Columbia require students receive instruction about HIV/AIDS (Guttmacher Institute, 2014). For states that do require sexual education in schools, most have similar requirements such as the provision of information that is medically accurate and age- or developmentally appropriate, and 26 states and the District of Columbia require the inclusion of skill development in the areas of healthy sexuality (including avoiding coerced sex), healthy decision making, and family communication, for example. Some states have either developed or are in the process of developing comprehensive and inclusive standards for the provision of sexual education, and recently, the FoSE (2014) developed nationwide standards. The NSES (FoSE, 2014) provides a national set of standards that represents best practices consistent with the most current research related to sexual education.

Despite the advances in sexual education across the nation, continued growth is imperative. Of particular note, all states do not require sexual or HIV/AIDS education be provided. Further, of states that do, only 18 states and the District of Columbia require information on contraception be provided in sexual education, 19 states require instruction on the importance of engaging in sexual activity only within marriage, and only 12 states require discussion of sexual orientation (with three requiring only instruction of "negative information" regarding sexual orientation). Finally, many state laws regarding sexual education (e.g., Alabama) are undeveloped and/or outdated, lacking both research-based practices and inclusive guidelines.

In Chapter 5, we underscored the importance of healthy sexual development across childhood and adolescence, with the recognition that sexual development begins in infancy. We also discussed ways to provide developmentally appropriate sexual health education for all youth, with an emphasis on using the NSES (FoSE, 2014) as a guide and multitiered systems of supports as a framework for delivering developmentally appropriate and culturally responsive sexual health education that is also inclusive of individuals with disabilities (Burns & Gibbons, 2012; Doll & Cummings, 2008).

Additional attention to supporting the sexual health needs of individuals with disabilities, as well as ethnic minority youth, especially Latino youth, is needed (Cardoza, Documét, Fryer, Gold, & Butler, 2012; Elster, Jarosik, VanGeest, & Fleming, 2003; Goesling, Colman, Trenholm, Terzian, & Moore, 2014; Larson, Sandelowski, & McQuistan, 2012; McNeely & Blanchard, 2009). In particular, we reemphasize that further research exploring the larger societal and political variables that could account for racial and ethnic differences in sexual risk behaviors be conducted. For instance, it may be beneficial to explore the extent to which disparities in access to adequate health care documented for ethnic minority youth may have an impact on access to sexual health services. Overall, to best meet the sexual health needs of all youth, we assert there needs to be specific focused attention and more concentrated efforts from policy makers, researchers, and preventionists and interventionists who work with diverse youth.

Although research around supporting the sexual health of youth in the LGBTQ community is just emerging and is still in great need, Chapter 6 highlighted some of the advances that will be critical as research and conversations continue. For example, Elia and Eliason (2010) delineate principles that can be used to frame the development and delivery of inclusive sexuality education. As another example, the CDC (2014) has developed a framework of school-based strategies that can be used to address HIV among young men who have sex with men. Although these advances are certainly promising, continued research and advocacy is absolutely necessary, as there is a glaring absence of inclusive sexual health programing designed to meet LGBT youths' physical and social-emotional needs (Kubicek, 2010).

Efforts at home play an essential role in the promotion of sexual health of youth (Chapter 7). In particular, effective family and youth communication, as well as parental monitoring, can work toward preventing youth engagement in sexual risk behaviors and promoting healthy sexual behaviors (Kirby & Lepore, 2007). Similar to the environmental risk and protective factors described in Chapter 3, communication and parental monitoring are considered "alterable" factors that, with supports and education, can be modified or enhanced (Sinclair et al., 2005). In particular, before and during youths' adolescence, parents and caregivers can learn not only effective and direct communication strategies but also factual information about youth sexual health and sexual risk behaviors. Further, research supports the impact of having multiple conversations that are open, frequent, and spontaneous, especially before youth have begun having romantic relationships or engaging in sexual activity (Eisenberg, Sieving, Bearinger, Swain, & Resnick, 2006; Hutchinson, J. Jemmott, L. Jemmott, Braverman, & Fong, 2003), and there are multiple ways in which preventionists/interventionists can be supportive of these efforts. Similarly, the protective impact of parental monitoring (e.g., Borawski, Ievers-Landis, Lovegreen, & Trapl, 2003; Huebner & Howell, 2003) and parent knowledge of youths' peer groups on youths' engagement in sexual risk behaviors has also been supported.

As noted in Chapter 8, schools also play a critical role in promoting sexual health of youth. In particular, given the roles schools play in youths' lives, schools are the structures where sexuality education would be most accessible in a comprehensive, systematic, and developmentally appropriate fashion for youth from childhood through adolescence. Further, recent advances provide much-needed supports for schools that do, or wish to, provide comprehensive sexuality education: the NSES (FoSE, 2014) and the CDC *Health Education Curriculum Analysis Tool* (CDC, 2012). In addition to the instruction of sexual health, the range of personnel in schools (from educators to healthcare providers and mental health professionals) can add an additional layer of support in the delivery and receipt of comprehensive sexuality education. Finally, with the recent passage of the ACA, including the PREP (CDC, 2010; SIECUS, 2010; Solomon-Fears, 2014), it is hopeful the provision of sexuality education in schools may be enhanced.

Despite the promise schools hold, however, the provision of sexuality education, especially comprehensive or inclusive sexuality education, is not required in all public schools, nor is it routinely provided if not required. Further, as covered in more detail in Chapter 4, states that do require that sexuality education be provided in schools vary in content requirements, and it is likely there is also variation in implementation across schools that do provide sexuality education. In addition, even when schools do wish to provide comprehensive sexuality education, they may be limited by funding restrictions (SIECUS, 2010), and some states may choose not to accept funding for comprehensive sexuality education (U.S. Administration for Children and Families/Office of Planning Research and Evaluation, 2014). Finally, schools that do wish to provide comprehensive sexuality education will need to carefully balance factors such as potentially conflicting community beliefs and supports, as well as educator readiness to teach comprehensive sexuality education, for example.

Finally, communities also play an instrumental role in promoting the sexual health of youth (Chapter 9). Specifically, as outlined by ACT for Youth (2015), careful development of successful community coalitions can ensure the voices of youth and the commitment of partners across the community and across disciplines. As such, the broader community is not simply invested in youths' health but also offers data-driven comprehensive care and supports at multiple levels that is more likely to reach more youth. For example, across disciplines and possibly geography, a successful community coalition could partly be developed through the coordinated inclusion of CBOs and healthcare providers (possibly through existing SBHCs), organizations that are typically already offering sexual health supports to youth (Fisher, Reece, Wright, Dodge, Sherwood-Laughlin, & Baldwin, 2012; New York State Department of Health's Adolescent Sexual Health Work Group, 2010; O'Leary et al., 2014; School-Based Health Alliance, 2015). Finally, although the study of faith-based organizations' role in promoting sexual health of youth is just emerging, some communities might find their faith-based organizations have an interest in supporting the community's efforts and in being strong allies and partners within a community coalition.

Though resources for successful community efforts abound, one area of needed growth in communities is the preparation of all healthcare providers, especially physicians, in supporting the sexual health of youth (Coleman et al., 2013; Criniti, Andelloux, Woodland, Montgomery, & Hartmann, 2014; Shindel & Parish, 2013). Given that sexual health is often first viewed in terms of one's physical health, physicians are often the first, or primary contact, for youth and their families. However, data show many practicing physicians feel unprepared to initiate or have conversations about sexual health with youth and that sexual health training for medical students and residents is currently lacking. As a result, recent attention has been directed to ways medical students and residents can be comprehensively trained in sexual health (Coleman et al., 2013; Criniti et al., 2014; Shindel & Parish, 2013).

Home, School, and Community Collaboration

Throughout this book (particularly in Chapter 8), we have provided examples of how multitiered system of supports (MTSS; Burns & Gibbons, 2012) and population-based mental health models (Doll & Cummings, 2008), models that have been typically applied in school contexts to promote adaptive academic, behavioral, and social-emotional functioning, can be used as a framework to promote sexual health of youth. In brief, the guiding principles of these models are the use of formative assessments to guide decision making about supports that are provided on a continuum of need. Specifically, a core curriculum is provided for all youth within the system (Tier 1), and universal screening assessment is conducted periodically with all youth to assess youth progress and determine which youth may benefit from additional, more focused supports often, but not necessarily, in the form of small group instruction designed to support specific skills (Tier 2), or intense, individualized supports (Tier 3). Youth who receive Tier 2 and Tier 3 supports also are assessed more frequently, so their progress can be closely monitored, and changes to the supports they are receiving may be more responsive. For example, with time, an adolescent may no longer need Tier 2 supports and may receive the core curriculum only, or assessment data may suggest the adolescent could benefit from additional supports (Tier 3). Readers are referred to Chapter 3 and Chapter 8, as well as Burns and Gibbons (2012) and Doll and Cummings (2008) for more detailed descriptions of the models.

A call to support sexual health of youth by understanding the multiple systems within which youth function and through an integrated and coordinated manner is not new (e.g., ASCD/CDC, 2014; Kotchick, Shaffer, Forehand, & Miller, 2001; Office of the Surgeon General, 2001). For example, Kotchick et al. (2001) proposed a valuable multisystemic perspective focused on three systems of influence (the self, family, and extrafamilial systems) situated within higher order sociocultural, economic, and political systems. In addition, the ASCD/CDC (2014) has emphasized the necessity of a public health and education collaboration to support youth's health needs and proposed a Whole School, Whole Community, Whole Child (WSCC) model.

We believe the adoption of a multitiered system of supports framework to promote the sexual health of youth complements the multisystemic perspective (Kotchick et al., 2001) and the WSCC model and provides a structure for continuous assessment and the implementation of data-driven, evidence-based interventions designed to meet the needs of *all* youth. Further, given that preventionists/interventionists in home, school, and community settings tend to separately, and at time informally, use these models, a coordinated approach across settings could enhance an integrative approach to supporting youth. As such, we propose a multitiered system of supports framework with youth can be applied not only in single structures or systems, such as schools, but systematically across the multiple settings of home, school, and community.

In closing and in consideration of this proposed model, let us revisit a case scenario initially presented in Chapter 7.

Trina, a Hispanic female, is a 15-year-old high school freshman who just transitioned to a large public high school of 3,600 students from her smaller Catholic middle school. The public high school is relatively diverse and includes a mixture of White (50%), Latino (30%), African American (15%), and students of Middle Eastern and Asian backgrounds (5%). Trina lives with her father (Marcus) and mother (Maria) and her 10-year-old younger brother (Isaac) in a northeastern mid-size city. Isaac is in fifth grade at the same Catholic school Trina attended. Trina's family emigrated from Mexico when she was a baby and is very close and tight-knit. Maria is a stay-at-home mom, while Marcus is a manager at a local car dealership and is a mechanic by training, but his hours have recently been cut back, and some financial challenges have ensued.

Trina's family is part of a larger extended family that lives in the same town comprised of aunts, uncles, and cousins who comprise the primary group with which Trina's family interacts. Both sets of grandparents still reside in Mexico. Maria and Marcus send money back to Mexico to financially support their parents. Spanish is spoken in the home, but Trina and Isaac have been instructed in English and are more comfortable with English. Marcus is also comfortable in English, but Maria is more comfortable speaking Spanish. The other social and community group the family interacts with are members of the local Catholic parish. For instance, the family is very involved in church events and activities. They attend church regularly. Trina's mother goes to mass daily. Trina's parents wanted her to attend a Catholic high school but were concerned about the financial implications of the tuition and are working hard to set money away for college tuition.

As Trina transitioned to high school, she has made many new friends on the high school soccer team and in her classes. Recently, she has met an older boy in his junior year on the soccer team. He has asked her to the fall Homecoming dance and would like to "hang out" with her at his house one day when his parents are at work. At this point, Trina has received no formal instruction in school about sexual risk behaviors, STIs/HIV, pregnancy prevention, or contraception, as health class is provided during the sophomore year and she did not receive instruction in sexual health while in the Catholic school. Trina approaches her school psychologist and begins asking questions about how one can avoid pregnancy. Although she does not think that her relationship will result in sexual activity or intercourse, she feels wholly unprepared to enter the world of dating and being in new social situations that involve dating and the presence of males. She wants to "hang out" with this boy, but she is afraid of being in an uncomfortable situation. She knows that she is not ready for sexual activity but also does not know where to turn for answers about questions. When she started menstruation a couple of years ago, her mother explained some things about her body and how her monthly cycle worked, but she felt that the conversation was awkward (Guzman, Golub, Caal, Hickman, & Ramos, 2013). Her mother also told her that she needed to "be careful" and "safe," and Trina believed that her mother was cautioning her to avoid sexual advances from boys, but she was nervous about asking more specific questions as to how she might actually do this. Trina mentioned to her mother that she would like to go to the fall Homecoming dance, and her mother consented and left it at that, focusing more on questions about what she should wear, how she will be transported there, and in general what needs to be done to prepare for the event because this was not a custom in Mexico. Maria felt that the discussion about Homecoming might have been a good opportunity to talk more about sexual activity and the risks for pregnancy and STIs, and contraception, but then dismissed this thought as she believed the conversation would be premature and perhaps give her daughter unspoken permission that sexual activity is okay (Rouvier, Campero, Walker, & Caballero, 2011). Trina approached the school psychologist for some assistance in how she can talk with her mom about her feelings and learn more about how to say "no" to sexual advances if such a situation would occur. Trina was very sure that she was not ready for sexual activity, but also felt that she did not have nearly the information that other peers had who have been exposed to health instruction in a public middle school. She was considering turning to her peers for advice, but also felt that her mom has always been supportive of her, and she is close to her mom. Trina also felt close to her dad, but from her perspective, she felt that her mom is the one to approach for "girl things" like this.

The analysis of this case scenario presented in Chapter 7 provided examples of how a multitiered system of supports could be applied specifically within the context of Trina's individual needs and those of her family. The analysis also incorporated examples of home–school collaboration efforts the school psychologist may consider (e.g., the development of a parent group designed to support the development of effective parent–child communication). Within the framework we are proposing that supporting Trina's sexual health, as well as that of her peers, would also include collaboration between the larger community, the school, and the home. In particular, given that Trina has not yet received formal sexuality education, the school does not offer sexuality education until the tenth grade, and national data show us youth are engaging in sexual risk behaviors as early as the middle school grades (see Chapter 2), the community and school may wish to coordinate efforts in considering options for developmentally appropriate and culturally responsive sexuality education earlier and throughout the curriculum. Specifically, to begin these conversations and to proceed in a coordinated and integrated fashion, the community may wish to develop a community coalition with youth, CBOs, healthcare providers, and business partners across the community (see Chapter 9). It is also possible that Trina's Catholic parish and other faith-based organizations may also wish to partner with the coalition. Together, partners in the coalition may then conduct a comprehensive community assessment, using a tool such as the YRBS as a universal screener and additional forms of data collection such as focus groups or interview, to determine the sexual health needs of youth in the community. In this example, it may be that the school district chooses to administer the middle school and high school YRBS, and then the coalition uses the data together to inform planning for evidence-based sexuality education programing inclusive of all students' needs (Tier 1) and works together to answer logistical questions such as where, when, how, and by whom will the programing be implemented. Although there are numerous advantages to providing sequenced programing across grade levels in schools, it may be that plans are made for community partners such as CBOs and faith-based organizations to also supplement school-based comprehensive sexuality education (an example of Tier 2). Further, for youth who need supports in addition to Tier 1 and Tier 2 supports, health professionals in the community may work in a coordinated effort to provide individualized, more intensive supports, such as wraparound supports (an example of Tier 3). With continued collaboration within the coalition, continued use of data to inform decision making regarding supports and implementation of inclusive supports with fidelity, it is hopeful that collaborative efforts such as these and others within a multitiered system of supports will better meet the sexual health needs of *all* youth within Trina's school district and may ultimately prevent engagement in sexual risk behaviors.

References

ACT for Youth Center of Excellence. (2015). *Community approaches to adolescent sexual health*. Retrieved from http://www.actforyouth.net/sexual_health/community

ASCD/CDC. (2014). *Whole school, whole community, whole child: A collaborative approach to learning and health*. Retrieved from http://www.ascd.org/ASCD/pdf/siteASCD/publications/wholechild/wscc-a-collaborative-approach.pdf

Borawski, E. A., Ievers-Landis, C., Lovegreen, L. D., & Trapl, E. S. (2003). Parental monitoring, negotiated unsupervised time and parental trust: The role of perceived parenting practices in adolescent health risk behaviors. *Journal of Adolescent Health, 33*, 60–70.

Burns, M. K., & Gibbons, K. (2012). *Implementing response-to-intervention in elementary and secondary schools: Procedures to assure scientific-based practice* (2nd ed.). New York, NY: Routledge.

Cardoza, V. J., Documét, P. I., Fryer, C. S., Gold, M. A., & Butler, J. (2012). Sexual health behavior interventions for U.S. Latino adolescents: A systematic review of the literature. *Journal of Pediatric Adolescent Gynecology, 25*, 136–149.

CDC. (2010). *Effective HIV/STD prevention program for youth: A summary of scientific evidence. CDC Division of Adolescent and School Health.* Retrieved from http://www.cdc.gov/healthyyouth/sexualbehaviors/pdf/effective_hiv.pdf

CDC. (2014). *HIV and young men who have sex with men.* Retrieved from Centers for Disease Control and Prevention Website at http://www.cdc.gov/HealthyYouth/sexualbehaviors/pdf/hiv_factsheet_ymsm.pdf

Centers for Disease Control and Prevention (CDC). (2012). *Health education curriculum analysis tool (HECAT).* Retrieved from http://www.cdc.gov/HECAT

Coleman, E., Elders, J., Satcher, D., Shindel, A., Parish, S., Kenagy, G., et al. (2013). Summit on medical school education in sexual health: Report of an expert consultation. *Journal of Sexual Medicine, 10*, 924–938.

Criniti, S., Andelloux, M., Woodland, M. B., Montgomery, O. C., & Hartmann, S. U. (2014). The state of sexual health education in U.S. medicine. *American Journal of Sexuality Education, 9*, 65–80.

Crosby, R. A., DiClemente, R. J., Wingood, G. M., Harrington, K., Davies, S., & Oh, M. K. (2002). Activity of African-American female teenagers in black organizations is associated with STD/HIV protective behaviours: A prospective analysis. *Journal of Epidemiological Community Health, 56*, 549–550.

Doll, B. A., & Cummings, J. A. (2008). *Transforming school mental health services: Population based approaches to promoting the competency and wellness of children.* Thousand Oaks, CA: Corwin Press/NASP.

Eisenberg, M. E., Sieving, R. E., Bearinger, L. H., Swain, C., & Resnick, M. D. (2006). Parents' communication with adolescents about sexual behavior: A missed opportunity for prevention? *Journal of Youth and Adolescence, 35*(6), 893–902.

Elia, J. P., & Eliason, M. (2010). Discourses of exclusion: Sexuality education's silencing of sexual others. *Journal of LGBT Youth, 7*, 29–48.

Elster, A., Jarosik, J., VanGeest, J., & Fleming, M. (2003). Racial and ethnic disparities in health care for adolescents: A systematic review of the literature. *Archives of Pediatric Adolescent Medicine, 157*(9), 867–874.

Fisher, C. M., Reece, M., Wright, E., Dodge, B., Sherwood-Laughlin, C., & Baldwin, K. (2012). The role of community-based organizations in adolescent sexual health promotion. *Health Promotion Practice, 13*(4), 544–552.

Ford, K., Sohn, W., & Lepkowski, J. (2001). Characteristics of adolescents' sexual partners and their association with the use of condoms and other contraceptive methods. *Family Planning Perspectives, 33*, 100–105, 132.

FoSE. (2014). *National Sexuality Education Standards: Core Content and Skills K-12.* Retrieved from http://www.futureofsexed.org/documents/josh-fose-standards-web.pdf

Goesling, B., Colman, S., Trenholm, C., Terzian, M., & Moore, K. (2014). Programs to reduce teen pregnancy, sexually transmitted infections, and associated sexual risk behaviors: A systematic review. *Journal of Adolescent Health, 54*, 499–507.

Guttmacher Institute. (2014). *State policies in brief: Sex and HIV education.* Retrieved from http://www.guttmacher.org/statecenter/spibs/spib_SE.pdf

Guzman, L., Golub, E., Caal, S., Hickman, S., & Ramos, M. (2013, November). *Let's (not) talk about sex: Communication and teen pregnancy prevention within Hispanic families.* Retrieved from http://www.childtrends.org/wp-content/uploads/2013/11/2013-50LetsNotTalkAboutSex.pdf

Huebner, A. J., & Howell, L. W. (2003). Examining the relationship between adolescent sexual risk taking and perceptions of monitoring, communication and parenting styles. *Journal of Adolescent Health, 33*(2), 71–78.

Hutchinson, M. K., Jemmott, J. B., Jemmott, L. S., Braverman, P., & Fong, G. T. (2003). The role of mother-daughter sexual risk communication in reducing sexual risk behavior among urban adolescent females: A prospective study. *Journal of Adolescent Health, 33*(2), 98–107. doi:10.1016/S1054.139X(03) 00183-6

Jaccard, J., & Dittus, P. J. (1993). Parent-adolescent communication about premarital pregnancy. *Families in Society, 74*, 329–343.

Kann, L., Kinchen, S., Shanklin, S. L., Flint, K. H., Hawkins, J., Harris, W. A., et al. (2014). Youth risk behavior surveillance – United States, 2013. *CDC Morbidity and Mortality Weekly Report, 63*(4), 1–168.

Kann, L., Olsen, E. O., McManus, T., Kinchen, S., Chyen, D., Harris, W. A., et al. (2011). Sexual identity, sex of sexual contacts, and health-risk behaviors among students in grades 9–12 – Youth risk behavior surveillance, selected sites, United States, 2001–2009. *CDC Morbidity and Mortality Weekly Report, 60*, 1–133.

Kirby, D., & Lepore, G. (2007). *Sexual risk and protective factors: Factors affecting teen sexual behavior, pregnancy, childbearing, and sexually transmitted disease: Which are important? Which can you change?* Washington, DC: The National Campaign to Prevent Teen and Unplanned Pregnancy.

Kotchick, B. A., Shaffer, A., Forehand, R., & Miller, K. S. (2001). Adolescent sexual risk behavior: A multisystem perspective. *Clinical Psychology Review, 21*(4), 493–519.

Kubicek, K. (2010). In the dark: Young men's stories of sexual initiation in the absence of relevant sexual health information. *Health Education Behavior, 37*(2), 243–263.

Larson, K., Sandelowski, M., & McQuiston, C. (2012). "It's a touchy subject": Latino adolescent sexual risk behaviors in the school context. *Applied Nursing Research, 25*, 231–238.

Manlove, J., Ryan, S., & Franzetta, K. (2004). Contraceptive use and consistency in US teenagers' most recent sexual relationships. *Perspectives on Sexual and Reproductive Health, 36*(6), 265–275.

Marin, B. V., Kirby, D. B., Hudes, E. S., Coyle, K. K., & Gomez, C. A. (2006). Boyfriends, girlfriends, and teenagers' risk of sexual involvement. *Perspectives on Sexual and Reproductive Health, 38*(2), 76–83.

Markham, C. M., Lormand, D., Gloppen, K. M., Peskin, M. F., Flores, B., Low, B., et al. (2010). Connectedness as a predictor of sexual and reproductive health outcomes for youth. *Journal of Adolescent Health, 46*, S23–S41.

McNeely, C., & Blanchard, J. (2009). *The teen years explained: A guide to healthy adolescent development.* Baltimore, MD: Center for Adolescent Health at Johns Hopkins Bloomberg School of Public Health.

McNeely, C. A., & Falci, C. (2004). School connectedness and the transition into and out of health risk behavior among adolescents: A comparison of social belonging and teacher support. *Journal of Adolescent Health, 74*(7), 284–293.

Morrison-Beedy, D., Xia, Y., & Passmore, D. (2013). SI-SRH Sexual risk factors of partner age-discordance in adolescent girls and their male partners. *Journal of Clinical Nursing, 22*, 3289–3299. doi.10.1111/jocn.12408

New York State Department of Health's Adolescent Sexual Health Work Group. (2010). *Guiding principles for sexual health education for young people: A guide for community-based organizations.* Retrieved from http://planaheadnewyork.com/publications/0206/index.htm

Office of the Surgeon General. (2001). *Surgeon General's call to action to promote sexual health and responsible sexual behavior.* Rockville, MD: Office of the Surgeon General.

O'Leary, S. T., Lee, M., Federico, S., Barnard, J., Lockhart, S., Albright, K., et al. (2014). School-based health centers as patient-centered medical homes. *Pediatrics, 134*(5), 957–964.

Patient Protection and Affordable Care Act of 2010, Pub. L. No. 111–148, 124 Stat. 119 (2010).

Paul, C., Fitzjohn, J., Herbison, P., & Dickson, N. (2000). The determinants of sexual intercourse before age 16. *Journal of Adolescent Health, 27*, 136–147.

Price, M., & Hyde, J. (2009). When two isn't better than one: Predictors of early sexual activity in adolescence using a cumulative risk model. *Journal of Youth and Adolescence, 38*(8), 1059–1071.

Resnick, M. D., Bearman, P. S., Blum, R. W., Bauman, K. E., Harris, K. M., Jones, J., et al. (1997). Protecting adolescents from harm: Findings from the National Longitudinal Study on Adolescent Health. *Journal of the American Medical Association, 278*(10), 823–832.

Rouvier, M., Campero, L., Walker, D., & Caballero, M. (2011). Factors that influence communication about sexuality between parents and adolescents in the cultural context of Mexican families. *Sex Education, 11*(2), 175–191. doi:10.1080/14681811.2011.558425

School-Based Health Alliance. (2015). *School-based health alliance: Redefining health for kids and teens.* Retrieved from http://www.sbh4all.org

Sexuality Information and Education Council of the United States (SIECUS). (2010). *A brief history of federal funding for sex education and related programs.* Retrieved from http://www.siecus.org/index.cfm?fuseaction=page.viewpage&pageid=1341&nodeid=1

Shindel, A. W., & Parish, S. J. (2013). Sexuality education in North American medical schools: Current status and future directions. *Journal of Sexual Medicine, 10*, 3–18.

Sinclair, M. F., Christenson, S. L., & Thurlow, M. L. (2005). Promoting school completion of urban secondary youth with emotional and behavioral disabilities. *Exceptional Children, 71*(4), 465–482.

Solomon-Fears, C. (2014). *Teenage pregnancy prevention: Statistics and programs (CRS report for congress).* Congressional Research Service. Retrieved from https://www.fas.org/sgp/crs/misc/RS20301.pdf

U.S. Administration for Children and Families, Office of Planning Research and Evaluation (OPRE). (2014, April). *Personal responsibility education program (PREP) evaluation.* Retrieved from http://www.acf.hhs.gov/sites/default/files/opre/prep_dis_brief_032814_edited.pdf

Whitaker, D. J., & Miller, K. S. (2000). Parent-adolescent discussions about sex and condoms: Impact on peer influences of sexual risk behaviors. *Journal of Adolescent Research, 15*(2), 251–273.

INDEX